D0856625

THE
DECADENT
CONSCIOUSNESS

A
HIDDEN ARCHIVE OF LATE
VICTORIAN LITERATURE

FORTY-TWO RARE AND IMPORTANT TITLES
PUBLISHED IN THIRTY-SIX VOLUMES

EDITED BY

IAN FLETCHER &
JOHN STOKES

GARLAND PUBLISHING

MIKE FLETCHER

George Moore

Garland Publishing, Inc., New York & London

1977

Bibliographical note:
This facsimile has been made from
a copy in the collection of
the Mercantile Library Association
(M515014)

Library of Congress Cataloging in Publication Data

Moore, George, 1852-1933.
   Mike Fletcher.

   (The Decadent consciousness)
   Reprint of the 1889 ed. published by Minerva
Pub. Co., New York.
   I.   Title.   II.   Series.
PZ3.M783Mi7 [PR5042]   823'.8   76-20121
ISBN 0-8240-2770-1

Printed in the United States of America

MIKE FLETCHER.

A Novel.

BY

GEORGE MOORE,

AUTHOR OF

"A MUMMER'S WIFE," "CONFESSIONS OF A YOUNG MAN," ETC.

PRESS OF

THE MINERVA PUBLISHING COMPANY,

10 WEST 23D STREET, NEW YORK.

1889.

PREFACE.

Has any reader of this book ever visited one of the dissecting-rooms in the great cities in Europe and listened to some eminent surgeon as with scalpel in hand he dexterously cuts open a cadaver, and in clear and concise language explains to his hearers the ravages of disease in the human body? If so, I am certain that all thoughts of the putrefying matter vanished before the eloquence of the learned professor. A similar comparison may be made concerning the author of "Mike Fletcher." He is the experienced surgeon before whose description, language, and diction all other thoughts disappear. Let those who are ever ready to find fault and to cast a stone raise their hands and eyes in orthodox fashion and condemn George Moore,—Moore, whom I unhesitatingly pronounce to be the greatest realistic writer of the present age, superior to Zola, inasmuch as the author of "Mike Fletcher" is always sincere and never vulgar. Let people with squeamish tastes disparage George Moore. Broad-minded people, generous people, people of the world, people who constitute the brains and sinews of society, will declare that "Mike Fletcher" is an imperishable masterpiece of the Anglo-Saxon tongue.

T. T. Timayenis.

MIKE FLETCHER.

CHAPTER I.

Oaths, vociferations, and the slamming of cab-doors. The darkness was decorated by the pink of a silk skirt, the crimson of an opera-cloak vivid in the light of a carriage-lamp, with women's faces, necks, and hair. The women sprang gaily from hansoms and pushed through the swing-doors. It was Lubini's famous restaurant. Within the din was deafening.

> " What cheer, 'Ria !
> 'Ria's on the job,"

roared thirty throats, all faultlessly clothed in the purest linen. They stood round a small bar, and two women and a boy endeavoured to execute their constant orders for brandies-and-sodas They were shoulder to shoulder, and had to hold their liquor almost in each other's faces. A man whose hat had been broken addressed reproaches to a friend, who cursed him for interrupting his howling.

Issued from this saloon a long narrow gallery set with a single line of tables, now all occupied by supping courtesans and their men. An odour of savouries, burnt cheese and vinegar met the nostrils, also the sharp smell of a patchouli-scented handker-

5

chief drawn quickly from a bodice; and a young man protested energetically against a wild duck which had been kept a few days over its time. Lubini, or Lubi, as he was called by his pals, signed to the waiter, and deciding the case in favour of the young man, he pulled a handful of silver out of his pocket and offered to toss three lords, with whom he was conversing, for drinks all round.

"Feeling awfully bad, dear boy; haven't been what I could call sober since Monday. Would you mind holding my liquor for me? I must go and speak to that chappie."

Since John Norton[1] had come to live in London, his idea had been to put his theory of life, which he had defined in his aphorism, "Let the world be my ·monastery," into active practice. He did not therefore refuse to accompany Mike Fletcher to restaurants and music-halls, and was satisfied so long as he was allowed to disassociate and isolate himself from the various women who clustered about Mike. But this evening he viewed the courtesans with more than the usual liberalism of mind, had even laughed loudly when one fainted and was upheld by anxious friends, the most zealous and the most intimate of whom bathed her white tragic face and listened in alarm to her incoherent murmurings of "Mike darling, oh, Mike!" John had uttered no word of protest until dear old Laura, who had never, as Mike said, behaved badly to anybody, and had been loved by everybody, sat down at their table, and the discussion turned on who was likely to be Bessie's first sweetheart, Bessie being her youngest sister whom she was "bringing out." Then he rose from the table and wished Mike good-night; but Mike's liking for John was sincere,

---

[1] See "A Mere Accident."

and preferring his company to Laura's, he paid the bill and followed his friend out of the restaurant; and as they walked home together he listened to his grave and dignified admonitions, and though John could not touch Mike's conscience, he always moved his sympathies. It is the shallow and the insincere that inspire ridicule and contempt, and even in the dissipations of the Temple, where he had come to live, he had not failed to enforce respect for his convictions and ideals.

In the Temple John had made many acquaintances and friends, and about him were found the contributors to the *Pilgrim*, a weekly newspaper devoted to young men, their doings, their amusements, their literature, and their art. The editor and proprietor of this organ of amusement was Escott. His editorial work was principally done in his chambers in Temple Gardens, where he lived with his friend, Mike Fletcher. Of necessity the newspaper drew like gravitation, art and literature, but the revelling lords who assembled there were a disintegrating influence, and made John Norton a sort of second centre; and Harding and Thompson and others of various temperaments and talents found their way to Pump Court. Like cuckoos, some men are only really at home in the homes of others; others are always ill at ease when taken out of the surroundings which they have composed to their ideas and requirements; and John Norton was never really John Norton except when, wrapped in his long dressing-gown and sitting in his high canonical chair, he listened to Harding's paradoxes or Thompson's sententious utterances. These artistic discussions—when in the passion of the moment, all the cares of life were lost and the soul battled in pure idea—were full of attraction and charm for John, and he often thought he had never been so happy. And then Harding's eyes would brighten, and his intelligence, eager as a wolf prowling for food, ran to and fro, seeking and sniffing in all John's interests and enthusiasms. He was at once fascinated by the scheme for the pessimistic poem and charmed with the projected voyage in Thibet and the book on the Great Lamas.

One evening a discussion arose as to whether Goethe had stolen from Schopenhauer, or Schopenhauer from Goethe, the comparison of man's life with the sun "which seems to set to our earthly eyes, but which in reality never sets, but shines on unceasingly." The conversation came to a pause, and then Harding said—

"Mike spoke to me of a pessimistic poem he has in mind; did he ever speak to you about it, Escott?"

"I think he said something once, but he did not tell me what it was about. He can speak of nothing now but a nun whom he has persuaded to leave her convent. I had thought of having some articles written about convents, and we went to Roehampton. While I was talking to my cousin, who is at school there, he got into conversation with one of the sisters. I don't know how he managed it, but he has persuaded her to leave the convent, and she is coming to see him to-morrow."

"You don't mean to say," cried John, "that he has persuaded one of the nuns at Roehampton to leave the convent and to come and see him in Temple Gardens? Such things should not be permitted. The Reverend Mother or some one is in fault. That man has been the ruin of hundreds, if not in fact, in thought. He brings an atmosphere of sensuality wherever he goes, and all must breathe it; even the most virtuous are contaminated. I have felt the pollution myself. If the woman is seventy she will look pleased and coquette if he notices her. The fascination is inexplicable !"

"We all experience it, and that is why we like Mike," said Harding. " I heard a lady, and a woman whose thoughts are not, I assure you, given to straying in that direction, say that the first time she saw him she hated him, but soon felt an influence like the fascination the serpent exercises over the bird stealing over her. We find but ourselves in all that we see, hear, and feel. The world is but our idea. All that women have of goodness, sweetness, gentleness, they keep for others. A woman would not speak to you of what is bad in her, but she would to Mike ; her sensuality is the side of her nature which she shows him, be she Messalina or St. Theresa ; the proportion, not the principle is altered. And this is why Mike cannot believe in virtue, and declares his incredulity to be founded on experience."

" No doubt, no doubt !"

Fresh brandies-and-sodas were poured out, fresh cigars were lighted, and John descended the staircase and walked with his friends into Pump Court, where they met Mike Fletcher.

" What have you been talking about to-night ?" he asked.

"We wanted Norton to read us the pessimistic poem he is writing, but he says it is in a too unfinished state. I told him you were at work on one on the same subject. It is curious that you who differ so absolutely on essentials should agree to sink your differences at the very point at which you are most opposed to principle and practice."

After a pause, Mike said—

" I suppose it was Schopenhauer's dislike of women that first attracted you. He used to call women the short-legged race, that were only admitted into society a hundred and fifty years ago."

" Did he say that? Oh, how good, and how true! I never could think a female figure as beautiful as a male. A male figure rises to the head, and is a symbol of the intelligence; a woman's figure sinks to the inferior parts of the body, and is expressive of generation."

As he spoke his eyes followed the line and balance of Mike's neck and shoulders, which showed at this moment upon a dark shadow falling obliquely along an old wall. Soft, violet eyes in which tenderness dwelt, and the strangely tall and lithe figure was emphasized by the conventional pose—that pose of arm and thigh which the Greeks never wearied of. Seeing him, the mind turned from the reserve of the Christian world towards the frank enjoyment of the Pagan; and John's solid, rhythmless form was as symbolic of dogma as Mike's of the grace of Athens.

As he ascended the stairs, having bidden his friends good-night, John thought of the unfortunate nun whom that man had persuaded to leave her convent, and he wondered if he were justified in living in such close communion of thought with those whose lives were set in all opposition to the principles on which he had staked his life's value. He was thinking and writing the same thoughts as Fletcher. They were swimming in the same waters; they were living the same life.

Disturbed in mind he walked across this room, his spectacles glimmering on his high nose, his dressing-gown floating. The manuscript of the poems caught his eyes, and he turned over the sheets, his hand trembling violently. And if they were antagonistic to the spirit of his teaching, if not to the doctrine that the Church in her eternal wisdom deemed healthful and wise, and conducive to the best attainable morality and heaven? What a fearful responsibility he was taking upon himself! He had learned in bitter experience that he must seek salvation rather in elimination than in acceptance of responsibilities. But his poems were all he deemed best in the world. For a moment John stood face to face with, and he looked into the eyes of, the Church. The dome of St. Peter's, a solitary pope, cardinals, bishops, and priests. Oh! wonderful symbolization of man's lust of eternal life!

Must he renounce all his beliefs? The wish so dear to him that the unspeakable spectacle of life might cease for ever; must he give thanks for existence because it gave him a small chance of gaining heaven? Then it were well to bring others into the world. . . . True it is that the Church does not advance into such sloughs of optimism, but how different is her teaching from that of the early fathers, and how different is such dull optimism from the severe spirit of early Christianity.

Whither lay his duty? Must he burn the poems? Far better that they should burn and he should save his soul from burning. A sudden vision of hell, a realistic mediæval hell full of black devils and ovens came upon him, and he saw himself thrust into flame. It seemed to him certain that his soul was lost—so certain, that the source of prayer died within him and he fell prostrate. He cursed with curses that seared his soul as he uttered them, Harding, that cynical atheist, who had striven to undermine his faith, and he shrank from thought of Fletcher, that dirty voluptuary.

He went out for long walks, hoping by exercise to

throw off the gloom and horror which were thickening in his brain. He sought vainly to arrive at some certain opinions concerning his poems, and he weighed every line, not now for cadence and colour, but with a view of determining their ethical tendencies; and this poor torn soul stood trembling on the verge of fearful abyss of unreason and doubt.

And when he walked in the streets, London appeared a dismal, phantom city. The tall houses vanishing in darkness, the unending noise, the sudden and vague figures passing; some with unclean gaze, others in mysterious haste, the courtesans springing from hansoms and entering their restaurant, lurking prostitutes, jocular lads, and alleys suggestive of crime. All and everything that is city fell violently upon his mind, jarring it, and flashing over his brow all the horror of delirium. His pace quickened, and he longed for wings to rise out of the abominable labyrinth.

At that moment a gable of a church rose against the sky. The gates were open, and one passing through seemed to John like an angel, and obeying the instinct which compels the hunted animal to seek refuge in the earth, he entered, and threw himself on his knees. Relief came, and the dread about his heart was loosened in the romantic twilight. One poor woman knelt amid the chairs; presently she rose and went to the confessional. He waited his turn, his eyes fixed on the candles that burned in the dusky distance.

" Father, forgive me, for I have sinned!"

The priest, an old man of gray and shrivelled mien, settled his cassock and mumbled some Latin.

" I have come to ask your advice, father, rather than to confess the sins I have committed in the last week. Since I have come to live in London I have been drawn into the society of the dissolute and the impure."

"And you have found that your faith and your morals are being weakened by association with these men?"

"I have to thank God that I am uninfluenced by them. Their society presents no attractions for me, but I am engaged in literary pursuits, and most of the young men with whom I am brought in contact lead unclean and unholy lives. I have striven, and have in some measure succeeded, in enforcing respect for my ideals; never have I countenanced indecent conversation, although perhaps I have not always set as stern a face against it as I might have."

"But you have never joined in it?"

"Never. But, father, I am on the eve of the publication of a volume of poems, and I am grievously afflicted with scruples lest their tendency does not stand in agreement with the teaching of our holy Church."

"Do you fear their morality, my son?"

"No, No!" said John in an agitated voice, which caused the old man to raise his eyes and glance inquiringly at his penitent; "the poem I am most fearful of is a philosophic poem based on Schopenhauer."

"I did not catch the name."

"Schopenhauer; if you are acquainted with his works, father, you will appreciate my anxieties, and will see just where my difficulty lies."

"I cannot say I can call to mind at this moment any exact idea of his philosophy; does it include a denial of the existence of God?"

"His teaching, I admit, is atheistic in its tendency, but I do not follow him to his conclusions. A part of his theory—that of the resignation of desire of life

—seems to me not only reconcilable with the traditions of the Church, but may really be said to have been original and vital in early Christianity, however much it may have been forgotten in these later centuries. Jesus Christ our Lord is the perfect symbol of the denial of the will to live."

"Jesus Christ our Lord died to save us from the consequences of the sin of our first parents. He died of His own free will, but we may not live an hour more than is given to us to live, though we desire it with our whole heart. We may be called away at any moment."

John bent his head before the sublime stupidity of the priest.

"I was anxious, father, to give you in a few words some accouut of the philosophy which has been engaging my attention, so that you might better understand my difficulties. Although Schopenhauer may be wrong in his theory regarding the will, the conclusions he draws from it, namely, that we may only find lasting peace in resignation, seems to me well within the dogma of our holy Church."

"It surprises me that he should hold such opinions, for if he does not acknowledge a future state, the present must be everything, and the gratification of the senses the only . . ."

"I assure you, father, no one can be more opposed to materialism than Schopenhauer. He holds the world we live in to be a mere delusion—the veil of Maya."

"I am afraid, my son, I cannot speak with any degree of certainty about either of those authors, but I think it my duty to warn you against inclining too willing an eart o the specious sophistries of German philosophers. It would be well if you were to turn to our Christian philosophers; our great cardinal—Cardinal Newman—has over and over again refuted the enemies of the Church. I have forgotten the name."

" Schopenhauer."

" Now I will give you absolution."

The burlesque into which his confession had drifted awakened new terrors in John and sensations of sacrilege. He listened devoutly to the prattle of the priest, and to crush the rebellious spirit in him he promised to submit his poems; and he did not allow himself to think the old man incapable of understanding them. But he knew he would not submit those poems, and turning from the degradation he faced a command which had suddenly come upon him. A great battle raged; and growing at every moment less conscious of all save his soul's salvation, he walked through the streets, his stick held forward like a church candle.

He walked through the city, seeing it not, and hearing all cruel voices dying to one—this: " I can only attain salvation by the elimination of all responsibilities. There is therefore but one course to adopt." Decision came upon him like the surgeon's knife. It was in the cold darkness of his rooms in Pump Court. He raised his face, deadly pale, from his hands; but gradually it went aflame with the joy and rapture of sacrifice, and taking his manuscript, he lighted it in the gas. He held it for a few moments till it was well on fire, and then threw it all blazing under the grate.

CHAPTER II.

An odour of spirits evaporated in the warm winds
of May which came through the open window. The
rich velvet sofa of early English design was littered
with proofs and copies of the *Pilgrim*, and the stamped
velvet was two shades richer in tone than the pale,
dead-red of the floorcloth. Small pictures in light
frames harmonized with a green paper of long inter-
lacing leaves. On the right, the grand piano and the
slender brass lamps ; and the impression of refinement
and taste was continued, for between the blue chintz
curtains the river lay soft as a picture of old Venice.
The beauty of the water, full of the shadows of hay
and sails, many forms of chimneys, wharfs, and warehouses, made panoramic and picturesque by the
motion of the great hay-boats, were surely wanted
for the windows of this beautiful apartment.

Mike and Frank stood facing the view, and talked of
Lily Young, whom Mike was momentarily expecting.

" You know as much about it as I do. It was only
just at the end that you spoke to your cousin and I
got in a few words."

" What did you say?"

" What could I say? Something to the effect that
the convent must be a very happy home."

" How did you know she cared for you?"

" I always know that. The second time we went
there she told me she was going to leave the convent.
I asked her what had decided her to take that step,
and she looked at me—that thirsting look which
women cannot repress. I said I hoped I should see

her when she came to London ; she said she hoped so too. Then I knew it was all right. I pressed her hand, and when we went again I said she would find a letter waiting for her at the post-office. Somehow she got the letter sooner than I expected, and wrote to say she'd come here if she could. Here is the letter. But will she come?"

" Even if she does, I don't see what good it will do you ; it isn't as if you were really in love with her."

" I believe I am in love ; it sounds rather awful, doesn't it? but she is wondrous sweet. I want to be true to her. I want to live for her. I'm not half so bad as you think I am. I have often tried to be constant, and now I mean to be. This ceaseless desire of change is very stupid, and it leads to nothing. I'm sick of change, and would think of none but her. You have no idea how I have altered since I have seen her. I used to desire all women. I wrote a ballad the other day on the women of two centuries hence. Is it not shocking to think that we shall lie mouldering in our graves while women are dancing and kissing? They will not even know that I lived and was loved. It will not occur to them to say as they undress of an evening, ' Were he alive to-day we might love him.'"

THE BALLADE OF DON JUAN DEAD.

My days for singing and loving are over,
    And stark I lie in my narrow bed,
I care not at all if roses cover,
    Or if above me the snow is spread ;
    I am weary of dreaming of my sweet dead,
All gone like me unto common clay.
Life's bowers are full of love's fair fray,
    Of piercing kisses and subtle snares ;
So gallants are conquered, ah, well away !—
    My love was stronger and fiercer than theirs.

O happy moths that now flit and hover
    From the blossom of white to the blossom of red,
Take heed, for I was a lordly lover
    Till the little day of my life had sped ;
    As straight as a pine-tree, a golden head,
And eyes as blue as an austral bay.
Ladies, when loosing your evening array,
    Reflect, had you lived in my years, my prayers
Might have won you from weakly lovers away—
    My love was stronger and fiercer than theirs.

Through the song of the thrush and the pipe of the plover
    Sweet voices come down through the binding lead ;
.O queens that every age must discover
    For men, that man's delight may be fed ;
    Oh, sister queens to the queens I wed.
For the space of a year, a month, a day,
No thirst but mine could your thirst allay ;
    And oh, for an hour of life, my dears,
To kiss you, to laugh at your lovers' dismay—
    My love was stronger and fiercer than theirs.

ENVOI.

Prince was I ever of festival gay,
And time never silvered my locks with gray ;
    The love of your lovers is as hope that despairs,
So think of me sometimes, dear ladies, I pray—
    My love was stronger and fiercer than theirs.

" It is like all your poetry—merely metricious glitter ; there is no heart in it. That a man should like to have a nice mistress, a girl he is really fond of, is simple enough, but lamentation over the limbo of unborn loveliness is, to my mind, sheer nonsense."

Mike laughed.

" Of course it is silly, but I cannot alter it ; it is the sex and not any individual woman that attracts me. I enter a ball-room and I see one, one whom I have never seen before, and I say, ' It is she whom I have sought, I can love her.' I am always disappointed, but hope is born again in every fresh face. Women are so common when they have loved you."

Startled by his words, Mike strove to measure the thought.

"I can see nothing interesting in the fact that it is natural to you to behave badly to every woman who gives you a chance of deceiving her. That's what it amounts to. At the end of a week you'll tire of this new girl as you did of the others. I think it a great shame. It isn't gentlemanly."

Mike winced at the word 'gentlemanly.' For a moment he thought of resentment, but his natural amiability predominated, and he said—

"I hope not. I really do think I can love this one; she isn't like the others. Besides, I shall be much happier. There is, I know, a great sweetness in constancy. I long for this sweetness." Seeing by Frank's face that he was still angry, he pursued his thoughts in the line which he fancied would be most agreeable; he did so without violence to his feelings. It was as natural to him to think one way as another. Mike's sycophancy was so innate that it did not appear and was therefore almost invariably successful. "I have been the lover of scores of women, but I never loved one. I have always hoped to love; it is love that I seek. I find love-tokens and I do not know who were the givers. I have possessed nothing but the flesh, and I have always looked beyond the flesh. I never sought a woman for her beauty. I dreamed of a companion, one who would share each thought; I have dreamed of a woman to whom I could bring my poetry, who could comprehend all sorrows, and with whom I might deplore the sadness of life until we forget it was sad, and I have been given some more or less imperfect flesh."

"I," said Frank, "don't care a rap for your blue stockings. I like a girl to look pretty and sweet in a muslin dress, her hair with the sun on it slipping over her shoulders, a large hat throwing a shadow over the garden of her face. I like her to come and sit on my knee in the twilight before dinner, to come behind me when I am working and put her hand on my forehead, saying, ' Poor old man, you are tired ! ' ''

" And you could love one girl all your life—Lizzie Baker, for instance ; and you could give up all women for one, and never wander again free to gather ?"

" It is always the same thing."

" No, that is just what it is not. The last one was thin, this one is fat ; the last one was tall, this one is tiny. The last one was stupid, this one is witty. Some men seek the source of the Nile, and the lace of a bodice. A new love is a voyage of discovery. What is her furniture like? What will she say ? What are her opinions of love? But when you have been a woman's lover a month you know her morally and physically. Society is based on the family. The family alone survives, it floats like an ark over every raging flood. But you may understand without being able to accept, and I cannot accept, although I understand and love family life. What promiscuity of body and mind ! The idea of never being alone fills me with horror to lose that secret self, which, like a shy bird, flies out of sight in the day, but is with you, oh, how intensely in the morning !"

" Nothing pleases you so much as to be allowed to talk nonsense about yourself."

Mike laughed.

" Let me have those opera-glasses. That woman sitting on the bench is like her."

The trees of the embankment waved along the laughing water, and in scores the sparrows flitted across the sleek green sward. The porter in his bright uniform, cocked hat, and brass buttons, explained the way out to a woman. Her child wore a red sash and stooped to play with a cat that came along the railings, its tail high in the air.

"They know nothing of Lily Young," Mike said to himself; and knowing the porter could not interfere, he wondered what he would think if he knew all. "If she comes nothing can save her, she must and shall be mine."

Waterloo Bridge stood high above the river, level and lovely. Over Charing Cross the brightness was full of spires and pinnacles, but Southwark shore was lost in flat dimness. Then the sun glowed and Westminster ascended tall and romantic, St. Thomas's and St. John's floating in pale enchantment, and beneath the haze that heaved and drifted, revealing coal-barges moored by the Southwark shore, lay a sheet of gold. The candour of the morning laughed upon the river; and there came a little steamer into the dazzling water, her smoke heeling over, coiling and uncoiling like a snake, and casting tremendous shadow—in her train a line of boats laden to the edge with deal planks. Then the haze heaved and London disappeared, became again a gray city, faint and far away—faint as spires seem in a dream. Again and again the haze wreathed and went out, discovering wharfs and gold inscriptions, uncovering barges aground upon the purple slime of the Southwark shore, their yellow yards pointing like birds with outstretched necks.

The smoke of the little steamer curled and rolled over, now like a great snake, now like a great bird hovering with a snake in its talons; and the little steamer made pluckily for Blackfriars. Carts and hansoms, vans and brewers' vans, all silhouetting. Trains slip past, obliterating with white whiffs the delicate distances, the perplexing distances that in London are delicate and perplexing as a spider's web.

Great hay-boats, yellow in the sun, brown in the shadow—great hay-boats came by, their sails scarce filled with the light breeze; standing high, they sailed slowly and picturesquely, with men thrown in all attitudes; somnolent in sunshine and pungent odour —one only at work, wielding the great rudder.

"Ah! if she would not disappoint me; if she would only come; I would give my life not to be disappointed . . . One o'clock! She said she would be here by one, if she came at all. I think I could love her—I am sure of it; it would be impossible to weary of her—so frail—a white blond. She said she would come, I know she wanted to . . . This waiting is agony! Oh, if I were only good-looking! Whatever power I have over women I have acquired; it was the desire to please women that gave me whatever power I possess; I was as soft as wax, and in the fingers of desire was modified and moulded. You did not know me when I was a boy—I was hideous. It seemed to me impossible that women could love men. Women seemed to me so beautiful and desirable, men so hideous and revolting. Could they touch us without a revulsion of feeling? Could they really desire us? That is why I could not bear to give women money, nor a present of any kind—no, not even a flower. If I did all my pleasure was gone; I could not help thinking it was for what they got out of me that they liked me. I longed to penetrate the mystery of woman's life. It seemed to me cruel that the differences between the sexes should never be allowed to dwindle, but should be strictly maintained through all the observances of life. There were beautiful beings walking by us of whom we knew nothing—irreparably separated from us. I wanted to be with this sex as a shadow is with its object."

" You didn't find many opportunities of gratifying your tastes in Cashel ?"

"No, indeed ! Of course the women about the town were not to be thought of." Unpleasant memories seemed to check his flow of words.

Without noticing his embarrassment, Frank said—

" After France it must have been a horrible change to come to Ireland. How old were you ?"

" About fourteen. I could not endure the place. Every day was so appallingly like the last. There was nothing for me to do but to dream ; I dreamed of everything. I longed to get alone and let my fancy wander—weaving tales of which I was the hero, building castles of which I was the lord."

" I remember always hearing of your riding and shooting. No one knew of your literary tastes. I don't mind telling you that Mount Rorke often suspected you of being a bit of a poacher."

Mike laughed.

" I believe I have knocked down a pheasant or two. I was an odd mixture—half a man of action, half a man of dreams. My position in Cashel was unbearable. My mother was a lady ; my father—you know how he had let himself down. You cannot imagine the yearnings of a poor boy ; you were brought up in all elegance and refinement. That beautiful park ! On afternoons I used to walk there, and I remember the very moments I passed under the foliage of the great beeches and lay down to dream. I used to wander to the outskirts of the wood as near as I dared to the pleasure-grounds, and looking on the towers strove to imagine the life there. The bitterest curses lie in the hearts of young men, who understanding refinement and elegance, see it for ever out of their reach. I used to watch the parade of dresses passing on the summer lawns between the firs and

flowering trees. What graceful and noble words
were spoken !—and that man walking into the poetry
of the laburnum gold, did he put his arm about her?
And I wondered what silken ankles moved beneath
her skirts. My brain was on fire, and I was crazed ;
I thought I should never hold a lady in my arms.
A lady ! all the delicacy of silk and lace, high-heeled
shoes, and the scent and colour of hair that a *coiffeur*
has braided."

" I think you are mad !"

Mike laughed and continued—

" I was so when I was sixteen. There was a girl
staying there. Her hair was copper, and her flesh
was pink and white. Her waist, you could span it.
I saw her walking one day on . . ."

" You must mean Lady Alice Hargood, a very tall
girl ?"

" Yes ; five feet seven, quite. I saw her walking
on the terrace with your uncle. Once she passed
our house, and I smarted with shame of it as of some
restless wound, and for days I remembered I was
little better than a peasant. Originally we came, as
you know, of good English stock, but nothing is vital
but the present. I cried and cursed my existence,
my father and the mother that bore me, and that
night I climbed out by my window and roved through
the dark about the castle so tall in the moonlight.
The sky that night was like a soft blue veil, and the
trees were painted quite black upon it. I looked
for her window, and I imagined her sleeping with
her copper hair tossed in the moonlight, like an
illustration in a volume of Shelley.

" You remember the old wooden statue of a nymph
that stood in the sycamores at the end of the terraces ;
she was the first naked woman I saw. I used to
wander about her, sometimes at night, and I have

often climbed about and hung round those shoulders, and ever since I have always met that breast of wood. You have been loved more truly; you have been possessed of woman more thoroughly than I. Though I clasp a woman in my arms, it is as if the Atlantic separated us. Did I never tell you of my first love affair? That was the romance of the wood nymph. One evening I climbed on the pedestal of my divinity, my cheek was pale . . .''

" For God's sake, leave out the poetics, and come to the facts.''

" If you don't let me tell my story in my own way I won't tell it at all. Out of my agony prayer rose to Alice, for now it pleased me to fancy there was some likeness between this statue and Lady Alice. The dome of leafage was sprinkled with the colour of the sunset, and as I pressed my lips to the wooden breast, I heard dead leaves rustling under a footstep. Holding the nymph with one arm, I turned and saw a lady approaching. She asked me why I kissed the statue. I looked away embarrassed, but she told me not to go, and she said, 'You are a pretty boy.' I said I had never seen a woman so beautiful. Again I grew ashamed, but the lady laughed. We stood talking in the stillness. She said I had pretty hands, and asked me if I regretted the nymph was not a real woman. She took my hands. I praised hers, and then I grew frightened, for I knew she came from the castle; the castle was to me what the Ark of the Covenant was to an Israelite. She put her arm about me, and my fears departed in the thrilling of an exquisite minute. She kissed me and said, ' Let us sit down.' ''

" I wonder who she was! What was her name? You can tell me.''

" No, I never mention names; besides, I am not certain she gave her right name.''

"Are you sure she was staying at the castle? For if so, there would be no use for her to conceal her name. You could easily have found it out."

" Oh, yes, she was staying at the castle; she talked about you all. Don't you believe me?"

"What, all about the nymph? I am certain you thought you ought to have loved her, and if what Harding says is right, that there is more truth in what we think than in what we do, I'm sure you might say that you had been on a wedding-tour with one of the gargoyles."

Mike laughed; and Frank did not suspect that he had annoyed him. Mike's mother was a French-woman, whom John Fletcher had met in Dublin and had pressed into a sudden marriage. At the end of three years of married life she had been forced to leave him, and strange were the legends of the pro-fanities of that bed. She fled one day, taking her son with her. Fletcher did not even inquire where she had gone; and when at her death Mike returned to Ireland, he found his father in a small lodging-house playing the flute. Scarcely deigning to turn his head, he said—" Oh! is that you, Mike?—sit down."

At his father's death, Mike had sold the lease of the farm for three hundred pounds, and with that sum and a volume of verse he went to London. When he had published his poems he wrote two comedies. His efforts to get them produced led him into various society. He was naturally clever at cards, and one night he won three hundred pounds. Journalism he had of course dabbled in—he was drawn towards it by his eager, impatient nature; he was drawn from it by his gluttonous and artistic nature. Only ten pounds for an article, whereas a successful " bridge" brought him ten times that amount, and he revolted against the column of platitudes that the hours whelmed in oblivion. There had been times, however, when he had been obliged to look to journalism for daily bread. The *Spectator*, always open to young talent, had published many of his poems; the *Saturday* had welcomed his paradoxes and strained eloquence; but whether he worked or whether he idled he never wanted money. He was one of those men who can always find five pounds in the streets of London.

We meet Mike in his prime—in his twenty-ninth year—a man of various capabilities, which an inveterate restlessness of temperament had left undeveloped—a man of genius, diswrought with passion, occasionally stricken with ambition.

"Let me have those glasses. There she is! I am sure it is she—there, leaning against the Embankment. Yes, yes, it is she. Look at her. I should know her figure among a thousand—those frail shoulders, that little waist; you could break her like a reed. How sweet she is on that background of flowing water, boats, wharves, and chimneys; it all rises about her like a dream, and all is as faint upon the radiant air as a dream upon happy sleep. So she is coming to see me. She will keep her promise. I shall love her. I feel at last that love is near me. Supposing I were to marry her?"

"Why shouldn't you marry her if you love her? That is to say, if this is more than one of your ordinary caprices, spiced by the fact that its object is a nun."

The men looked at each other for a moment doubtful. Then Mike laughed.

"I hope I don't love her too much, that is all. But perhaps she will not come. Why is she standing there?"

" I should laugh if she turned on her heel and walked away right under your very nose."

A cloud passed over Mike's face.

" That's not possible," he said, and he raised the glass. " If I thought there was any chance of that I should go down to see her."

" You couldn't force her to come up. She seems to be admiring the view."

Then Lily left the Embankment and turned towards the Temple.

" She is coming!" Mike cried, and laying down the opera-glass he took up the scent and squirted it about the room. " You won't make much noise like a good fellow, will you? I shall tell her I am here alone."

" I shall make no noise—I shall finish my article. I am expecting Lizzie about four; I will slip out and meet her in the street. Good-bye."

Mike went to the head of the staircase, and looking down the prodigious height, he waited. It occurred to him that if he fell, the emparadised hour would be lost for ever. If she were to pass through the Temple without stopping at No. 2! The sound of little feet and the colour of a heliotrope skirt dispersed his fears, and he watched her growing larger as she mounted each flight of stairs, when she stopped to take breath; he thought of running down and carry-ing her up in his arms, but he did not move and she did not see him until the last flight.

" Here you are at last!"

" I am afraid I have kept you waiting. I was not certain whether I should come."

" And you stopped to look at the view instead?"

" Yes; but how did you know that?"

" Ah! that's telling; come in."

The girl went in shyly.

"So this is where you live? How nicely you have arranged the room. I never saw a room like this before. How different from the convent! What would the nuns think if they saw me here? What strange pictures!—those ballet-girls; they remind me of the pantomime. Did you buy those pictures?"

"No; they are wonderful, aren't they? A friend of mine bought them in France."

"Mr. Escott?"

"Yes; I forgot you knew him—how stupid of me! Had it not been for him I shouldn't have known you —I was thinking of something else."

"Where is he now? I hope he will not return while I am here. You did not tell him I was coming?"

"Of course not; he is away in France."

"And those portraits—it is always the same face."

"They are portraits of a girl he is in love with."

"Do you believe he is in love?"

"Yes, rather; head over heels. What do you think of the painting?"

Lily did not answer. She stood puzzled, striving to separate the confused notions the room conveyed to her. She wore on her shoulders a small black lace shawl and held a black silk parasol. She was very slender, and her features were small and regular, and so white was her face that the blue eyes seemed the only colour. There was, however, about the cheek-bones just such tint as mellow as a white rose.

"How beautiful you are to-day. I knew you would be beautiful when you discarded that shocking habit; but you are far more beautiful than I thought. Let me kiss you."

"No, you will make me regret that I came here. I wanted to see where you lived, so that when I was

away I could imagine you writing your poems. Have
you nothing more to show me? I want to see
everything."

"Yes, come, I will show you our dining-room.
Mr. Escott often gives dinner parties. You must get
your mother to bring you."

"I should like to. But what a good idea to have
book-cases in the passages, they furnish the walls so
well. And what are those rooms?"

"Those belong to Escott. Here is where I sleep."

"What a strange room!" Discountenanced by
the great Christ, she turned her head.

"That crucifix is a present from Frank. He
bought it in Paris. It is superb expression of the
faith of the Middle Ages."

"Old ages, I should think; it is all worm-eaten.
And that Virgin? I did not know you were so
religious."

"I do not believe, but I think Christ is picturesque
—the one bit of nakedness in Christianity."

"Christ is very beautiful. When I prayed to Him
an hour passed like a little minute. It always seemed
to me more natural to pray to Him than to the
Virgin Mary. But is that your bed?"

Upon a trellis supported by lion's claws a feather
bed was laid. The sheets and pillows were covered
with embroidered cloth, the gift of some unhappy
lady, and about the twisted columns heavy draperies
hung in apparent disorder. Lily sat down on the
pouff ottoman. Mike took two Venetian glasses,
poured out some champagne, and sat at her feet.
She sipped the wine and nibbled a biscuit.

"Tell me about the convent," he said. "That is
now a thing over and done."

"Fortunately I was not professed; had I taken
vows I could not have broken them."

"Why not? A nun cannot be kept imprisoned nowadays."

"I should not have broken my vows."

"It was I who saved you from them—if you had not fallen in love with me . . ."

"I never said I had fallen in love with you; I liked you, that was all."

"But it was for me you left the convent?"

"No; I had made up my mind to leave the convent long before I saw you. So you thought it was love at first sight."

"On my part, at least, it was love at first sight. How happy I am!—I can scarcely believe I have got you. To have you here by me seems so unreal, so impossible. I always loved you. I want to tell you about myself. You were my ideal when I was a boy; I had already imagined you; my poems were all addressed to you. My own sweet ideal that none knew of but myself. You shall come and see me all the summer through, in this room—our room. When will you come again?"

"I shall never come again—it is time to go."

"To go! Why, you haven't kissed me yet!"

"I do not intend to kiss you."

"How cruel of you! You say you will never come and see me again; you break and destroy my dream."

"How did you dream of me?"

"I dreamed the world was buried in snow, barred with frost—that I never went out, but sat here waiting for you to come. I dreamed that you came to see me on regular days. I saw myself writing poems to you, looking up to see the clock from time to time. Tea and wine were ready, and the room was scented with your favourite perfume. Ting! How the bell thrilled me, and with what precipitation I rushed to the door! There I found you. What pleasure to lead you to the great fire, to help you to take off your pelisse!"

The girl looked at him, her eyes full of innocent wonderment.

"How can you think of such things? It sounds like a fairy tale. And if it were summer-time?"

"Oh! if it were summer we should have roses in the room, and only a falling rose-leaf should remind us of the imperceptible passing of the hours. We should want no books, the picturesqueness of the river would be enough. And holding your little palm in mine, so silken and delicately moist, I would draw close to you."

Knowing his skin was delicate to the touch, he took her arm in his hand, but she drew her arm away, and there was incipient denial in the withdrawal. His face clouded. But he had not yet made up his mind how he should act, and to gain time to think, he said—

"Tell me why you thought of entering a convent?"

"I was not happy at home, and the convent, with its prayers and duties, seemed preferable. But it was not quite the same as I had imagined, and I couldn't learn to forget that there was a world of beauty, colour, and love."

"You could not but think of the world of men that awaited you."

"I only thought of Him."

"And who was he?"

"Ah! He was a very great saint, a greater saint than you'll ever be. I fell in love with Him when I was quite a little girl."

"What was his name?"

"I am not going to tell you. It was for Him I went into the convent; I was determined to be His bride in heaven. I used to read His life, and think of

Him all day long. I had a friend who was also in love, but the reverend mother heard of our conversations, and we were forbidden to speak any more of our saints."

"Tell me his name? Was he anything like me?"

"Well, perhaps there is a something in the eyes."

The conversation dropped, and he laid his hand gently upon her foot. Drawing it back she spilt the wine.

"I must go."

"No, dearest, you must not."

She looked round, taking the room in one swift circular glance, her eyes resting one moment on the crucifix.

"This is cruel of you," he said. "I dreamed of you madly, and why do you destroy my dream? What shall I do?—where shall I go?—how shall I live if I don't get you?"

"Men do not mind whom they love; even in the convent we knew that."

"You seem to have known a good deal in that convent; I am not astonished that you left it."

"What do you mean?" She settled her shawl on her shoulders.

"Merely this: you are in a young man's room alone, and I love you."

"Love! You profane the word; loose me, I am going."

"No, you are not going, you must remain." There was an occasional nature in him, that of the vicious dog, and now it snarled. "If you did not love me, you should not have come here," he said interposing, getting between her and the door.

Then she entreated him to let her go. He laughed at her; then suddenly her face flamed with a passion he was unprepared for, and her eyes danced with

strange lights. Few words were spoken, only a few
ejaculatory phrases such as "How dare you?" "Let
me go!" she said, as she strove to wrench her arms
from his grasp. She caught up one of the glasses;
but before she could throw it Mike seized her hand;
he could not take it from her, and unconscious of
danger (for if the glass broke both would be cut to
the bone), she clenched it with a force that seemed
impossible in one so frail. Her rage was like wild-
fire. Mike grew afraid, and preferring that the glass
should be thrown than it should break in his hand,
he loosed his fingers. It smashed against the opposite
wall. He hoped that Frank had not heard; that he
had left the chambers. He seized the second glass.
When she raised her arm, Mike saw and heard the
shattered window falling into the court below. He
anticipated the porter's steps on the staircase and his
knock at the door, and it was with an intense relief
and triumph that he saw the bottle strike the curtain
and fall harmless. He would win yet. Lily screamed
piercingly.

"No one will hear," he said, laughing hoarsely.

She escaped him and she screamed three times.
And now quite like a mad woman, she snatched a
light chair and rushed to the window. Her frail
frame shook, her thin face was swollen, and she
seemed to have lost control over her eyes. If she
should die! If she should go mad! Now really
terrified, Mike prayed for forgiveness. She did not
answer; she stood clenching her hands, choking.

"Sit down," he said, "drink something. You need
not be afraid of me now—do as you like, I am your
servant. I will ask only one thing of you—forgiveness. If you only knew!"

"Don't speak to me!" she gasped, "don't!"

"Forgive me, I beseech you; I love you better than all the world."

"Don't touch me! How dare you? Oh! how dare you?"

Mike watched her quivering. He saw she was sublime in her rage, and torn with desire and regret he continued his pleadings. It was some time before she spoke.

"And it was for this," she said, "I left my convent, and it was of him I used to dream! Oh! how bitter is my awakening!"

She grasped one of the thin columns of the bed, and her attitude bespoke the revulsion of feeling that was passing in her soul; beneath the heavy curtains she stood pale all over, thrown by the shock of too coarse a reality. His perception of her innocence was a goad to his appetite, and his despair augmented at losing her. Now, as died the fulgurant rage that had supported her, and her normal strength being exhausted, a sudden weakness intervened, and she couldn't but allow Mike to lead her to a seat.

"I am sorry; words cannot tell you how sorry I am. Why do you tremble so? You are not going to faint, say—drink something." Hastily he poured out some wine and held it to her lips. "I never was sorry before; now I know what sorrow is—I am sorry, Lily. I am not ashamed of my tears; look at them, and strive to understand. I never loved till I saw you. Ah! that lily face, when I saw it beneath the white veil, love leaped into my soul. Then I hated God, and I longed to scale the sky to dispossess Him of that which I held the one sacred and desirable thing—you! My soul! I would have given it to Him to burn for ten thousand years for one kiss, one touch of these snow-coloured hands. When I saw, or thought I saw, that you loved me, I was God.

I said on reading your sweet letter, ' My life shall not pass without kissing at least once the lips of my ideal.' ''

Words and images rose in his mind without sensation or effort, and experiencing the giddiness and exultation of the orator, he strove to win her with eloquence. And all his magnetism was in his hands and eyes—deep blue eyes full of fire and light were fixed upon her—hands, soft yet powerful hands held hers, sometimes were clenched on hers, and a voice which seemed his soul rose and fell, striving to sting her with passionate sound ; but she remained absorbed in, and could not be drawn out of, angry thought.

" Now you are with me," he said, " nearly mine ; here I see you like a picture that is mine. Around us is mighty London. I saved you from God, am I to lose you to man? This was the prospect that faced me, that faces me, that drove me mad. All I did was to attempt to make you mine. I hold you by so little—I could not bear the thought that you might pass from me. A ship sails away, growing indistinct, and then disappears in the shadows ; in London a cab rattles, appears and disappears behind other cabs, turns a corner and is lost for ever. I failed, but had I succeeded you would have come back to me ; I failed, is not that punishment enough? You will go from me ; I shall not get you—that is sorrow enough for me ; do not refuse me forgiveness. Ah! if you knew what it is to have sought love passionately, the high hopes entertained, and then the depth of every deception, and now the supreme grief of finding love and losing. Seeing love leave me without leaving one flying feather for token, I strove to pluck one—that is my crime. Go, since you must go, but do not go unforgiving, lest perhaps you might regret."

Lily did not cry. Her indignation was vented in broken phrases, the meaning of which she did not seem to realize, and so jarred and shaken were her nerves that without being aware of it her talk branched into observations on her mother, her home life, the convent, and the disappointments of child-hood. So incoherently did she speak that for a moment Mike feared her brain was affected, and his efforts to lead her to speak of the present were fruit-less. But suddenly, waxing calm, her inner nature shining through the eyes like light through porcelain, she said—

"I was wrong to come here, but I imagined men different. We know so little of the world in the convent . . . Ah, I should have stayed there. It may be but a poor delusion, but it is better than such wickedness."

" But I love you."

" Love me ! . . . You say you have sought love ; we find love in contemplation and desire of higher things. I am wanting in experience, but I know that love lives in thought, and not in violent passion ; I know that a look from the loved one on entering a room, a touch of a hand at most will suffice, and I should have been satisfied to have seen your windows, and I should have gone away, my heart stored with impressions of you, and I should have been happy for weeks in the secret possession of such memories. So I have always understood love ; so we understood love in the convent."

They were standing face to face in the faint twi-light and scent of the bedroom. Through the gauze blind the river floated past, decorative and grand ; the great hay-boats rose above the wharves and steamers; one lay in the sun's silver casting a black shadow; a barge rowed by one man drifted round and round in the tide.

" When I knelt in the choir I lifted my heart to the saint I loved. How far was he from me? Millions of miles!—and yet he was very near. I dreamed of meeting him in heaven, of seeing him come robed in white with a palm in his hand, and then in a little darkness and dimness I felt him take me to his breast. I loved to read of the miracles he performed, and one night I dreamed I saw him in my cell—or was it you?"

All anger was gone from her face, and it reflected the play of her fancy. " I used to pray to you to come down and speak to me."

" And now," said Mike, smiling, " now that I have come to you, now that I call you, now that I hold my arms to you—you the bride-elect—now that the hour has come, shall I not possess you?"

" Do you think you can gain love by clasping me to your bosom? My love, though separated from me by a million miles, is nearer to me than yours has ever been."

" Did you not speak of me as the lover of your prayer, and you said that in ecstasy the nuns—and indeed it must be so—exchange a gibbeted saint for some ideal man? Give yourself; make this afternoon memorable."

" No; good-bye! Remember your promises. Come; I am going."

" I must not loose you," he cried, drunk with her beauty and doubly drunk with her sensuous idealism. " May I not even kiss you?"

" Well, if you like—once, just here," she said, pointing where white melted to faint rose.

Mastered, he followed her down the long stairs;

but when they passed into the open air he felt he
had lost her irrevocably.   The river was now tinted
with setting light, the balustrade of Waterloo Bridge
showed like lace-work, the glass roofing of Charing
Cross station was golden, and each spire distinct
upon the moveless blue.   The splashing of a steamer
sounded strange upon his ears.   The "Citizen"
passed!   She was crowded with human beings, all
apparently alike.   Then the eye separated them.
An old lady making her way down the deck, a young
man in gray clothes, a red soldier leaning over the
rail, the captain walking on the bridge.

Mike called a hansom; a few seconds more and
she would pass from him into London.   He saw the
horse's hoofs, saw the cab appear and disappear
behind other cabs; it turned a corner, and she was
gone.

CHAPTER III.

SEVEN hours had elapsed since he had parted from
Lily Young, and these seven hours he had spent in
restaurants and music-halls, seeking in dissipation sur-
cease of sorrow and disappointment.   He had dined
at Lubi's, and had gone on with Lord Muchross and
Lord Snowdown to the Royal, and they had returned
in many hansoms and with many courtesans to drink
at Lubi's.   But his heart was not in gaiety, and feeling he could neither break a hat joyously nor allow
his own to be broken good-humouredly, nor even
sympathize with Dicky, the driver, who had not been
sober since Monday, he turned and left the place.

" This is why fellows marry," he said, when he
returned home, and sat smoking in the shadows—he

had lighted only one lamp—depressed by the loneliness of the apartment.   And more than an hour
passed before he heard Frank's steps.   Frank was in
evening dress ; he opened his cigarette-case, lighted
a cigarette, and sat down willing to be amused.   Mike
told him the entire story with gestures and descrip-
tive touches; on the right was the bed with its curtains hanging superbly, on the left the great hay-boats
filling the window ; and by insisting on the cruelest aspects, he succeeded in rendering it almost unbearable.
But Frank had dined well, and as Lizzie had promised
to come to breakfast he was in excellent humour, and
on the whole relished the tale.   He was duly impressed and interested by the subtlety of the fancy
which made Lily tell how she used to identify her
Divine lover while praying to Him, Him with the
human ideal which had led her from the cloister, and
which she had come to seek in the world.   He was
especially struck with, and he admired the conclusion
of, the story, for Mike had invented a dramatic and
effective ending.

" Well-nigh mad, drunk with her beauty and the
sensuous charm of her imagination, I threw my arms
about her.   I felt her limbs against mine, and I said,
' I am mad for you ; give yourself to me, and make this
afternoon memorable.'   There was a faint smile of
reply in her eyes.   They laughed gently, and she said,
' Well, perhaps I do love you a little.' "

Frank was deeply impressed by Mike's tact and
judgment, and they talked of women, discussing each
shade of feminine morality through the smoke of
innumerable cigarettes ; and after each epigram they
looked in each others' eyes astonished at their genius
and originality.   Then Mike spoke of the paper and
the articles that would have to be written on the

morrow. He promised to get to work early, and they said good-night.

When Frank left Southwick two years ago and pursued Lizzie Baker to London, he had found her in straitened circumstances and unable to obtain employment. The first night he took her out to dinner and bought her a hat, on the second he bought her a gown, and soon after she became his mistress. Henceforth his days were devoted to her; they were seen together in all popular restaurants, and in the theatres. One day she went to see some relations, and Frank had to dine alone. He turned into Lubini's, but to his annoyance the only table available was one which stood next where Mike Fletcher was dining. "That fellow dining here," thought Frank, "when he ought to be digging potatoes in Ireland." But the accident of the waiter seeking for a newspaper forced him to say a few words, and Mike talked so agreeably that at the end of dinner they went out together and walked up and down, talking on journalism and women.

Suddenly the last strand of Frank's repugnance to make a friend of Mike broke, and he asked him to come up to his rooms and have a drink. They remained talking till daybreak, and separated as friends in the light of the empty town. Next day they dined together, and a few days after Frank and Lizzie breakfasted with Mike at his lodgings. But during the next month they saw very little of him, and this pause in the course of dining and journalistic discussion, indicating, as Frank thought it did, a coolness on Mike's part, determined the relation of these two men. When they ran against each other in the corridor of a theatre, Frank eagerly button-holed Mike, and asked him why he had not been to dine at Lubini's, and not suspecting that he dined there only

when he was in funds, was surprised at his evasive
answers.   Mistress and lover were equally anxious to
know why they had not been able to find him in any
of the usual haunts; he urged a press of work, but
it transpired he was harassed by creditors, and was
looking out for rooms.   Frank told him he was
thinking of moving into the Temple.

" Lucky fellow! I wish I could afford to live there."

" I wish you could. . . .   The apartment I have in
mind is too large for me, you might take the half of it."

Mike knew where his comforts lay, and he accepted
his friend's offer.   There they founded, and there they
edited the *Pilgrim*, a weekly sixpenny paper devoted
to young men, their doings, their amusements, their
literature and their art.   Under their dual editorship
this journal had prospered; it now circulated five
thousand a week, and published twelve pages of advertisements.   Frank, whose bent was hospitality, was
therefore able to entertain his friends as it pleased
him, and his rooms were daily and nightly filled with
revelling lords, comic vocalists, and chorus girls.
Mike often craved for other amusements and other
society.   Temple Gardens was but one page in the
book of life, and every page in that book was equally
interesting to him.   He desired all amusements, to
know all things, to be loved by every one, and longing
for new sensations of life he often escaped to the
Cock tavern for a quiet dinner with some young
barristers, and a quiet smoke afterwards with them in
their rooms.   It was there he had met John Norton.

The *Pilgrim* was composed of sixteen columns of
paragraphs in which society, art, and letters were
dealt with—the form of expression preferred being
the most exaggerated. Indeed, the formula of criticism
that Mike and Frank, guided by Harding, had developed, was to consider as worthless all that the

world held in estimation, and to laud as best all that the world had agreed to discard. John Norton's views regarding Latin literature had been adopted, and Virgil was declared to be the great old bore of antiquity, and some three or four quite unknown names, gathered amid the Fathers, were upon occasion trailed in triumph with adjectives of praise.

What painter of Madonnas does the world agree to consider as the greatest? Raphael—Raphael was therefore descried as being scarcely superior to Sir Frederick Leighton; and one of the early Italian painters, Francesco Bianchi, whom Vasari exhumes in some three or four lines, was praised as possessing a subtle and mysterious talent very different indeed from the hesitating smile of La Jaconde. There is a picture of the Holy Family by him in the Louvre, and of it Harding wrote—"This canvas exhales for us the most delicious emanations, sorrowful bewitchments, insidious sacrileges, and troubled prayers."

All institutions, especially the Royal Academy, St. Paul's Cathedral, Drury Lane Theatre, and Eton College, were held to be the symbols of man's earthiness, the bar-room and music-hall as certain proof of his Divine origin; actors were scorned and prizefighters revered; the genius of courtesans, the folly of education, and the poetry of pantomime formed the themes on which the articles which made the centre of the paper were written. Insolent letters were addressed to eminent people, and a novel by Harding, the hero of which was a butler and the heroine a cook, was in course of publication.

Mike was about to begin a series of articles in this genial journal, entitled *Lions of the Season*. His first lion was a young man who had invented a pantomime, *Pierrot murders his Wife*, which he was acting with success in fashionable drawing-rooms. A mute brings

Pierrot back more dead than alive from the cemetery, and throws him in a chair. When Pierrot recovers he re-acts the murder before a portrait of his wife—how he tied her down and tickled her to death. Then he begins drinking, and finally sets fire to the curtains of the bed and is burnt.

It was the day before publishing-day, and since breakfast the young men had been drinking, smoking, telling tales, and writing paragraphs; from time to time the page-boy brought in proofs, and the narrators made pause till he had left the room. Frank continued reading Mike's manuscript, now and then stopping to praise a felicitous epithet.

At last he said—" Harding, what do you think of this?—' The Sphynx is representative of the grave and monumental genius of Egypt, the Faun of the gracious genius of Rome, the Pierrot of the fantastic genius of the Renaissance. And, in this one creation, I am not sure that the seventeenth does not take the palm from the earlier centuries. Pierrot!— there is music, there is poetry in the name. The soul of an epoch lives in that name, evocative as it is of shadowy trees, lawny spaces, brocade, pointed bodices, high heels and guitars. And in expression how much more perfect is he than his ancestor, the Faun! His animality is indicated without coarse or awkward symbolism; without cloven hoof or hirsute ears—only a white face, a long white dress with large white buttons, and a black skull-cap; and yet, somehow, the effect is achieved. The great white creature is not quite human—hereditary sin has not descended upon him; he is not quite responsible for his acts.' "

" I like the paragraph," said Harding; " you finish up, of course, with the apotheosis of pantomimists, and announce him as one of the lions of the season. Who are your other lions and lionesses?"

" The others will be far better," said Mike. He took a cigarette from a silver box on the table, and, speaking as he puffed at it, entered into the explanation of his ideas.

Mademoiselle D'Or, the *première danseuse* who had just arrived from Vienna, was to be the lioness of next week. Mike told how he would translate into words the insidious poetry of the blossom-like skirt that the pink body pierces like a stem, the beautiful springing, the lifted arms, then the flight from the wings; the posturing, the artificial smiles; this art a survival of oriental tradition; this art at once so carnal and so enthusiastically ideal. " A prize-fighter will follow the *danseuse*. And I shall gloat in Gautier-like cadence—if I can catch it—over each superb muscle and each splendid development. But my best article will be on Kitty Carew. Since Laura Bell and Mabel Grey our courtesans have been but a mediocre lot."

" You must not say that in the *Pilgrim*—we should offend all our friends," Harding said, and he poured himself out a brandy-and-soda.

Mike laughed, and walking up and down the room, he continued—

" That it should be so is inexplicable, that it is so is certain; we have not had since Mabel Grey died a courtesan with whom a foreign prince, passing London, would visit as a matter of course as he would visit St. Paul's or Westminster Abbey; and yet London has advanced enormously in all that constitutes wealth and civilization. In Paris, as in ancient Greece, courtesans are rich, brilliant, and depraved; here in London the women are poor, stupid, and almost virtuous. Kitty is revolution. I know for a fact that she has had as much as £1000 from a foreign potentate, and she spends in one day upon her

tiger-cat what would keep a poor family in affluence
for a week. Nor can she say half-a-dozen words
without being witty. What do you think of this?
We were discussing the old question, if it were well
for a woman to have a sweetheart. Kitty said, 'London has given me everything but that. I can always find a man who will give me five-and-twenty
guineas, but a sweetheart I can't find.' "

Every pen stopped, and expectation was on every
face. After a pause Mike continued—

" Kitty said, ' In the first place he must please me,
and I am very difficult to please ; then I must please
him, and sufficiently for him to give up his whole
time to me. And he must not be poor, for although
he would not give me money, it would cost him
several hundreds a year to invite me to dinner and
send me flowers. And where am I to find this
combination of qualities?' Can't you hear her saying
it, her sweet face like a tea-rose, those innocent blue
eyes all laughing with happiness? The great stock-
broker, who has been with her for the last ten years,
settled fifty thousand pounds when he first took her
up. She was speaking to me about him the other
day, and when I said, ' Why didn't you leave him
when the money was settled?' she said, ' Oh no, I
wouldn't do a dirty trick like that ; I contented
myself simply by being unfaithful to him.' "

" This is no doubt very clever, but if you put all
you have told us into your article, you'll certainly have
the paper turned off the book-stalls."

The conversation paused. Every one finished his
brandy-and-soda, and the correction of proofs was
continued in silence, interrupted only by an occasional
oath or a word of remonstrance from Frank, who
begged Drake, a huge-shouldered man, whose hand
was never out of the cigarette-box, not to drop the

lighted ends on the carpet. Mike was reading Harding's article.

" I think we shall have a good number this week," said Mike. " But we want a piece of verse. I wonder if you could get something from John Norton. What do you think of Norton, Harding ?"

" He is one of the most interesting men I know. His pessimism, his Catholicism, his yearning for ritual, his very genuine hatred of women, it all fascinates me."

" What do you think of that poem he told us of the other night?"

" Intensely interesting ; but he will never be able to complete it. A man may be full of talent and yet be nothing of an artist; a man may be far less clever than Norton, and with a subtler artistic sense. If a seal had really something to say, I believe it would find a way of saying it ; but has John Norton really got any idea so overwhelmingly new and personal that it would force a way of utterance where none existed ? The Christian creed with its tale of Mary must be of all creeds most antipathetic to his natural instincts, he nevertheless accepts it. . . . If you agitate a pool from different sides you must stir up mud, and this is what occurs in Norton's brain ; it is agitated equally from different sides, and the result is mud."

Mike looked at Harding inquiringly, for a moment wondered if the novelist understood him as he seemed to understand Norton.

A knock was heard, and Norton entered. His popularity was visible in the pleasant smiles and words which greeted him.

" You are just the man we want," cried Frank. " We want to publish one of your poems in the paper this week."

"I have burnt my poems," he answered, with something more of sacerdotal tone and gesture than usual.

All the scribblers looked up. "You don't mean to say seriously that you have burnt your poems?"

"Yes; but I do not care to discuss my reasons. You do not feel as I do."

"You mean to say that you have burnt *The Last Struggle*—the poem you told us about the other night?"

"Yes, I felt I could not reconcile its teaching, or I should say the tendency of its teaching, to my religion. I do not regret—besides I had to do it; I felt I was going off my head. I should have gone mad. I have been through agonies. I could not think. Thought and pain and trouble were as one in my brain. I heard voices. . . . I had to do it. And now a great calm has come. I feel much better."

"You are a curious chap."

Then at the end of a long silence John said as if he wished to change the conversation—

"Even though I did burn my pessimistic poem, the world will not go without one. You are writing a poem on Schopenhauer's philosophy. It is hard to associate pessimism with you."

"Only because you take the ordinary view of the tendency of pessimistic teaching," said Mike. "If you want a young and laughing world, preach Schopenhauer at every street corner; if you want a sober utilitarian world, preach Comte."

"Doesn't much matter what the world is as long as it is not sober," chuckled Platt, the paragraph-writing youth at the bottom of the table.

"Hold your tongue!" cried Drake, and he lighted another cigarette preparatory to fixing his whole attention on the paradox that Mike was about to enounce.

"The optimist believes in the regeneration of the race, in its ultimate perfectibility, the synthesis of humanity, the providential idea, and the path of the future; he therefore puts on a shovel hat, cries out against lust and depreciates prostitution."

"Oh, the brute!" chuckled the wizen youth, "without prostitutes and public houses! what a world to live in!"

"The optimist counsels manual labour for all. The pessimist believes that forgetfulness and nothingness is the whole of man. He says, 'I defy the wisest of you to tell me why I am here, and being here, what good is gained by my assisting to bring others here.' The pessimist is therefore the gay Johnny, and the optimist is the melancholy Johnny. The former drinks champagne and takes his 'tart' out to dinner, the latter says that life is not intended to be happy in—that there is plenty of time to rest when you are dead."

John laughed loudly; but a moment after, reassuming his look of admonition, he asked Mike to tell him about his poem.

"The subject is astonishingly beautiful," said Mike; "I only speak of the subject; no one, not even Victor Hugo or Shelley, ever conceived a finer theme. But they had execution, I have only the idea. I suppose the world to have ended; but ended, how? Man has at last recognized that life is in equal parts, misery and abomination, and has resolved that it shall cease. The tide of passion has again risen, and lashed by repression to tenfold fury, the shores of life have again been strewn with new victims; but knowledge—calm, will-less knowledge—has gradually invaded all hearts, and that the restless, shifting sea (which is passion) shrinks to its furthest limits.

" There have been Messiahs, there have been per-
secutions, but the Word has been preached uninter-
mittently. Crowds have gathered to listen to the
wild-eyed prophets. You see them on the desert
promontories, preaching that human life must cease ;
they call it a disgraceful episode in the life of one of
the meanest of the planets—you see them hunted and
tortured as were their ancestors, the Christians of the
reign of Diocletian. You see them entering cottage
doors and making converts in humble homes. The
world, grown tired of vain misery, accepts oblivion.

" The rage and the seething of the sea is the image
I select to represent the struggle for life. The
dawn is my image for the diffusion and triumph of
sufficient reason. In a couple of hundred lines I
have set my scene, and I begin. It is in the plains
of Normandy ; of countless millions only two friends
remain. One of them is dying. As the stars recede
he stretches his hand to his companion, breathes
once more, looking him in the face, joyous in the
attainment of final rest. A hole is scraped, and the
last burial is achieved. Then the man, a young beautiful man with the pallor of long vigils and spiritual
combat upon his face, arises.

" The scene echoes strangely the asceticism that
produced it. Rose-garden and vineyard are gone ;
there are no fields, nor hedgerows, nor gables seen
picturesquely on a sky, human with smoke mildly
ascending. A broken wall that a great elm tears and
rends, startles the silence ; apple-orchards spread no
flowery snow, and the familiar thrushes have deserted
the moss-grown trees, in other times their trees ; and
the virgin forest ceases only to make bleak place for
marish plains with lonely pools and stagnating
streams, where perchance a heron rises on blue and
heavy wings.

" All the beautiful colours the world had worn when she was man's mistress are gone, and now, as if mourning for her lover and lord, she is clad only in sombre raiment. Since her lord departed she bears but scanty fruit, and since her lover left her, she that was glad has grown morose; her joy seems to have died with his; and the feeling of gloom is heightened, when at the sound of the man's footsteps a pack of wild dogs escape from a ruin, where they have been sleeping, and wake the forest with lugubrious yelps and barks. About the dismantled porches no single rose—the survival of roses planted by some fair woman's hand—remain to tell that man was once there—worked there for his daily bread, seeking a goodness and truth in life which was not his lot to attain.

" There are few open spaces, and the man has to follow the tracks of animals. Sometimes he comes upon a herd of horses feeding in a glade ; they turn and look upon him in a round-eyed surprise, and he sees them galloping on the hilsides, their manes and tails floating in the wind.

" Paris is covered with brushwood, and trees and wood from the shore have torn away the bridges, of which only a few fragments remain. Dim and desolate are those marshes now in the twilight shedding.

" The river swirls through multitudinous ruins, lighted by a crescent moon ; clouds hurry and gather and bear away the day. The man stands like a saint of old, who, on the last verge of the desert, turns and smiles upon the world he conquered.

" The great night collects and advances in shadow ; and wandering vapour, taking fire in the darkness, rolls, tumbling over and over like fiery serpents through loneliness and reeds.

" But in the eternal sunshine of the South flowers

have not become extinct; winds have carried seeds hither and thither, and the earth has waxed lovely, and the calm of the spiritual evenings of the Adriatic descend upon eternal perfume and the songs of birds. Symbol of pain or joy there is none, and the august silence is undisturbed by tears. From rotting hangings in Venice rats run, and that idle wave of palace-stairs laps in listless leisure the fallen glories of Veronese. As it is with painters so it is with poets, and wolf-cubs tear the pages of the last *Divine Comedy* in the world. Rome is his great agony, her shameful history falls before his eyes like a painted curtain. All the inner nature of life is revealed to him, and he sees into the heart of things as did Christ in the Garden of Gethsemane—Christ, that most perfect symbol of the denial of the will to live; and, like Christ, he cries that the world may pass from him.

" But in resignation, hatred and horror vanish, and he muses again on the more than human redemption, the great atonement that man has made for his shameful life's history; and standing amid the orange and almond trees, amid a profusion of bloom that the world seems to have brought for thank-offering, amid an apparent and glorious victory of inanimate nature, he falls down in worship of his race that had freely surrendered all, knowing it to be nothing, and in surrender had gained all.

" In that moment of intense consciousness a cry breaks the stillness, and searching among the marbles he finds a dying woman. Gathering some fruit, he gives her to eat, and they walk together, she considering him as saviour and lord, he wrapped in the contemplation of the end. They are the end, and all paling fascination, which is the world, is passing from them, and they are passing from it. And the splendour of gold and red ascends and spreads—crown and raiment of a world that has regained its primal beauty.

" ' We are alone. The woman says the world is ours ; we are as king and queen, and greater than any king or queen.'

" Her dark olive skin changes about the neck like a fruit near to ripen, and the large arms, curving deeply, fall from the shoulder in superb indolences of movement, and the hair, varying from burnt up black to blue, curls like a fleece adown the shoulders. She is large and strong, a fitting mother of man, supple in the joints as the young panther that has just bounded into the thickets ; and her rich almond eyes, dark, and moon-like in their depth of mystery, are fixed on him. Then he awakes to the danger of the enchantment ; but she pleads that they, the last of mankind, may remain watching over each other till the end ; and seeing his eyes flash, her heart rejoices. And out of the glare of the moon they passed beneath the sycamores. And listening to the fierce tune of the nightingales in the dusky daylight there, temptation hisses like a serpent ; and the woman listens, and drawing herself about the man, she says—

" ' The world is ours ; let us make it ours for ever ; let us give birth to a new race more great and beautiful than that which is dead. Love me, for I am love ; all the dead beauties of the race are incarnate in me. I am the type and epitome of all. Was the Venus we saw yesterday among the myrtles more lovely than I ? '

" But he casts her from him, asking in despair (for he loves her) if they are to renew the misery and abomination which it required all the courage and all the wisdom of all the ages to subdue ? He calls names from love's most fearful chronicle—Cleopatra, Faustina, Borgia. A little while and man's shameful life will no longer disturb the silence of the heavens. But no perception of life's shame touches the heart of the woman. 'I am love,' she cries again. 'Take me, and make me the mother of men. In me is incarnate all the love songs of the world. I am Beatrice; I am Juliet. I shall be all love to you— Fair Rosamond and Queen Eleanor. I am the rose! I am the nightingale!'

"She follows him in all depths of the forests where-. ever he may go. In the white morning he finds her kneeling by him, and in blue and rose evening he sees her whiteness crouching in the brake. He has fled to a last retreat in the hills where he thought she could not follow, and after a long day of travel lies down. But she comes upon him in his first sleep, and with amorous arms uplifted, and hair shed to the knee, throws herself upon him. It is in the soft and sensual scent of the honeysuckle. The bright lips strive, and for an instant his soul turns sick with famine for the face; but only for an instant, and in a supreme revulsion of feeling he beseeches her, crying that the world may not end as it began, in blood. But she heeds him not, and to save the generations he dashes her on the rocks.

"Man began in bloodshed, in bloodshed he has ended.

"Standing against the last tinge of purple, he gazes for a last time upon the magnificence of a virgin world, seeing the tawny forms of lions in the shadows, watching them drinking at the stream."

"Adam and Eve at the end of the world," said Drake. "A very pretty subject; but I distinctly object to an Eve with black hair. Eve and golden hair have ever been considered inseparable things."

"That's true," said Platt ; "the moment my missis went wrong her hair turned yellow."

Mike joined in the jocularity, but at the first pause he asked Escott what he thought of his poem.

"I have only one fault to find. Does not the *dénouement* seem too violent ? Would it not be better if the man were to succeed in escaping from her, and then vexed with scruples to return and find her dead ? What splendid lamentations over the body of the last woman !—and as the man wanders beneath the waxing and waning moon he hears nature lamenting the last woman. Mountains, rocks, forests, speak to him only of her."

"Yes, that would do . . . But no—what am I saying? Such a conclusion would be in exact contradiction to the philosophy of my poem. For it is man's natural and inveterate stupidity (Schopenhauer calls it Will), that forces man to live and continue his species. Reason is the opposing force. As time goes on reason becomes more and more complete, until at last it turns upon the will and denies it, like the scorpion, which, if surrounded by a ring of fire, will turn and sting itself to death. Were the man to escape, and returning find the woman dead, it would not be reason but accident which put an end to this ridiculous world."

Seeing that attention was withdrawn from him, Drake filled his pockets with cigarettes, split a soda with Platt, and seized upon the entrance of half-a-dozen young men as an excuse for ceasing to write paragraphs. Although it had only struck six they were all in evening dress. They were under thirty, and in them elegance and dissipation were equally evident. Lord Muchross, a clean-shaven Johnnie, walked at the head of the gang, assuming by virtue of his greater volubility a sort of headship. Dicky, the driver, a stout commoner, spoke of drink; and a languid blond, Lord Snowdown, leaned against the chimney-piece displaying a thin figure. The others took seats and laughed whenever Lord Muchross spoke.

"Here we are, old chappie, just in time to drink to the health of the number. Ha, ha, ha! What damned libel have you in this week? Ha, ha!"

"Awful bad head, a heavy day yesterday," said Dicky—"drunk blind."

"Had to put him in a wheelbarrow, wheeled him into a greengrocer's shop, put a carrot in his mouth, and rang the bell," shouted Muchross.

"Ha, ha, ha!" shouted the others.

"Had a rippin' day all the same, didn't we, old Dicky? Went up the river in Snowdown's launch. Had lunch by Tag's Island, went as far as Datchet. There we met Dicky; he tooted us round by Staines. There we got in a fresh team, galloped all the way to Houndslow. Laura brought her sister. Kitty was with us. Made us die with a story she told us of a fellow she was spoony on. Had to put him under the bed . . . Ghastly joke, dear boy; the other fellow remained till two o'clock next day."

Amid roars of laughter Dicky's voice was heard—

"She calls him Love's martyr; he nearly died of bronchitis, and became a priest. Kitty swears she'll go to confession to him one of these days."

"By Jove, if she does I'll publish it in the *Pilgrim.*"

"Too late this week," Mike said to Frank.

"We got to town by half-past six, went round to the Cri. to have a sherry-and-bitters, dined at the Royal, went on to the Pav., and on with all the girls in hansoms, four in each, to Snowdown's."

"See me dance the polka, dear boy," cried the

languid lord, awaking suddenly from his indolence, and as he pranced across the room most of his drink went over Drake's neck; and amid oaths and laughter Escott besought of the revellers to retire.

" We are still four columns short, we must get on." And for an hour and a half the scratching of the pens was only interrupted by the striking of a match and an occasional damn. At six they adjourned to the office. They walked along the Strand swinging their sticks, full of consciousness of a day's work done. Drake and Platt, who had avenged some private wrongs in their paragraphs, were disturbed by the fear of libel; Harding gnawed the end of his moustache, and reconsidered his attack on a contemporary writer, pointing his gibes afresh.

They trooped up-stairs, the door was thrown open. It was a small office, and at the end of the partitioned space a clerk sat in front of a ledger on a high stool, his face against the window. Lounging on the counter, turning over the leaves of back numbers, they discussed the advertisements. They stood up when Lady Helen entered.[1] She had come to speak to Frank about a poem, and she only paused in her rapid visit to shake hands with Harding, and she asked Mike if his poems would be published that season.

The contributors to the *Pilgrim* dined together on Wednesday, and spent four shillings a head in an old English tavern, where unlimited joint and vegetables could be obtained for half-a-crown. The old-fashioned boxes into which the guests edged themselves had not been removed, and about the mahogany bar, placed in the passage in front of the proprietress's parlour, two dingy barmaids served actors from the

---

[1] See *A Modern Lover.*

adjoining theatre with whisky-and-water. The contributors to the *Pilgrim* had selected a box, and were clamouring for food. Smacking his lips, the head-waiter, an antiquity who cashed cheques and told stories about Mr. Dickens and Mr. Thackeray, stopped in front of this table.

"Roast beef, very nice—a nice cut, sir; saddle of mutton just up."

All decided for saddle of mutton.

"Saddle of mutton, number three."

Greasy and white the carver came, and as if the meat were a delight the carver sliced it out. Some one remarked this.

"That is nothing," said Thompson; you should hear Hopkins grunting as he cuts the venison on Tuesdays and Fridays, and how he sucks his lips as he ladles out the gravy. We only enjoy a slice or two, whereas his pleasure ends only with the haunch."

The evening newspapers were caught up, glanced at, and abused as worthless rags, and the editors covered with lively ridicule.

The conversation turned on Boulogne, where Mike had loved many solicitors' wives, and then on the impurity of the society girl and the prurient purity of her creation—the "English" novel.

"I believe that it is so," said Harding; "and in her immorality we find the reason for all this bewildering outcry against the slightest licence in literature. Strange that in a manifestly impure age there should be a national tendency towards chaste literature. I am not sure that a moral literature does not of necessity imply much laxity in practical morality. We seek in art what we do not find in ourselves, and it would be true to nature to represent an unfortunate woman delighting in reading of such purity as her own life daily insulted and contradicted; and the novel is the rag in which this leper age coquettes before the mirror of its hypocrisy, rehearsing the deception it would practise on future time."

"You must consider the influence of impure literature upon young people," said John.

"No, no; the influence of a book is nothing; it is life that influences and corrupts. I sent my story of a drunken woman to Randall, and the next time I heard from him he wrote to say he had married his mistress, and he knew she was a drunkard."

"It is easy to prove that bad books don't do any harm; if they did, by the same rule good books would do good, and the world would have been converted long ago," said Frank.

Harding thought how he might best appropriate the epigram, and when the influence of the liberty lately acquired by girls had been discussed—the right to go out shopping in the morning, to sit out dances on dark stairs; in a word, the decadence and overthrow of the chaperon, the conversation again turned on art.

"It is very difficult," said Harding, "to be great as the old masters were great. A man is great when every one is great. In the great ages if you were not great you did not exist at all, but in these days everything conspires to support the weak."

Out of deference to John, who had worn for some time a very solid look of disapproval, Mike ceased to discourse on half hours passed on staircases, and in summer-houses when the gardener had gone to dinner, and he spoke about naturalistic novels and an exhibition of pastels.

"As time goes on, poetry, history, philosophy, will so multiply that the day will come when the learned will not even know the names of their predecessors. There is nothing that will not increase out of all reckoning except the naturalistic novel. A man may write twenty volumes of poetry, history, and philosophy. But the naturalistic novel is the essence of a phase of life that the writer has lived in and assimilated. If you take into consideration the difficulty of observing twice, of the time an experience takes to ripen in you, you will easily understand *à priori* that the man will never be born who will write three."

Coffee and cigars were ordered, and Harding extolled the charm and grace of pastels.

Thompson said—" I keep pastels for my hours of idleness—cowardly hours, when I have no heart to struggle with nature, and may but smile and kiss my hand to her at a distance. For dreaming I know nothing like pastel; it is the painter's opium pipe. . . . Latour was the greatest pastellist of the eighteenth century, and he never attempted more than a drawing heightened with colour. But how suggestive, how elegant, how well-bred !"

Then in reply to some flattery on the personality of his art, Thompson said, " It is strange, for I assure you no art was ever less spontaneous than mine. What I do is the result of reflection and study of the great masters; of inspiration, spontaneity, temperament—temperament is the word—I know nothing. When I hear people talk about temperament, it always seems to me like the strong man in the fair, who straddles his legs, and asks some one to step upon the palm of his hand."

Drake joined in the discussion, and the chatter that came from this enormous man was as small as his head, which sat like a pin's-head above his shoulders. Platt drifted from the obscene into the incomprehensible. The room was fast emptying, and the waiter loitered, waiting to be paid.

"We must be getting off," said Mike, "it is nearly eleven o'clock, and we have still the best part of the paper to read through."

"Don't be in such a damned hurry," said Frank, authoritatively.

Harding bade them good-night at the door, and the editors walked down Fleet Street. To pass up a rickety court to the printer's, or to go through the stage-door to the stage, produced similar sensations in Mike. The white-washed wall, the glare of the raw gas, the low monotonous voice of the reading-boy, like one studying a part, or perhaps like the murmur of the distant audience ; the boy coming in asking for "copy" or proof, like the call-boy, with his "curtain's going up, gentlemen." Is there not analogy between the preparation of the paper that will be before the public in the morning, and the preparation of the play that will be before its eyes in the evening?

From the glass closet where they waited for the "pages," they could see the compositors bending over the forms. The light lay upon a red beard, a freckled neck, the crimson of the volutes of an ear.

In the glass closet there were three wooden chairs, a table, and an ink-stand ; on the shelf by the door a few books—the *London Directory*, an *English Diction-ary*, a *French Dictionary*—the titles of the remaining books did not catch the eye. As they waited, for no "pages" would be ready for them for some time, Mike glanced at stray numbers of two trade journals. It seemed to him strange that the same compositors who set up these papers should set up the *Pilgrim*.

Presently the "pages" began to come in, but long delays intervened, and it transpired that some of the "copy" was not yet in type. Frank grew weary, and he complained of headache, and asked Mike to see the paper through for him. Mike thought Frank selfish, but there was no help for it. He could not refuse, but must wait in the paraffin-like smell of the ink, listening to the droning voice of the reading-boy. If he could only get the proof of his poem he could kill time by correcting it; but it could not be obtained. Two hours passed, and he still sat watching the red beard of a compositor, and the crimson volutes of an ear. At last the printer's devil, his short sleeves rolled up, brought in a couple of pages. Mike read, following the lines with his pen, correcting the literals, and he cursed when the "devil" told him that ten more lines of copy were wanting to complete page nine. What should he write?

About two o'clock, holding her ball-skirts out of the dirt, a lady entered.

"How do you do, Emily?" said Mike. "Just fancy seeing you here, and at this hour!" He was glad of the interruption; but his pleasure was dashed by the fear that she would ask him to come home with her.

"Oh, I have had such a pleasant party; So-and-so sang at Lady Southey's. Oh, I have enjoyed myself! I knew I should find you here; but I am interrupting. I will go." She put her arm round his neck. He looked at her diamonds, and congratulated himself that she was a lady.

"I am afraid I am interrupting you," she said again.

"Oh no, you aren't, I shall be done in half-an-hour; I have only got a few more pages to read through, Escott went away, selfish brute that he is, and has left me to do all the work."

She sat by his side contentedly reading what he

had written. At half-past two all the pages were passed for press, and they descended the spiral iron staircase, through the grease and vinegar smell of the ink, in view of heads and arms of a hundred compositors, in hearing of the drowsy murmur of the reading-boy. Her brougham was at the door. As she stepped in Mike screwed up his courage and said good-bye.

" Won't you come?" she said, with disappointment in her eyes.

" No, not to-night. I have been slaving at that paper for the last four hours. Thanks; not to-night. Good-bye; I'll see you next week."

The brougham rolled away, and Mike walked home. The hands of the clocks were stretching towards three, and only a few drink-disfigured creatures of thirty-five or forty lingered; so horrible were they that he did not answer their salutations.

CHAPTER IV.

MIKE was in his bath when Frank entered.

" What, not dressed yet?"

" All very well for you to talk. You left me at eleven to get the paper out as best I could. I did not get away from the printer's before half-past two."

" I'm very sorry, but you've no idea how ill I felt. I really couldn't have stayed on. I heard you come in. You weren't alone."

The room was pleasant with the Eau de Lubin, and Mike's beautiful figure appealed to Frank's artistic sense; and he noticed it in relation to the twisted oak columns of the bed. The body, it was smooth and white as marble ; and the pectoral muscles were especially beautiful when he leaned forward to wipe a lifted leg.   He turned, and the back narrowed like a leaf, and expanded in shapes as subtle.   He was really a superb animal as he stepped out of his bath.

"I wish to heavens you'd dress.   Leave off messing yourself about.   I want breakfast.   Lizzie's waiting.   What are you putting on those clothes for? Where are you going ?"

"I am going to see Lily Young.   She wrote to me this morning saying she had her mother's permission to ask me to come."

"She won't like you any better for all that scent and washing."

"Which of these neckties do you like ?"

"I don't know. . . . I wish you'd be quick.   Come on !"

As he fixed his tie with a pearl pin he whistled the 'Wedding March.'   Catching Frank's eyes he laughed and sang at the top of his voice as he went down the passage.

Lizzie was reading in one of the arm-chairs that stood by the high chimney-piece tall with tiles and blue vases.   The stiffness and glare of the red cloth in which the room was furnished, contrasted with the soft colour of the tapestry which covered one wall. The round table shone with silver, and an agreeable smell of coffee and sausages pervaded the room. Lizzie looked up astonished ; but without giving her time to ask questions, Mike seized her and rushed her up and down.

"Let me go ! let me go !" she exclaimed.   "Are you mad ?"

Frank caught up his fiddle.   At last Lizzie wrenched herself from Mike.

"What do you mean? . . . Such nonsense!"

Laughing, Mike placed her in a chair, and uncovering a dish, said—

"What shall I give you this happy day?"

"What do you mean? I don't like being pulled about."

"You know what tune that is? That's the 'Wedding March.'"

"Who's going to be married? Not you."

"I don't know so much about that. At all events I am in love. The sensation is delicious—like an ice, or a glass of Chartreuse. Real love—all the others were coarse passions—I feel it here, the genuine article. You would not believe that I could fall in love."

"Listen to me," said Lizzie. "You wouldn't talk like that if you were in love."

"I always talk; it relieves me. You have no idea how nice she is; so frail, so white—a white blonde, a Seraphita. But you haven't read Balzac; you do not know those white women of the north. '*Plus blanche que la blanche hermine*,' etc. So pure is she that I cannot think of kissing her without sensations of sacrilege. My lips are not pure enough for hers. I would I were chaste. I never was chaste."

Mike laughed and chattered of everything. Words came from him like flour from a mill.

The *Pilgrim* was published on Wednesday. Wednesday was the day, therefore, for walking in the Park; for lunching out; for driving in hansoms. Like a fish on the crest of a wave he surveyed London—multitudinous London, circulating about him; and he smiled with pleasure when he caught sight of trees spreading their summer green upon the curling whiteness of the clouds. He loved the Park. The Park had always been his friend; it had given

him society when no door was open to him ; it had
been the inspiration of all his ambitions ; it was the
Park that had first showed him ladies and gentlemen
in all the gaud and charm of town leisure. There he
had seen for the first time the panorama of slanting
sunshades, patent leather shoes, horses cantering in
the dusty sunlight, or proudly grouped, the riders
flicking the flies away with gold-headed whips. He
loved the androgynous attire of the horsewomen—
collars, silk hats, and cravats. The Park appealed to
him intensely and strangely as nothing else did. He
loved the Park for the great pasture it afforded to his
vanity. It was in the Park he saw the fashionable
procuress driving—she who would not allow him to
pay even for champagne in her house; it was in the
Park he met the little actress who looked so beseech-
ingly in his face ; it was in the Park he met fashionable
ladies who asked him to dinner and took him to the
theatre ; it was in the Park he had found life and
fortune, and, saturated with happiness, with health,
tingling with consciousness of his happiness, Mike
passed among the various crowd, which in its listless-
ness seemed to balance and air itself like a many-
petalled flower. But much as the crowd amused
and pleased him, he was more amused and pleased
with the present vision of his own personality,
which in a long train of images and stories passed
within him. He loved to dream of himself ; in
dreams he entered his soul like a temple, seeing himself in various environment, and acting in manifold
circumstances.

" Here am I—a poor boy from the bogs of Ireland—
poor people (the reflection was an unpleasant one,
and he escaped from it); at all events a poor boy
without money or friends. I have made myself what
I am. . . . I get the best of everything—women,

eating, clothes; I live in beautiful rooms surrounded with pretty things. True, they are not mine, but what does that matter?—I haven't the bother of looking after them. . . . If I could only get rid of that cursed accent, but I haven't much; Escott has nearly as much, and he was brought up at an English school. How pleasant it is to have money! Heigho! How pleasant it is to have money! Six pounds a week from the paper, and I could make easily another four if I choose. Sometimes I don't get any presents; women seem as if they were going to chuck it up, and then they send all things—money, jewelry, and comestables. I am sure it was Ida who sent that hundred pounds. What should I do if it ever came out? But there's nothing to come out. I believe I am suspected, but nothing can be proved against me.

"Why do they love me? I always treat them badly. Often I don't even pretend to love them, but it makes no difference. Pious women, wicked women, stupid women, clever women, high-class women, low-class women, it is all the same—all love me. That little girl I picked up in the Strand liked me before she had been talking to me five minutes. And what sudden fancies! I come into a room, and every feminine eye fills with sudden appetite. I wonder what it is. My nose is broken, and my chin sticks out like a handle. And men like me just as much as women do. It is inexplicable. True, I never say disagreeable things; and it is so natural to me to wheedle. I twist myself about them like a twining plant about a window. Women forgive me everything, and are glad to see me after years. But they are never wildly jealous. Perhaps I have never been really loved. . . . I don't know though—Lady Seely loved me. There was an old lady at Margate, sixty if she was a day (of course there was nothing improper), and she worshipped me. How nicely she used to smile when she said, 'Come round here that I may look at you!'—and her husband was quite as bad; he'd run all over the place after me. So-and-so was quite offended because I didn't rush to see him; he'd put me up for six months. . . Servants hate Frank; for me they'd do anything. I never was in a lodging-house in my life that the slavey didn't fall in love with me. People dislike me; I speak to them for five minutes, and henceforth they run after me. I make friends everywhere.

"Those Americans wanted me to come and stay six months with them in New York. How she did press me to come! . . . The Brookes, they want me to come and stay in the country with them; they'd give me horses to ride, guns to shoot, and I'd get the girls besides. They looked rather greedily at me just now. How jealous poor old Emily is of them! She says, 'I'd go to the end of the earth for them'—and would not raise a little finger for her. Dear old Emily, she wasn't a bit cross the other night when I wouldn't go home with her. I must go and see her. She says she loved me—really loved me! . . . She used to lie and dream of pulling me out of burning houses. I wonder why I am liked! How intangible, and yet how real! What a wonderful character I would make in a novel!"

At that moment he saw Mrs. Byril in the crowd; but notwithstanding his kind thoughts of her, he prayed she might pass without seeing him. Perceiving Lady Helen walking with her husband and Harding, he followed her slim figure with his eyes, remembering what Seymour's good looks had brought him, for he envied all love, desiring to be himself all that women desire. Then his thoughts wandered. The decoration

of the Park absorbed him—the nobility of a group
of horses, the attractiveness of some dresses; and
amid all this elegance and parade he dreamed of
tragedy—of some queen blowing her brains out for
him—and he saw the fashionable dress and the blood
oozing from the temple, trickling slowly through the
sand. Then Lords Muchross and Snowdown passed,
and they passed without acknowledging him!

"Cads, cads, damn them!" His face changed expression. "I may rise to any height, queens may fall
down and worship me, but I may never undo my
birth. Not to have been born a gentleman! That is to
say, of a long line—a family with a history. Not to be
able to whisper, 'I may lose everything, all troubles
may be mine, but the fact remains that I was born
a gentleman!' Those two men who cut me are lords.
What a delight in one's life to have a name all to
one's self!" And then Mike lost himself in a maze of
little dreams. A gleam of mail; escutcheons and
castles; a hawk flew from fingers fair; a lady clasped
her hands when the lances shivered in the tourney;
and Mike was the hero that persisted in the course
of this shifting little dream.

The Brookes—Sally and Maggie—stopped to speak
to him, and he went to lunch with them. His interest
in all they did and said was unbounded, and that he
might not be able to reproach himself with waste of
time, he contrived by hint and allusion to lay the
foundation for a future intrigue with one of the
girls.

Lily Young, however, had never been forgotten;
she had been as constantly present in his mind as
this sense of the sunshine and his own happy condition. She had been parcel of and one with these;
but now, as he drove to see her, he separated her

from the morning phenomena of his life, and began to think definitely of her.

Smiling, he called himself a brute, and regretted his failure. But in her presence his cynicism was evanescent. She sat on a little sofa, covered with an Indian shawl; behind her was a great bronze, the celebrated gift of a celebrated Rajah to her mother. Mrs. Young had been on a tour in the East with her husband, and ever since her house had been frequented by decrepit old gentlemen interested in Arabi, and other matters which they spoke of as Eastern questions. Lily wore a gray dress, and once as she crossed them he saw her slim legs.

Lily looked at Mike under her eyes as she passed across the room to get him some tea, and they talked a little while. Then some three or four great and very elderly historians entered, and she had to leave him; and feeling he could not prolong his visit he went, conscious of sensations of purity and some desire of goodness, if not for itself, for the grace that goodness brings. He paid many visits in this house, but conversations with learned Buddhists seemed the only result; a *tête-à-tête* with Lily seemed impossible. To his surprise he never met her in society, and his heart beat fast when one evening he heard she was expected; and for the first time forgetful of the multitude, and nervous as a school-boy in search of his first love, he sought her in the crowd. He feared to remain with her, and it seemed to him he had accomplished much in asking her to come down to supper. When talking to others his thoughts were with her, and his eyes followed her. An inquisitive woman noted his agitation, and suspecting the cause said, "I see, I see, and I think something may come of it." Even when Lily left he did not recover his ordinary humour, and about two in the morning, in sullen weariness and disappointment, he offered to drive Lady Helen home.

Should he make love to her? He had often wished to. Here was an opportunity.

"You did not see that I was looking at you to-night; you did not guess what I was thinking of."

"Yes, I did; you were looking at and thinking of my arms."

Should he pass his arm round her? Lady Helen knew Lily, and might tell; he did not dare it, and instead, spoke of her contributions to the paper. Then the conversation branched into a description of the Wednesday night festivities in Temple Gardens—the shouting and cheering of the lords, the comic vocalists, the inimitable Arthur, the extraordinary Bessie. He told, with fits of laughter, of Muchross's stump speeches, and how he had once got on the supper-table and sat down in the very centre, regardless of plates and dishes. Mike and Lady Helen nearly died of laughter when he related how on one occasion Muchross and Snowdown, both crying drunk, had called in a couple of sweeps. "You see," he said, "the look of amazement on their faces, and the black 'uns were forced into two chairs, and were waited upon by the lords, who tucked their napkins under their arms."

"Oh don't, oh don't!" said Lady Helen, leaning back exhausted.

But Mike went on, though he was hardly able to speak, and told how Muchross and Snowdown had danced the can-can, kicking at the chandelier from time to time, the sweeps keeping time with their implements on the sideboard; the revel finishing up with a wrestling match, Muchross taking the big sweep, and Snowdown the little one.

"You should have seen them rolling over under the

dining-room table ; I shall never forget Snowdown's shirt."

" I should like to see one of these entertainments. Do you ever have a ladies' night ? If you do, and the ladies are not supposed to wrestle with the laundresses in the early light, I should like to come."

" Oh, yes, do come ; Frank will be delighted. I'll see that things are kept within bounds." The conversation fell, and he regretted he must forego this very excellent opportunity to make love to her.

Next day, changed in his humour, but still thinking of Lily, he went to see Mrs. Byril, and he stopped a few days with her. He was always strict in his own room, and if Emily sought him in the morning he reprimanded her.

She was one of those women who, having much heart, must affect more ; a weak intelligent woman, honest and loyal—one who could not live without a lover. And with her arms about his neck, she listened to his amours, and learnt his poetry by heart. Mike was her folly, and she would never have thought of another if, as she said, he had only behaved decently to her. "I am sorry, darling, I told you anything about it, but when I got your beastly letter I wrote to him. Tell me you'll come and stay with me next month, and I'll put him off. . . . I hate this new girl ; I am jealous because she may influence you, but for the others—the Brookes and their friends—the half-hours spent in summer-houses when the gardener is at dinner, I care not one jot." So she spoke as she lay upon his knees in the black satin arm-chair in the drawing-room.

But her presence at breakfast—that invasion of the morning hours—was irritating ; he hated the request to be in to lunch, and the duty of spending the evening in her drawing-room, instead of in club or bar-room. He desired freedom to spend each minute as the caprice of the moment prompted. Were he a rich man he would not have lived with Frank; to live with a man was unpleasant; to live with a woman was intolerable. In the morning he must be alone to dream of a book or poem; in the afternoons, about four, he was glad to æstheticize with Harding or Thompson, or abandon himself to the charm of John's aspirations.

John and he were often seen walking together, and they delighted in the Temple. The Temple is escapement from the omniscient domesticity which is so natural to England; and both were impressionable to its morning animation—the young men hurrying through the courts and cloisters, the picturesqueness of a wig and gown passing up a flight of steps. It seemed that the old hall, the buttresses and towers, the queer tunnels leading from court to court, turned the edge of the commonplace of life. Nor did the Temple ever lose for them its quaint and primitive air, and as they strolled about the cloisters talking of art or literature, they experienced a delight that cannot be quite put into words; and were strangely glad as they opened the iron gates, and looked on all the many brick entanglements with the tall trees rising, spreading the delicate youth of leaves upon the weary red of the tiles and the dim tones of the dear walls.

> " A gentel Manciple there was of the Temple
> Of whom achatours mighten take ensample
> For to ben wise in bying of vitaille."

The gentle shade of linden trees, the drip of the fountain, the monumented corner where Goldsmith rests, awake even in the most casual and prosaic a fleeting touch of romance. And the wide steps with balustrades sweeping down in many turnings to the gardens, cause vagrant and hurrying steps to pause, and wander about the library and through the gardens, which lead with such charm of way to the open spaces of the King's Bench walk.

There, there is another dining-hall and another library. The clock is ringing out the hour, and the place is filled with young men in office clothes, hurrying on various business with papers in their hands ; and such young male life is one of the charms of the Temple ; and the absence of women is refreshment to the eye wearied of their numbers in the streets. The Temple is an island in the London sea. Immediately you pass the great doorway, studded with great nails, you pass out of the garishness of the merely modern day, unhallowed by any associations, into a calmer and benigner day, over which floats some shadow of the great past. The old staircases lighted by strange lanterns, the river of lingering current, bearing in its winding so much of London into one enchanted view. The church built by the Templars more than seven hundred years ago, now stands in the centre of the inn all surrounded, on one side yellowing smoke-dried cloisters, on another side various closes, feebly striving in their architecture not to seem too shamefully out of keeping with its beauty. There it stands in all the beauty of its pointed arches and triple lancet windows, as when it was consecrated by the patriarch of Jerusalem in the year 1185.

But in 1307 a great ecclesiastical tribunal was held in London, and it was proved that an unfortunate knight, who had refused to spit upon the cross, was haled from the dining-hall and drowned in a well, and testimony of the secret rites that were held there, and in which a certain black idol was worshipped, was forthcoming. The Grand Master was burnt at the stake, the knights were thrown into prison, and their property was confiscated. Then the forfeited estate of the Temple, presenting ready access by water, at once struck the advocates of the Court of Common Pleas at Westminster, and the students who were candidates for the privilege of pleading therein, as a most desirable retreat, and interest was made with the Earl of Lancaster, the king's first cousin, who had claimed the forfeited property of the monks by escheat, as the immediate lord of the fee, for a lodging in the Temple, and they first gained a footing there as his lessees.

Above all, the church with its round tower-like roof was very dear to Mike and John, and they often spoke of the splendid spectacle of the religious warriors marching in procession, their white tunics with red crosses, their black and white banner called Beauseant. It is seen on the circular panels of the vaulting of the side aisles, and on either side the letters BEAUSEANT. There stands the church of the proud Templars, a round tower-like church, fitting symbol of· those soldier monks, at the west end of a square church, the square church engrafted upon the circular so as to form one beautiful fabric. The young men lingered around the timeworn porch, lovely with foliated columns, strange with figures in prayer, and figures holding scrolls. And often without formulating their intentions in words they entered the church. Beneath the groined ribs of the circular tower lie the mail-clad effigies of the knights, and through beautiful gracefulness of grouped pillars the painted panes shed bright glow upon the tessellated pavement. The young men passed beneath the pointed arches and waited, their eyes raised to the celestial blueness of the thirteenth century window, and then in silence stole back whither the knights sleep so grimly, with hands clasped on their breasts and their long swords.

And seeing himself in those times, clad in armour, a knight templar walking in procession in that very church, John recited a verse of Tennyson's *Sir Galahad*—

> " Sometimes on lonely mountain meres
>   I find a magic bark ;
>   I leap on board ; no helmsman steers :
>   I float till all is dark.
>
> " A gentle sound, an awful light !
>   Three angels bear the holy Grail ;
>   With folded feet, in stoles of white,
>   On sleeping wings they sail.
>
> " Ah, blessed vision ! blood of God !
>   My spirit beats her mortal bars,
>   As down dark tides the glory slides,
>   And star-like mingles with the stars."

" Oh ! very beautiful. ' On sleeping wings they sail.' Say it again."

John repeated the stanza, his eyes fixed upon the knight.

Mike said—

" How different to-day the girls of the neighbourhood, their prayer-books and umbrellas ! Yet I don't think the anachronism displeases me."

" You say that to provoke me ; you cannot think that all the dirty little milliners' girls of the neighbourhood are more dignified than these Templars marching in procession and taking their places with iron clangour in the choir."

" So far as that is concerned," said Mike, who loved to " draw " John, " the little girls of the neighbourhood in all probability wash themselves a great deal oftener than the Templars ever did. And have you forgotten the accusations that were brought against them before the ecclesiastical tribunal assembled in London ? What about the black idol with shining eyes and gilded head ?"

" Their vices were at least less revolting than the disgustful meanness of to-day ; besides, nothing is really known about the reasons for the suppression of the Templars. Men who forswear women are open to all contumely. Oh! the world is wondrous, just wondrous well satisfied with its domestic ideals."

The conversation came to a pause, and then Mike spoke of Lily Young, and extolled her subtle beauty and intelligence.

" I never liked any one as I do her. I am ashamed of myself when I think of her purity."

" The purity of . . . Had she been pure she would have remained in her convent."

" If you had heard her speak of her temptations . . ."

" I do not want to hear her temptations. But it was you who tempted her to leave her convent. I cannot but think that you should marry her. There is nothing for you but marriage. You must change your life. Think of the constant sin you are living in."

" But I don't believe in sin."

With a gesture that declared a non-admission of such a state of soul, John hesitated, and then he said—

" The beastliness of it !"

" We have to live," said Mike, " since nature has so willed it, but I fully realize the knightliness of your revolt against the principle of life."

John continued his admonitions, and Mike an amused and appreciative listener.

" At all events, I wish you would promise not to indulge in improper conversation when I am present. It is dependent upon me to beg of you to oblige me in this. It will add greatly to your dignity to refrain ; but that is your concern ; I am thinking now only of myself. Will you promise me this ?"

" Yes, and more ; I will promise not to indulge in

such conversation, even when you are not present. It is, as you say, lowering. . . . I agree with you. I will strive to mend my ways."

And Mike was sincere; he was determined to become worthy of Lily. And now the best hours of his life—hours strangely tense and strangely personal—were passed in that Kensington drawing-room. She was to him like the light of a shrine; he might kneel and adore from afar, but he might not approach. The goddess had come to him like the moon to Endymion. He knew nothing, not even if he were welcome. Each visit was the same as the preceding. A sweet but exasperating changelessness reigned in that drawing-room—that pretty drawing-room where mother and daughter sat in sweet naturalness, removed from the grossness and meanness of life as he knew it. Neither illicit whispering nor affectation of reserve, only the charm of strict behaviour; unreal and strange was the refinement, material and mental, in which they lived. And for a time the charm sufficed; desire was at rest. But she had been to see him, however at variance such a visit, such event seemed with her present demeanour. And she must come again!

In increasing restlessness he conned all the narrow chances of meeting her, of speaking to her alone. But no accident varied the even tenor of their lives, the calm lake-like impassibility of their relations, and in last resort he urged Frank to give a dance or an At Home. And how ardently he pleaded, one afternoon, sitting face to face with mother and daughter. Inwardly agitated, but with outward calm, he impressed upon them many reasons for their being of the party. The charm of the Temple, the river, and glitter of light, the novel experience of bachelors' quarters. . . . They promised to come.

CHAPTER V.

MIKE leaned forward to tie his white cravat.   He was slight, and white and black, and he thought of Lily, of the exquisite pleasure of seeing her and lead-ing her away.   And he was pleased and surprised to find that his thoughts of her were pure.

The principal contributors to the *Pilgrim* had been invited, and a selection had been made from the fast and fashionable gang—those who could be trusted to become neither drunk nor disorderly.   It had been decided, but not without misgivings, to ask Muchross and Snowdown.

The doors were open, servants could be seen passing with glasses and bottles.   Frank, who had finished dressing, called from the drawing-room and begged Mike to hasten ; for the housemaid was waiting to arrange his room, for it had been decided that this room should serve as a lounge where dancers might sit between the waltzes.

" She can come in now," he shouted.   He folded the curtains of his strange bed ; he lighted a silver lamp, re-arranged his palms, and smiled, thinking of the astonished questions when he invited young ladies to be seated among the numerous cushions.   And Mike determined he would say that he considered his bed-room far too sacred to admit of any of the base wants of life being performed there.

It was well-dressed Bohemia, with many markings and varied with contrasting shades.   The air was as sugar about the doorway with the scent of gardenias ; young lords shrank from the weather-stained cloth of doubtful journalists, and a lady in long puce

Cashmere provoked a smile. Frank received his guests with laughter and epigram.

The emancipation of women is marked by the decline of the chaperon, and it was not clear under whose protection the young girls had come. Beneath double rows of ruche-rose feet passed, and the soft glow of lamps shaded with large leaves of pale glass bathed the women's flesh in endless half tints; the reflected light of copper shades flushed the blond hair on Lady Helen's neck to auroral fervencies.

In one group a fat man with white hair and faded blue eyes talked to Mrs. Bentham and Lewis Seymour. A visit to the Haymarket Theatre being arranged, he said—

" May I hope to be permitted to form one of the party ?"

Harding overheard the remark. He said, " It is difficult to believe, but I assure you that that Mr. Senbrook was one of the greatest Don Juans that ever lived.".

" We have in this room Don Juan in youth, middle age, and old age—Mike Fletcher, Lewis Seymour, and Mr. Senbrook."

" Did Seymour, that fellow with the wide hips, ever have success with women? How fat he has grown !"

" Rather;[1] don't you know his story? He came up to London with a few pounds. When we knew him first he was starving in Lambeth. You remember, Thompson, the day he stood us a lunch ? He had just taken a decorative panel to a picture-dealer's, for which he had received a few pounds, and he told us how he had met a lady (there's the lady, the woman with the white hair, Mrs. Bentham) in the picture-dealer's shop. She fell in love with him, and

---

[1] See *A Modern Lover.*

took him down to her country house to decorate it. She sent him to Paris to study, and it was said employed a dealer for years to buy his pictures."

" And he dropped her for Lady Helen?"

" Not exactly. Lady Helen dragged him away from her. He never seized or dropped anything."

" Then what explanation do you give of his success?" said a young barrister.

" His manner was always gentle and insinuating. Ladies found him pretty to look upon, and very soothing. Mike is just the same; but of course Seymour never had any of Mike's brilliancy or enthusiasm."

" Do you know anything of the old gentleman— Senbrook's his name?"

" I have heard that those watery eyes of his were once of entrancing violet hue, and I believe he was wildly enthusiastic in his love. His life has been closely connected with mine."

" I didn't know you knew him."

" I do not know him. Yet he poisoned my happiest years; he is the upas tree in whose shade I slept. When I was in Paris I loved a lady; and I used to make sacrifices for this lady, who was, needless to say, not worthy of them; but she had loved Senbrook in her earliest youth, and it appears when a woman has once loved Senbrook, she can love none other. You wouldn't think it, to look at him now, but I assure you it is so. France is filled with the women he once loved. The provincial towns are dotted with them. I know eight—eight exist to my personal knowledge. Sometimes a couple live together, united by the indissoluble fetter of a Senbrook betrayal. They know their lives are broken, and they are content that their lives should be broken. They have loved Senbrook, therefore there is nothing to do but retire to France. You may think I am joking, but I'm not. It is comic, but that is no reason why it shouldn't be true. And these ladies neither forget nor upbraid; and they will attack you like tigers if you dare say a word against him. This creation of faith is the certain sign of Don Juan! No matter how cruelly the real Don Juan behaves, the women he has deceived are ready to welcome him. After years they meet him in all forgetfulness of wrong. Examine history, and you will find that the love inspired by the real Don Juan ends only with death. Nor am I sure that the women attach much importance to his infidelities; they accept them, his infidelities being a consequential necessity of his being, the eons and the attributes of his godhead. Don Juan inspires no jealousy; Don Juan stabbed by an infuriated mistress is a psychological impossibility."

"I have heard that Seymour used to drive Lady Helen crazy with jealousy."

"Don Juan disappears at the church-door. He was her husband. The most unfaithful wife is wildly jealous of her husband."

A sudden silence fell, and a young girl was borne out fainting.

"Nothing more common than for young girls to faint when he is present. Go," said Harding, "and you will hear her calling his name." Then, picking up the thread of the paradox, he continued—"But you can't have Don Juan in this century, our civilization has wiped him out; not the vice of which he is representative—that is eternal—but the spectacle of adventure of which he is the hero. No more fascinating idea. Had the age admitted of Don Juan, I should have written out his soul long ago. I love the idea. With duelling and hose picturesqueness has gone out of life. The mantle and the rapier are essential; and angry words . . ."

" Are angry words picturesque ?"

" Angry words mean angry attitudes; and they are picturesque."

The young men smiled at the fascinating eloquence, and feeling an appreciative audience about him, Harding continued—

"See Mike Fletcher, know him, understand him, and imagine what he would have been in the eighteenth century, the glory of adventure he would have gathered. His life to-day is a mean parody upon an easily realizable might-have-been. So vital is the idea in him that his life to-day is the reflection of a life that burned in another age too ardently to die with death. In another age Mike would have outdone Casanova. Casanova !—what a magnificent Casanova he would have been! Casanova is to me the most fascinating of characters. He was everything—a frequenter of taverns and palaces, a necromancer. His audacity and unscrupulousness, his comedies, his immortal memoirs ! What was that delightful witty remark he made to some stupid husband who lay on the ground, complaining that Casanova hadn't fought fairly? You remember? it was in an avenue of chestnut trees, approaching a town. Ha! I have forgotten. Mike has all that this man had—love of adventure, daring, courage, strength, beauty, skill. For Mike would have made a unique swordsman. Have you ever seen him ride? Have you ever seen him shoot? I have seen him knock a dozen pigeons over in succession. Have you ever seen him play billiards? He made a break of a hundred two years ago. Have you ever seen him play tennis? He is the best man we have in the Temple. And a poet! Have you ever heard him tell of the poem he is writing? The most splendid subject. He says that neither Goethe nor Hugo ever thought of a better."

"You may include self-esteem in your list of his qualities."

"A platitude! Self-esteem is synonymous with genius. Still, I do not suppose he would in any circumstances have been a great poet; but there is enough of the poet about him to enhance and complete his Don Juan genius."

"You would have to mend his broken nose before you could cite him as a model Don Juan."

"On the contrary, by breaking his nose chance emphasized nature's intention; for a broken nose is the element of strangeness so essential in modern beauty, or shall I say modern attractiveness? But see that slim figure in hose, sword on thigh, wrapped in rich mantle, arriving on horseback with Leporello! Imagine the castle balcony, and the pale sky, green and rose, pensive as her dream, languid as her attitude. Then again, the grand staircase with courtiers bowing solemnly; or maybe the wave lapping the marble, the gondola shooting through the shadow! What encounters, what assignations, what disappearances, what sudden returnings! So strong is the love idea in him, that it has suscitated all that is inherent and essential in the character. It sent him to Boulogne so that he might fight a duel; and the other day a nun left her convent for him. Curious atavism, curious recrudescence of a dead idea of man! Say is it his fault if his pleasures are limited to clandestine visits; his fame to a summons to appear in a divorce case; his danger to that most pitiful of modern ignominies—five shillings a week? . . . Bah! this age has much to answer for."

"But Casanova was a marvellous necromancer, an extraordinary gambler."

"I know no more enthusiastic gambler than Mike. Have you ever seen him play whist? At Boulogne he cleaned them all out at baccarat."

"And lost heavily next day, and left without paying."

"The facts of the case have not been satisfactorily established. Have you seen him do tricks with cards? He used to be very fond of card tricks; and, by Jove! now I remember, there was a time when ladies came to consult him. He had two pieces of paper folded up in the same way. He gave one to the lady to write her question on; she placed it in a cleft stick and burnt it in a lamp; but the stick was cleft at both ends, and Mike managed it so that she burnt the blank sheet, while he read what she had written. Very trivial; inferior of course to Casanova's immense cabalistic frauds, but it bears out my contention . . . Have you ever read the *Memoirs?* What a prodigious book! Do you remember when the Duchesse de Chartres comes to consult the *cabale* in the little apartment in the Palais Royal as to the best means of getting rid of the pimples on her face? . . . and that scene (so exactly like something Wycherley might have written) when he meets the rich farmer's daughter travelling about with her old uncle, the priest?"

Mike was talking to Alice Barton, who was chaperoning Lily. Though she knew nothing of his character she had drawn back instinctively, but her strictness gradually crumbled and sank in his persuasiveness, and when he rose to go out of the room with Lily, she was astonished that she had pleasure in his society.

Lily was more beautiful than usual, the heat and

the pleasure of seeing her admirer having flushed her cheeks. He was penetrated with her sweetness, and the hand laid on his arm thrilled him. Where should he take her? Unfortunately the staircase was in stone; servants were busy in the drawing-room.

"How beautifully Mr. Escott plays the violin!"

The melodious strain reeked through the doorways filling the passage.

"That is Stradella's 'Chanson d'Eglise.' He always plays it; I'm sick of it."

"Yes, but I'm not. Do not let us go far, I should like to listen."

"I thought you would have preferred to talk with me."

Her manner did not encourage him to repeat his words, and he waited, uncertain what he should say or do. When the piece was over, he said—

"We had to turn my bedroom into a retiring-room. I'm afraid we shall not be alone."

"That does not matter; my mother does not approve of young girls sitting out dances."

"But your mother isn't here."

"I should not think of doing anything I knew she did not wish me to do."

The conversation was interrupted by the entrance of Muchross with several lords, and he was with difficulty dissuaded from an attempt to swarm up the columns of the wonderful bed. The room was full of young girls and barristers gathered from the various courts. Some had stopped before the great Christ. A girl had touched the suspended silver lamp and spoken of "dim religious light"; but by no word or look did Lily admit that she had been there before, and Mike felt it would be useless to remind her that she had. She was the same as she was every Wednesday in her mother's drawing-room.

And the party had been given solely with a view of withdrawing her from its influence. What was he to say to this girl? Was he to allow all that had passed between them to slip? Never had he felt so ill at ease. At last, fixing his eyes upon her, he said—

"Let us cease this trifling. Perhaps you do not know how painful it is to me. Tell me, will you come and see me? Do not let us waste time. I never see you alone now."

"I could not think of coming to see you; it would not be right."

"But you did come once."

"That was because I wanted to see where you lived. Now that I know, there would be no reason for coming again."

"You have not forgiven me. If you knew how I regret my conduct! Try and understand that it was for love of you. I was so fearful of losing you. I have lost you; I know it!"

He cursed himself for the irresolution he had shown. Had he made her his mistress she would now be hanging about his neck.

"I forgive you. But I wish you would not speak of love in connection with your conduct; when you do, all my liking for you dies."

"How cruel! Then I shall never kiss you again. Was my kiss so disagreeable? Do you hate to kiss me?"

"I don't know that I do, but it is not right. If I were married to you it would be different."

The conversation fell. Then realizing that he was compromising his chances, he said—

"How can I marry you? I haven't a cent in the world."

"I am not sure I would marry you if you had every cent in the world."

Mike looked at her in despair. She was adorably frail and adorably pale.

" This is very cruel of you." Words seemed very weak, and he feared that in the restlessness and pain of his love he had looked at her foolishly. So he almost welcomed Lady Helen's intrusion upon their *tête-à-tête.*

"And this is the way you come for your dance, Mr. Fletcher, is it ?"

" Have they begun dancing? I did not know it. I beg your pardon."

" And I too am engaged for this dance. I promised it to Mr. Escott," said Lily.

" Let me take you back."

He gave her his arm, assuring himself that if she didn't care for him there were hundreds who did. Lady Helen was one of the handsomest women in London, and he fancied she was thinking of him. And when he returned he stood at the door watching her as she leaned over the mantelpiece reading a letter. She did not put it away at once, but continued reading and playing with the letter as one might with something conclusive and important. She took no precaution against his seeing it, and he noticed that it was in a man's handwriting, and began *Ma chère amie.* The room was now empty, and the clatter of knives and forks drowned the strains of a waltz.

" You seemed to be very much occupied with that young person. She is very pretty. I advise you to take care."

" I don't want to marry. I shall never marry. Did you think I was in love with Miss Young ?"

" Well, it looked rather like it."

" No ; I swear you are mistaken. I say, if you don't care about dancing we'll sit down and talk. So you thought I was in love with Miss Young ?

How could I be in love with her while you are in the room? You know, you must have seen, that I have only eyes for you. The last time I was in Paris I went to see you in the Louvre."

"You say I am like Jean Gougon's statue."

"I think so, so far as a pair of stays allows me to judge."

Lady Helen laughed, but there was no pleasure in her laugh; it was a hard, bitter laugh.

"If only you knew how indifferent I am! What does it matter whether I am like the statue or not? I am indifferent to everything."

"But I admire you because you are like the statue."

"What does it matter to me whether you admire me or not? I don't care."

He had not asked her for the dance; she had sought him of her free will. What did it mean?

"Why should I care? What is it to me whether you like me or whether you hate me? I know very well that three months after my death every one will have ceased to think of me; three months hence it will be the same as if I had never lived at all."

"You are well off; you have talent and beauty. What more do you want?"

"The world cannot give me happiness. You find happiness in your own heart, not in worldly possessions. . . I am a pessimist. I recognize that life is a miserable thing—not only a miserable thing, but a useless thing. We can do no good; there is no good to be done; and life has no advantage except that we can put it off when we will. Schopenhauer is wrong when he asserts that suicide is no solution of the evil; so far as the individual is concerned suicide is a perfect solution, and were the race to cease to-morrow, nature would instantly choose another type and force it into consciousness. Until this earth resolves itself to ice or cinder, matter will never cease to know itself."

"My dear," said Lewis Seymour, who entered the room at that moment, "I am feeling very tired; I think I shall go home, but do not mind me. I will take a hansom—you can have your brougham. You will not mind coming home alone?"

"No, I shall not mind. But do you take the brougham. It will be better so. It will save the horse from cold; I'll come back in a hansom."

Mike noticed a look of relief or of pleasure on her face, he could not distinguish which. He pressed the conversation on wives, husbands, and lovers, striving to lead her into some confession. At last she said—

"I have had a lover for the last four years."

"Really!" said Mike. He hoped his face did not betray his great surprise. This was the first time he had ever heard a lady admit she had had a lover.

"We do not often meet; he doesn't live in England. I have not seen him for more than six months."

"Do you think he is faithful to you all that time?"

"What does it matter whether he is or not? When we meet we love each other just the same."

"I have never known a woman like you. You are the only one that has ever interested me. If you had been my mistress or my wife you would have been happier; you would have worked, and in work, not in pleasure, we may cheat life. You would have written your books, I should have written mine."

"I don't want you to think I am whining about my lot. I know what the value of life is; I'm not deceived, that is all."

"You are unhappy because your present life affords no outlet for your talent. Ah! had you had to fight the battle! How happy it would have made me to fight life with you! I wonder you never thought of leaving your husband, and throwing yourself into the battle of work."

" Supposing I wasn't able to make my living. To give up my home would be running too great a risk."

" How common all are when you begin to know them," thought Mike.

They spoke of the books they had read. She told him of *Le Journal d'Amiel*, explaining the charm that that lamentable record of a narrow, weak mind, whose power lay in an intense consciousness of its own failure, had for her. She spoke savagely, tearing out her soul, and flinging it as it were in Mike's face, frightening him not a little.

" I wish I had known Amiel; I think I could have loved him."

" Did he never write anything but this diary?"

" Oh, yes; but nothing of any worth. The diary was not written for publication. A friend of his found it among his papers, and from a huge mass extricated two volumes." Then speaking in praise of the pessimism of the Russian novels, she said— " There is no pleasure in life—at least none for me; the only thing that sustains me is curiosity."

" I don't speak of love, but have you no affection for your friends?—you like me, for instance."

" I am interested in you—you rouse my curiosity; but when I know you, I shall pass you by just like another."

" You are frank, to say the least of it. But like all other women, I suppose you like pleasure, and I adore you; I really do. I have never seen any one like you. You are superb to-night; let me kiss you." He took her in his arms.

" No, no; loose me. You do not love me, I do not love you; this is merely vice."

He pleaded she was mistaken. They spoke of indifferent things, and soon after went in to supper.

"What a beautiful piece of tapestry!" said Lady Helen.

"Yes, isn't it? But how strange!" he said, stopping in the doorway. "See how exquisitely real is the unreal—that is to say, how full of idea, how suggestive! Those blue trees and green skies, those nymphs like unswathed mummies, colourless but for the red worsted of their lips,—that one leaning on her bow, pointing to the stag that the hunters are pursuing through a mysterious yellow forest,—are to my mind infinitely more real than the women bending over their plates. At this moment the real is mean and trivial, the ideal is full of evocation."

"The real and the ideal; why distinguish as people usually distinguish between the words? The real is but the shadow of the ideal, the ideal but the shadow of the real."

The table was in disorder of cut pineapple, scattered dishes, and drooping flowers. Muchross, Snowdown, Dicky the driver, and others were grouped about the end of the table, and a waiter who styled them "most amusing gentlemen," supplied fresh bottles of champagne. Muchross had made several speeches, and now jumping on a chair, he discoursed on the tapestry, drawing outrageous parallels, and talking unexpected nonsense. The castle he identified as the cottage where he and Jenny had spent the summer; the bleary-eyed old peacock was the chicken he had dosed with cayenne pepper, hoping to cure its rheumatism; the pool with the white threads for sunlight was the water-butt into which Tom had fallen from the tiles—"those are the hairs out of his own old tail." The nymphs were Laura, Maggie, Emily, &c. Mike asked Lady Helen to come into the dancing-room, but she did not appear to hear, and her laughter encouraged Muchross to further excesses. The riot had reached its height, and dancers were beginning to come from the drawing-room to ask what it was all about.

" All about!" shouted Muchross; " I don't care any more about nymphs—I only care about getting drunk and singing. 'What cheer, 'Ria!'"

" Don't you care for dancing?" said Lady Helen, with tears running down her cheeks

" Ra-ther; see me dance the polka, dear girl." And they went banging through the dancers. Snowdown and Dicky shouted approval.

> " What cheer, 'Ria!
>   'Ria's on the job,
> What cheer, 'Ria!
>   Speculate a bob.
> 'Ria is a toff, and she is immensikoff—
> And we all shouted,
> What cheer, 'Ria!"

Amid the uproar Lady Helen danced with Lily Young. Insidious fragilities of eighteen were laid upon the plenitudes of thirty! Pure pink and cream-pink floated on the wind of the waltz, fading out of colour in shadowy corners, now gliding into the glare of burnished copper, to the quick appeal of the 'Estudiantina.' A life that had ceased to dream smiled upon one which had begun to dream. Sad eyes of Summer, that may flame with no desire again, looked into the eyes of Spring, where fancies collect like white flowers in the wave of a clear fountain.

Mike and Frank turned shoulder against shoulder across the room, four legs following in intricate unison to the opulent rhythm of the ' Blue Danube'; and when beneath ruche-rose feet died away in little exhausted steps, the men sprang from each other, and

the rhythm of sex was restored—Mike with Lily, and
Frank with Helen, yielding hearts, hands, and feet in
the garden enchantment of Straus' waltz.

*   *   *   *   *

The smell of burnt-out and quenched candle-ends
pervaded the apartment, and slips of gray light appeared between the curtains. The day, alas! had
come upon them. Frank yawned; and pale with
weariness he longed that his guests might leave him.
Chairs had been brought out on the balcony. Muchross and his friends had adjourned from the supper-
room, bringing champagne and an hysterical lady
with them. Snowdown and Platt were with difficulty
dissuaded from attempting acrobatic feats on the
parapet; and the city faded from deep purple into a
vast grayness. Strange was the little party ensconced
in the stone balcony high above the monotone of the
river.

Harding and Thompson, for pity of Frank, had
spoken of leaving, but the lords and the lady were
obdurate. Her husband had left in despair, leaving
Muchross to bring her home safely to Notting Hill.
As the day broke even the "bluest" stories failed to
raise a laugh. At last some left, then the lords left;
ten minutes after Mike, Frank, Harding, and Thompson were alone.

"Those infernal fellows wouldn't go, and now I'm
not a bit sleepy."

"I am," said Thompson. "Come on, Harding; you
are going my way."

"Going your way!"

"Yes; you can go through the Park. The walk
will do you good."

"I should like a walk," said Escott, "I'm not a bit
sleepy now."

"Come on then; walk with me as far as Hyde Park Corner."

"And come home alone! Not if I know it—I'll go if Mike will come."

"I'll go," said Mike. "You'll come with us, Harding?"

"It is out of my way, but if you are all going. . . . Where's John Norton?"

"He left about an hour ago."

"Let's wake him up."

As they passed up the Temple towards the Strand entrance, they turned into Pump Court, intending to shout. But John's window was open, and he stood, his head out, taking the air.

"What!—not gone to bed yet?"

"No; I have bad indigestion, and cannot sleep."

"We are going to walk as far as Hyde Park Corner with Thompson. Just the thing for you; you'll walk off your indigestion."

"All right. Wait a moment; I'll put my coat on. . . ."

"I never pass a set of street-sweepers without buttoning up," said Harding, as they went out of the Temple into the Strand. "The glazed shoes I don't mind, but the tie is too painfully significant."

"The old signs of City," said Thompson, as a begging woman rose from a door-step, and stretched forth a miserable arm and hand.

About the closed wine-shops and oyster-bars of the Haymarket a shadow of the dissipation of the night seemed still to linger; and a curious bent fig-ure passed picking with a spiked stick cigar-ends out of the gutter; significant it was, and so too was the starving dog which the man drove from a bone. The city was mean and squalid in the morning, and conveyed a sense of derision and reproach—the

sweep-carriage-road of Regent Street; the Royal
Academy, pretentious, aristocratic; the Green Park
still presenting some of the graces of a preceding
century. There were but three cabs on the rank.
The market-carts rolled along long Piccadilly, the
great dray-horses shuffling, raising little clouds of
dust in the barren street, the men dozing amid the
vegetables.

They were now at Hyde Park Corner. Thompson
spoke of the *improvements*—the breaking up of the
town into open spaces; but he doubted if anything
would be gained by these imitations of Paris. His
discourse was, however, interrupted by a porter from
the Alexandra Hotel asking to be directed to a certain street. He had been sent to fetch a doctor immediately—a lady just come from an evening party
had committed suicide.

"What was she like?" Harding asked.

"A tall woman."

"Dark or fair?"

He couldn't say, but thought she was something
between the two. Prompted by a strange curiosity,
feeling, they knew not why, but still feeling that it
might be some one from Temple Gardens, they went
to the hotel, and obtained a description of the suicide from the head-porter. The lady was very tall,
with beautiful golden hair. For a description of her
dress the housemaid was called.

"I hope," said Mike, "she won't say she was
dressed in cream-pink, trimmed with olive ribbons."
She did. Then Harding told the porter he was
afraid the lady was Lady Helen Seymour, a friend of
theirs, whom they had seen that night in a party
given in Temple Gardens by this gentleman, Mr.
Frank Escott. They were conducted up the desert
staircase of the hotel, for the lift did not begin

working till seven o'clock. The door stood ajar, and servants were in charge. On the left was a large bed, with dark-green curtains, and in the middle of the room a round table. There were two windows. The toilette-table stood between bed and window, and in the bland twilight of closed Venetian blinds a handsome fire flared loudly, throwing changing shadows upon the ceiling, and a deep, glowing light upon the red panels of the wardrobe. So the room fixed itself for ever on their minds. They noted the crude colour of the Brussels carpet, and even the oilcloth around the toilette-table was remembered. They saw that the round table was covered with a red tablecloth, and that writing materials were there, a pair of stays, a pair of tan gloves, and some withering flowers. They saw the ball-dress that Lady Helen had worn thrown over the arm-chair; the silk stockings, the satin shoes—and a gleam of sunlight that found its way between the blinds fell upon a piece of white petticoat. Lady Helen lay in the bed, thrown back low down on the pillow, the chin raised high, emphasizing a line of strained white throat. She lay in shadow and firelight, her cheek touched by the light. Around her eyes the shadows gathered, and as a landscape retains for an hour some impression of the day which is gone, so a softened and hallowed trace of life lingered upon her.

Then the facts of the case were told. She had driven up to the hotel in a hansom. She had asked if No. 57 was occupied, and on being told it was not, said she would take it; mentioning at the same time that she had missed her train, and would not return home till late in the afternoon. She had told the housemaid to light a fire, and had then dismissed her. Nothing more was known; but as the porter explained, it was clear she had gone to bed so as to make sure of shooting herself through the heart.

" The pistol is still in her hand; we never disturb anything till after the doctor has completed his examination."

Each felt the chill of steel against the naked side, and seeing the pair of stays on the table, they calculated its resisting force.

Harding mused on the ghastly ingenuity, withal so strangely reasonable. Thompson felt he would give his very life to make a sketch. Mike wondered what her lover was like. Frank was overwhelmed in sentimental sorrow. John's soul was full of strife and suffering. He had sacrificed his poems, and had yet ventured in revels which had led to such results! Then as they went down-stairs, Harding gave the porter Lewis Seymour's name and address, and said he should be sent for at once.

CHAPTER VI.

" I DON'T say we have never had a suicide here before, sir," said the porter in reply to Harding as they descended the steps of the hotel; " but I don't see how we are to help it. Whenever the upper classes want to do away with themselves they choose one of the big hotels—the Grosvenor, the Langham, or ourselves. Indeed they say more has done the trick in the Langham than 'ere, I suppose because it is more central ; but you can't get behind the motives of such people. They never think of the trouble and the harm they do us ; they only think of themselves."

London was now awake ; the streets were a-clatter with cabs ; the pick of the navvy resounded ; night loiterers were disappearing and giving place to hurrying early risers. In the resonant morning the young men walked together to the Corner. There they stopped to bid each other good-bye. John called a cab, and returned home in intense mental agitation.

"It really is terrible," said Mike. "It isn't like life at all, but some shocking nightmare. What could have induced her to do it?"

"That we shall probably never know," said Thompson; "and she seemed brimming over with life and fun. How she did dance! . . ."

"That was nerves. I had a long talk with her, and I assure you she quite frightened me. She spoke about the weariness of living;—no, not as we talk of it, philosophically; there was a special accent of truth in what she said. You remember the porter mentioned that she asked if No. 57 was occupied. I believe that is the room where she used to meet her lover. I believe they had had a quarrel, and she went there intent on reconciliation, and finding him gone determined to kill herself. She told me she had had a lover for the last four years. I don't know why she told me—it was the first time I ever heard a lady admit she had had a lover; but she was in an awful state of nerve excitement, and I think hardly knew what she was saying. She took the letter out of her bosom and read it slowly. I couldn't help seeing it was in a man's handwriting; it began, '*Ma chère amie.*' I heard her tell her husband to take the brougham; that she would come home in a cab. However, if my supposition is correct, I hope she burnt the letter."

"Perhaps that's what she lit the fire for. Did you notice if the writing materials had been used?"

"No, I didn't notice," said Mike. "And all so elaborately planned! Just fancy—shooting herself in a nice warm bed! She was determined to do it effectually. And she must have had the revolver in her pocket the whole time. I remember now, I had gone out of the room for a moment, and when I came back she was leaning over the chimney-piece, looking at something."

"I have often thought," said Harding, "that suicide is the culminating point of a state of mind long preparing. I think that the mind of the modern suicide is generally filled, saturated with the idea. I believe that he or she has been given for a long time preceding the act to considering, sometimes facetiously, sometimes sentimentally, the advantages of oblivion. For a long time an infiltration of desire of oblivion, and acute realization of the folly of living precedes suicide, and, when the mind is thoroughly prepared, a slight shock or interruption in the course of life produces it, just as an odorous wind, a sight of the sea, results in the poem which has been collecting in the mind."

"I think you might have the good feeling to forbear," said Frank; "the present is hardly, I think, a time for epigrams or philosophy. I wonder how you can talk so. . . ."

"I think Frank is quite right. What right have we to analyze her motives?"

"Her motives were simple enough; sad enough too, in all conscience. Why make her ridiculous by forcing her heart into the groove of your philosophy? The poor woman was miserably deceived; abominably deceived. You do not know what anguish of mind she suffered."

"There is nothing to show that she went to the Alexandra to meet a lover beyond the fact of a statement made to Mike in a moment of acute nervous excitement. We have no reason to think that she ever had a lover. I never heard her name mentioned in any such way. Did you, Escott?"

"Yes; I have heard that you were her lover."

"I assure you I never was; we have not even been on good terms for a long time past."

"You said just now that the act was generally preceded by a state of feeling long preparing. It was you who taught her to read Schopenhauer."

"I am not going to listen to nonsense at this hour of the morning. I never take nonsense on an empty stomach. Come, Thompson, you are going my way."

Mike and Frank walked home together. The clocks had struck six, and the milkmen were calling their ware; soon the shop-shutters would be coming down, and in this first flush of the day's enterprise, a last belated vegetable-cart jolted towards the market. Mike's thoughts flitted from the man who lay a-top taking his ease, his cap pulled over his eyes, to the scene that was now taking place in the twilight bedroom. What would Seymour say? Would he throw himself on his knees? Frank spoke from time to time; his thoughts growled like a savage dog, and his words bit at his friend. For Mike had incautiously given an account in particular detail of his *tête-à-tête* with Lady Helen.

"Then you are in a measure answerable for her death."

"You said just now that Harding was answerable; we can't both be blameworthy."

Frank did not reply. He brooded in silence, losing all perception of the truth in a stupid and harsh hatred of those whom he termed the villains that ruined women. When they reached Leicester Square, to escape from the obsession of the suicide, Mike said—

"I do not think that I told you that I have

sketched out a trilogy on the life of Christ. The first play *John*, the second *Christ*, the third *Peter*. Of course I introduce Christ into the third play. You know the legend. When Peter is flying from Rome to escape crucifixion, he meets Christ carrying His cross."

" Damn your trilogy—who cares. You have behaved abominably. I want you to understand that I cannot—that I do not hold with your practice of making love to every woman you meet. In the first place it is beastly, in the second it is not gentlemanly. Look at the result !"

" But I assure you I am in no wise to blame in this affair. I never was her lover."

" But you made love to her."

" No, I didn't ; we talked of love, that was all. I could see she was excited, and hardly knew what she was saying. You are most unjust. I think it quite as horrible as you do ; it preys upon my mind, and if I talk of other things it is because I would save myself the pain of thinking of it. Can't you understand that ?"

The conversation fell, and Mike thrust both hands into the pockets of his overcoat.

At the end of a long silence, Frank said—

" We must have an article on this—or, I don't know—I think I should like a poem. Could you write a poem on her death ?"

" I think so. A prose poem. I was penetrated with the modern picturesqueness of the room—the Venetian blinds."

" If that's the way you are going to treat it, I would sooner not have it—the face in the glass, a lot of repetitions of words, sentences beginning with 'And,' then a mention of shoes and silk stockings.

If you can't write feelingly about her, you had better not write at all."

"I don't see that a string of colloquialisms constitutes feelings," said Mike.

Mike kept his temper; he did not intend to allow it to imperil his residence in Temple Gardens, or his position in the newspaper; but he couldn't control his vanity, and ostentatiously threw Lady Helen's handkerchief upon the table, and admitted to having picked it up in the hotel.

"What am I to do with it? I suppose I must keep it as a relic," he added with a laugh, as he opened his wardrobe.

There were there ladies' shoes, scarves, and chemises; there were there sachets and pincushions; there were there garters, necklaces, cotillion favours, and a tea-gown.

Again Frank boiled over with indignation, and having vented his sense of rectitude, he left the room without even bidding his friend good-night or good-morning. The next day he spent the entire afternoon with Lizzie, for Lady Helen's suicide had set his nature in active ferment.

In the story of every soul there are times of dissolution and reconstruction in which only the generic forms are preserved. A new force had been introduced, and it was disintegrating that mass of social fibre which is modern man, and the decomposition teemed with ideas of duty, virtue, and love. He interrupted Lizzie's chit-chat constantly with reflections concerning the necessity of religious belief in women.

About seven they went to eat in a restaurant close by. It was an old Italian chop-house that had been enlarged and modernized, but the original marble tables where customers ate chops and steaks at low prices were retained in a remote and distant corner.

Lizzie proposed to sit there. They were just seated when a golden-haired girl of theatrical mien entered.

"That's Lottie Rilly," exclaimed Lizzie. Then lowering her voice she whispered quickly, "She was in love with Mike once; he was the fellow she left her 'ome for. She's on the stage now, and gets four pounds a week. I haven't seen her for the last couple of years. Lottie, come and sit down here."

The girl turned hastily. "What, Lizzie, old pal, I have not seen you for ages."

"Not for more than two years. Let me introduce you to my friend, Mr. Escott—Miss Lottie Rilly of the Strand Theatre."

"Very pleased to make your acquaintance, sir; the editor of the *Pilgrim*, I presume?"

Frank smiled with pleasure, and the waiter interposed with the bill of fare. Lottie ordered a plate of roast beef, and leaned across the table to talk to her friend.

"Have you seen Mike lately?" asked Lizzie.

"Swine!" she answered, tossing her head. "No; and don't want to. You know how he treated me. He left me three months after my baby was born."

"Have you had a baby?"

"What, didn't you know that? It is seven months old; 'tis a boy, that's one good job. And he hasn't paid me one penny piece. I have been up to Barber and Barber's, but they advised me to do nothing. They said that he owed them money, and that they couldn't get what he owed them—a poor look-out for me. They said that if I cared to summons him for the support of the child, that the magistrate would grant me an order at once."

"And why don't you?" said Frank; you don't like the *exposé* in the newspapers."

" That's it."

" Do you care for him still?"

" I don't know whether I do, or don't. I shall never love another man, I know that. I saw him in front about a month ago. He was in the stalls, and he fixed his eyes upon me; I didn't take the least notice, he was so cross. He came behind after the first act. He said, 'How old you are looking!' I said, 'What do you mean?' I was very nicely made up too, and he said, 'Under the eyes.' I said, 'What do you mean?' and he said, 'You are all wrinkles.' I said, 'What do you mean?' and he went downstairs. . . . Swine!"

" He isn't good-looking," said Frank, reflectively, —a broken nose, a chin thrust forward, and a mop of brown curls twisted over his forehead. Give me a pencil, and I'll do his caricature."

" Every one says the same thing. The girls in the theatre all say, 'What in the world do you see in him?' I tell them that if he chose—if he were to make up to them a bit, they'd go after him just the same as I did. There's a little girl in the chorus, and she trots about after him; she can't help it. There are times when I don't care for him. What riles me is to see other women messing him about."

" I suppose it is some sort of magnetism, electrobiology, and he can't help exercising it any more than you women can resist it. Tell me, how did he leave you?"

" Without a word or a penny. One night he didn't come home, and I sat up for him, and I don't know how many nights after. I used to doze off and awake up with a start, thinking I heard his footstep on the landing. I went down to Waterloo Bridge to drown myself. I don't know why I didn't; I almost wish I had, although I have got on pretty well since, and get a pretty tidy weekly screw."

"What do you get?"

"Three ten. Mine's a singing part. Waiter, some cheese and celery."

"What a blackguard he is; I'll never speak to him again; he shall edit my paper no more. To-night I'll give him the dirty kick-out."

Mike remained the topic of conversation until Lottie said—

"Good Lord, I must be 'getting'—it is past seven o'clock."

Frank paid her modest bill, and still discussing Mike, they walked to the stage-door. Quick with desire to possess Lizzie wholly beyond recall, and obfuscated with notions concerning the necessity of placing women in surroundings in harmony with their natural goodness, Frank walked by his mistress's side. At the end of a long silence, she said—

"That's the way you'll desert me one of these days. All men are brutes."

"No, darling, they are not. If you'll act fairly by me, I will by you—I'll never desert you."

Lizzie did not answer.

"You don't think me a brute like that fellow Fletcher, do you?"

"I don't think there's much difference between any of you."

Frank ground his teeth, and at that moment he only desired one thing—to prove to Lizzie that men were not all vile and worthless. They had turned into the Temple; the old places seemed dozing in the murmuring quietude of the evening. Mike was coming up the pathway, his dress distinct in the delicate gray light, his light-gray overcoat hanging over his arm.

"What a toff he is!" said Lizzie. His appearance and what it symbolized—an evening in a boudoir or at the gaming table—jarred on Frank, suggesting as it did a difference in condition from that of the wretched girl he had abandoned ; and as Mike prided himself that scandalous stories never followed upon his loves, the unearthing of this mean and obscure liaison annoyed him exceedingly. Above all, the accusation of paternity was disagreeable ; but determined to avoid a quarrel, he was about to pass by, when Frank noticed Lady Helen's pocket-handkerchief sticking out of his pocket.

"You blackguard," he said, "you are taking that handkerchief to a gambling-hell."

Then realizing that the game was up, he turned and would have struck his friend had not Lizzie interposed. She threw herself between the men, and called a policeman, and the quarrel ended in Mike's dismissal from the staff of the *Pilgrim*.

Frank had therefore to sit up writing till one o'clock, for the whole task of bringing out the paper was thrown upon him. Lizzie sat by him sewing. Noticing how pale and tired he looked, she got up, and putting her arm about his neck, said—

"Poor old man, you are tired ; you had better come to bed."

He took her in his arms affectionately, and talked to her.

"If you were always as kind and as nice as you are to-night . . . I could love you."

"I thought you did love me."

"So I do ; you will never know how much." They were close together, and the pure darkness seemed to separate them from all worldly influences.

"If you would be a good girl, and think only of him who loves you very dearly."

" Ah, if I only had met you first !"

" It would have made no difference, you'd have only been saying this to some one else."

" Oh, no ; if you had known me before I went wrong."

" Was he the first ?"

" Yes ; I would have been an honest little girl, trying to make you comfortable."

Throwing himself on his back, Frank argued prosaically :

" Then you mean to say you really care about me more than any one else ?"

She assured him that she did ; and again and again the temptations of women were discussed.   He could not sleep, and stretched at length on his back, he held Lizzie's hand.

She was in a communicative humour, and told him the story of the waiter, whom she described as being " a fellow like Mike, who made love to every woman." She told him of three or four other fellows, whose rooms she used to go to.   They made her drink ; she didn't like the beastly stuff ; and then she didn't know what she did.   There were stories of the landlady in whose house she lodged, and the woman who lived upstairs.   She had two fellows ; one she called Squeaker—she didn't care for him ; and another called Harry, and she did care for him ; but the landlady's daughter called him a ——, because he seldom gave her anything, and always had a bath in the morning.

" How can a girl be respectable under such circumstances ?" Lizzie asked, pathetically.   " The landlady used to tell me to go out and get my living !"

" Yes ; but I never let you want.   You never wrote to me for money that I didn't send it."

" Yes ; I know you did, but sometimes I think she

stopped the letters. Besides, a girl cannot be respectable if she isn't married. Where's the use?"

He strove to think, and failing to think, he said—

"If you really mean what you say, I will marry you." He heard each word; then a sob sounded in the dark, and turning impulsively he took Lizzie in his arms.

"No, no," she cried, "it would never do at all. Your family—what would they say? They would not receive me."

"What do I care for my family? What has my family ever done for me?"

For an hour they argued, Lizzie refusing, declaring it was useless, insisting that she would then belong to no set; Frank assuring her that hand-in-hand and heart-to-heart they would together, with united strength and love, win a place for themselves in the world. They dozed in each other's arms.

Rousing himself, Frank said—

"Kiss me once more, little wifie; good-night, little wife . . ."

"Good-night, dear."

"Call me little husband; I shan't go to sleep until you do."

"Good-night, little husband."

"Say little hussy."

"Good-night, little hussy."

Next morning, however, found Lizzie violently opposed to all idea of marriage. She said he didn't mean it; he said he did mean it, and he caught up a bible and swore he was speaking the truth. He put his back against the door, and declared she should not leave until she had promised him—until she gave him her solemn oath that she would become his wife. He was not going to see her go to the dogs—no, not

if he could help it ; then she lost her temper and tried
to push past him.　He restrained her, urging again
and again, and with theatrical emphasis, that he
thought it right, and would do his duty.　Then they
argued, they kissed, and argued again.

That night he walked up and down the pavement
in front of her door ; but the servant-girl caught sight
of him through the kitchen-window and the area-rail-
ings, and ran up-stairs to warn Miss Baker, who was
taking tea with two girl friends.

" He is a-walking up and down, Miss, 'is great-coat
flying behind him."

Lizzie slapped his face when he burst into her
room ; and scenes of recrimination, love, and rage
were transferred to and fro between Temple Gardens
and Winchester Street.　Her girl friends advised her
to marry, and the landlady when appealed to said,
" What could you want better than a fine gentleman
like that ?"

Frank was conscious of nothing but her, and every
vision of Mount Rorke that had risen in his mind
he had unhesitatingly swept away.　All prospects
were engulfed in his desire ; he saw nothing but the
white face, which like a star led and allured him.

One morning the marriage was settled, and like a
knight going to the crusade, Frank set forth to find
out when it could be.　They must be married at
once ; therefore a religious marriage was not to be
thought of.　Lizzie might again change her mind ;
and a registrar's office fixed itself in his thought.

It was a hot day in July when he set forth on his
quest.　He addressed the policeman at the corner,
and was given the name of the street and the number.　He hurried through the heat, irritated by the
sluggishness of the passers-by, and at last found himself in front of a red building.　The windows were

full of such general announcements as—Working
Men's Peace Preservation, Limited Liability Company, New Zealand, etc. The marriage office looked
like a miniature bank; there were desks, and a brass
railing a foot high preserved the inviolability of the
documents. A fat man with watery eyes rose from
the leather arm-chair in which he had been dozing,
and Frank intimated his desire to be married as soon
as possible; that afternoon if it could be managed.
It took the weak-eyed clerk some little time to order
and grasp the many various notions which Frank
urged upon him; but he eventually roused a little
(Frank had begun to shout at him), and explained
that no marriage could take place after two o'clock,
and later on it transpired that due notice would
have to be given.

Very much disappointed, Frank asked him to in-
scribe his name. The clerk opened a book, and then
it suddenly cropped up that this was the registry
office, not for Pimlico, but for Kensington.

"Great Scott!" exclaimed Frank, "and where is
the registry office for Pimlico in Kensington?"

"That I cannot tell you; it may be anywhere; you
will have to find out."

"How am I to find out, damn it?"

"I really can't tell you, but I must beg of you to
remember where you are, sir, and to moderate your
language," said the clerk, with some faint show of
hieratic dignity. "And now, ma'am, what can I do
for you?" he said, turning to a woman who smelt of
the kitchen, and whose black dress was bursting in
front.

Frank was furious; he appealed again to the casual
policeman, who, although reluctantly admitting he
could give him no information, sympathized with him
in his diatribe against the stupidities of the authori-

ties.   The policeman had himself been married by
the registrar, and some time was lost in vain reminiscences; he at last suggested that inquiry could
be made at a neighbouring church.

Frank hurried away, and had a long talk with a
charwoman whom he discovered in the desert of the
chairs.   She thought the office was situated some-
where in a region unknown to Frank, which she
called St. George-of-the-Fields; her daughter, who
had been shamefully deserted, had been married
there.   The parson, she thought, would know, and
she gave him his address.

The heat was intolerable.   There were few people
in the streets.   The perspiration collected under his
hat, and his feet ached so in his patent leather shoes
that he was tempted to walk after the water-cart and
bathe them in the sparkling shower.   Several hansoms
passed, but they were engaged.   Nor was the parson
at home.   The maidservant sniggered, but having
some sympathy with what she discovered was his
mission, summoned the housekeeper, who eyed him
askance, and directed him to Bloomsbury; and after
a descent into a grocer's shop, and an adventure
which ended in an angry altercation in a servants'
registry office, he was driven to a large building which
adjoined the parish infirmary and workhouse.

Even there he was forced to make inquiries, so
numerous and various were the offices.   At last an
old man in gray clothes declared himself the registrar's attendant, and offered to show him the way;
but seeing himself now within range of his desire, he
distanced the old chap up the four flights of stairs,
and arrived wholly out of breath before the brass
railing which guarded the hymeneal documents.   A
clerk equally slow of intellect as the first, and even

more somnolent, approached and leaned over the counter.

Feeling now quite familiar with a registrar's office, Frank explained his business successfully. The fat clerk, whose red nose had sprouted into many knobs, balanced himself leisurely, evidently giving little heed to what was said ; but the broadness of the brogue saved Frank from losing his temper.

"What part of Oireland do ye come from ? Is it Tipperary ?"

"Yes."

"I thought so ; Cashel, I'm thinking."

"Yes ; do you come from there ?"

"To be sure I do. I knew you when you were a boy ; and is his lordship in good health ?"

Frank replied that Lord Mount Rorke was in excellent health, and feeling himself obliged to be civil, he asked the clerk his name, and how long it was since he had been in Ireland.

"Well, this is odd," the clerk began, and then in an irritating undertone Mr. Scanlon proceeded to tell how he and four others were driving through Portarlington to take the train to Dublin, when one of them, Michael Carey he thought it was, proposed to stop the car and have some refreshment at the Royal Hotel.

Frank tried several times to return to the question of the licence, but the imperturbable clerk was not to be checked.

"I was just telling you," he interposed.

"It seemed hard luck that he should find a native of Cashel in the Pimlico registrar's office. He had intended so keep his marriage a secret, as did Willy Brookes, and for a moment the new danger thrilled him. It was intolerable to have to put up with this creature's idle loquacity, but not wishing to offend him he endured it a little longer.

When the clerk paused in his narrative of the four gentlemen who had stopped the car to have some refreshment, he made a resolute stand against any fresh developments of the story, and succeeded in extracting some particulars concerning the marriage laws. And within the next few days all formalities were completed, and Frank's marriage fixed for the end of the week—for Friday, at a quarter to eleven. He slept lightly that night, was out of bed before eight, and mistaking the time, arrived at the office a few minutes before ten. He met the old man in gray clothes in the passage, and this time he was not to be evaded.

" Are you the gentleman who's come to be married by special licence, sir?"

" Yes."

" Neither Mr. Southey—that is the Registrar—nor Mr. Freeman—that's the Assistant-Registrar—has yet arrived, sir."

" It is very extraordinary they should be late. Do they never keep their appointments?"

" They rarely arrives before ten, sir."

" Before ten! What time is it now?"

" Only just ten. I am the regular attendant. I'll see yer through it; no necessity to hagitate yerself. It will be done quietly in a private room—a very nice room too, fourteen feet by ten high—them's the regulations; all the chairs covered with leather; a very nice comfortable room. Would yer like to see the room? Would yer like to sit down there and wait? There's a party to be married before you. But they won't mind you. He's a butcher by trade."

" And what is she?"

"I think she's a tailoress; they lives close by here, they do."

"And who are you, and where do you live?"

"I'm the regular attendant; I lives close by here."

"Where close by?"

"In the work'us; they gives me this work to do."

"Oh, you are a pauper, then?"

"Yease; but I works here; I'm the regular attendant. No need to be afraid, sir; it's all done in a private room; no one will see you. This way, sir; this way."

The sinister aspect of things never appealed to Frank, and he was vastly amused at the idea of the pauper Mercury, and had begun to turn the subject over, seeing how he could use it for a queer story for the *Pilgrim*. But time soon grew horribly long, and to kill it he volunteered to act as witness to the butcher's marriage, one being wanted. The effects of a jovial night, fortified by some matutinal potations, were still visible in the small black eyes of the rubicund butcher—a huge man, apparently of cheery disposition; he swung to and fro before the shiny oak table as might one of his own carcasses. His bride, a small-featured woman, wrapped in a plaid shawl, evidently fearing that his state, if perceived by the Registrar, might cause a postponement of her wishes, strove to shield him. His pal and a stout girl, with the air of the coffee-shop about her, exchanged winks and grins, and at the critical moment, when the Registrar was about to read the declaration, the pal slipped behind some friends and, catching the bridegroom by the collar, whispered, "Now then, old man, pull yourself together." The Registrar looked up, but his spectacles did not appear to help him; the Assistant-Registrar, a tall, languid young man, who wore a carnation in his button-hole, yawned and called for order. The room was lighted by a skylight, and the light fell diffused on the hands and faces; and alternately and in combination the whiskied breath and the carnation's scent assailed the nostrils. Suddenly the silence was broken by the Registrar, who began to read the declarations. " I hereby declare that I, James Hicks, know of no impediment whereby I may not be joined in matrimony with Matilde, Matilde—is it Matilde or Matilda?"

" I calls her Tilly when I am a-cuddling of her; when she riles me, and gets my dander up, I says, 'Tilder, come here!'" and the butcher raised his voice till it seemed like an ox's bellow.

" I really must beg," exclaimed the Registrar, "that the sanctity of—the gravity of this ceremony is not disturbed by any foolish frivolity. You must remember. . ." But at that moment the glassy look of the butcher's eyes reached the old gentleman's vision, and a heavy hiccup fell upon his ears. " I really think, Mr. Freeman, that that gentleman, one of the contracting parties I mean, is not in a fit state —is in a state bordering on inebriation. Will you tell me if this is so?"

" I didn't notice it before," said Mr. Freeman, stifling a yawn, " but now you mention it, I really think he is a little drunk, and hardly in a fit . . ."

" I ne—ver was more jolly, jolly dog in my life (hiccup)—when you gentlemen have made it (hiccup) all squ—square between me and my Tilly" (a violent hiccup), catching her round the waist, he hugged her so violently that Matilda could not forbear a scream, " I fancy I shall be, just be a trifle more jolly still. . . If any of you ge—gen'men would care to join us— most 'appy, Tilly and me."

Lizzie, who had discovered a relation or two—a disreputable father and a nondescript brother—now appeared on the threshold. Her presence reminded

Frank of his responsibility, so forthwith he proceeded to bully the Registrar and allude menacingly to his newspaper.

"I'm sure, sir, I am very sorry you should have witnessed such a scene. Never, really, in the whole course of my life . . ."

"There is positively no excuse for allowing such people . . ."

"I will not go on with the marriage," roared the Registrar; "really, Mr. Freeman, you ought to have seen. You know how shortsighted I am. I will not proceed with this marriage."

"Oh, please, sir, Mr. Registrar, don't say that," exclaimed Matilda. "If you don't go on now, he'll never marry me; I'll never be able to bring 'im to the scratch again. Indeed, sir, 'e's not so drunk as he looks. 'Tis mostly the effect of the morning hair upon him."

"I shall not proceed with the marriage," said the Registrar, sternly. "I have never seen anything more disgraceful in my life. You come here to enter into a most solemn, I may say a sacred, contract, and you are not able to answer to your names; it is disgraceful."

"Indeed I am, sir; my name is Matilda, that's the English of it, but my poor mother kept company with a Frenchman, and he would have me christened Matilde; but it is all the same, it is the same name, indeed it is, sir. Do marry us; I shan't be able to get him to the scratch again. For the last five years . . ."

"Potter, Potter, show these people out; how dare you admit people who were in a state of inebriation?"

"I didn't 'ear what you said, sir."

"Show these people out, and if you ever do it again, you'll have to remain in the workhouse."

"This way, ladies and gentlemen, this way. I'm the regular attendant."

"Come along, Tilly dear, you'll have to wait another night afore we are churched. Come, Tilly; do you hear me? Come, Tilda."

Frightened as she was, the words "another night" suggested an idea to poor Matilde, and turning with supplicating eyes to the Registrar, she implored that they might make an appointment for the morrow. After some demur the Registrar consented, and she went away tearful, but in hope that she would be able to bring him on the morrow, as he put it, "fit to the post." This matter having been settled, the Registrar turned to Frank. Never in the course of his experience had the like occurred. He was extremely sorry that he (Mr. Escott) had been present. True, they were not situated in a fashionable neighbourhood, the people were ignorant, and it was often difficult to get them to sign their names correctly; but he was bound to admit that they were orderly, and seemed to realize, he would say, the seriousness of the transaction.

"It is," said the Registrar, "our object to maintain the strictly legal character of the ceremony—the contract, I should say—and to avoid any affectation of ritual whatsoever. I regret that you, sir, a representative of the press . . ."

"The nephew and heir to Lord Mount Rorke," suggested the clerk.

The Registrar bowed, and murmured that he did not know he had that honour. Then he spoke for some time of the moral good the registry offices had effected among the working classes; how they had allowed the poor—for instance, the person who has been known for years in the neighbourhood as Mrs.

Thompson, to legalize her cohabitation without scandal.

But Frank thought only of his wife, when he should clasp her hand, saying, "Dearest wife!" He had brought his dramatic and musical critics with him. The dramatic critic—a genial soul, well known to the shop-girls in Oxford Street, without social prejudices—was deep in conversation with the father and brother of the bride; the musical critic, a mild-faced man, adjusted his spectacles, and awaking from his dream reminded them of an afternoon concert that began unusually early, and that his presence there was indispensable. When the declarations were over, Frank asked when he should put the ring on.

"Some like to use the ring, some don't; it isn't necessary; all the best people of course do," said the Assistant-Registrar, who had not yawned once since he had heard that Frank's uncle was Lord Mount Rorke.

"I am much obliged to you for the information, but I should like to have my question answered— When am I to put on the ring?"

The dramatic critic tittered, and Frank authoritatively expostulated. But the Registrar interposed, saying—

"It is usual to put the ring on when the bride has answered to the declarations."

"Now all of ye can kiss the bride," exclaimed the clerk from Cashel.

Frank was indignant; the Registrar explained that the kissing of the bride was an old custom still retained among the lower classes, but Frank was not to be mollified, and the unhappy clerk was ordered to leave the room.

The wedding party drove to the Temple, where champagne was awaiting them; and when health and happiness had been drunk the critics left and the party became a family one.

Mike was in his bedroom; he was too indolent to move out of Escott's rooms, and by avoiding him he hoped to avert expulsion and angry altercations. The night he spent in gambling, the evening in dining; and some hours of each afternoon were devoted to the composition of his trilogy. Now he lay in his arm-chair smoking cigarettes, drinking lemonade, and thinking. He was especially attracted by the picture he hoped to paint in the first play of John and Jesus; and from time to time his mind filled with a picture of Herod's daughter. Closing his eyes slightly he saw her breasts, scarce hidden beneath jewels, and precious scarves floated from her waist as she advanced in a vaulted hall of pale blue architecture, slender fluted columns, and pointed arches. He sipped his lemonade, enjoying his soft, changing, and vague dream. But now he heard voices in the next room, and listening attentively he could distinguish the conversation.

"The drivelling idiot!" thought Mike. "So he's gone and married her—that slut of a barmaid! Mount Rorke will never forgive him. I wouldn't be surprised if he married again. The idiot!

The reprobate father declared he had not hoped to see such a day, so let bygones be bygones, that was his feeling. She had always been a good daughter; they had had differences of opinion, but let bygones be bygones. He had lived to see his daughter married to a gentleman, if ever there was one; and his only desire was that God might spare him to see her Lady Mount Rorke. Why should she not be Lady Mount Rorke? She was as pretty a girl as there was in London, and a good girl too; and now that she was married to a gentleman, he hoped they would both remember to let bygones be bygones.

"And he'll have to live with her for," thought Mike, "the next thirty years, watching her growing fat, old, and foolish. And that father!—won't he give trouble! What a pigstye the fellow has made of his life!"

Lizzie asked her father not to cry. Then came a slight altercation between Lizzie and her husband, in which it was passionately debated if Harry, the brother, was fitted to succeed Mike on the paper.

"Great Scott! how the fellow has done for himself! A nice sort of paper they'll bring out."

A cloud passed over Mike's face when he thought it would probably be this young gentleman who would continue his articles—*Lions of the Season.*

"You have quarrelled with Mike," said Lizzie, "and you say you aren't going to make it up again. You'll want some one, and Harry writes very nicely indeed. When he was at school his master always praised his writing. When he is in love he writes off page after page. I should like you to see the letters he wrote to . . ."

"Now, Liz, I really—I wish you wouldn't . . ."

"I am sure he would soon get into it."

"Quite so, quite so; I hope he will; I'm sure Harry will get into it—and the way to get into it is for him to send me some paragraphs. I will look over his 'copy,' making the alterations I think necessary. But for the moment, until he has learned the trick of writing paragraphs he would be of no use to me in the office. I should never get the paper out. I must have an experienced writer by me."

Then he dropped his voice, and Mike heard nothing till Frank said—

"That cad Fletcher is still here; we don't speak, of course; we passed each other on the staircase the other night. If he doesn't clear out soon I'll have to turn him out. You know who he is—a farmer's son, and used to live in a little house about a mile from Mount Rorke Castle, on the side of the road."

Mike thrilled with rage and hatred.

"You brute! you fool! you husband of a bar-girl! —you'll never be Lord Mount Rorke! He that came from the palace shall go to the garret; he that came from the little house on the roadside shall go to the castle, you brute!"

And Mike vowed that he would conquer sloth and lasciviousness, and outrageously triumph in the gaudy, foolish world, and insult his rival with riches and even honour. Then he heard Lizzie reproach Frank for refusing her first request, and the foolish fellow's expostulations suscitated feelings in Mike of intense satisfaction. He smiled triumphantly when he heard the old man's talents as accountant referred to.

"Father never told you about his failure," said Lizzie. Then the story with all its knots was laboriously unravelled.

"But," said the old man, "my books were declared to be perfect; I was complimented on my books; I was proud of them books."

"The brother as sub-editor, the father as book-keeper, the sister as wife—it would be difficult to imagine anything more complete. I'm sorry for the paper, though;—and my series, what a hash they'll make of it!" Taking the room in a glance, and realizing the others and every piece of furniture and every picture, he thought—"I give him a year, and then these rooms will be for sale. I shall get them; but I must clear out."

He had won four hundred pounds within the last

week, and this and his share in a play which was doing fairly well in the provinces, had run up his balance at the bank higher than it had ever stood—to
nearly a thousand pounds.

As he considered his good fortune, a sudden desire
of change of scene suddenly sprang upon him, and in
full revulsion of feeling his mind turned from the
long hours in the yellow glare of lamp-light, the staring faces, the heaps of gold and notes, and the cards
flying silently around the empty space of green baize;
from the long hours spent correcting and manipulat-
ing sentences; from the heat and turmoil and dirt
of London; from Frank Escott and his family; from
stinking, steamy restaurants; from the high flights
of stairs, and the prostitution of the Temple. And
like butterflies above two flowers, his thoughts hov-
ered in uncertain desire between the sanctity of a
honeymoon with Lily Young in a fair enchanted
pavilion on a terrace by the sea, near, but not too
near, white villas, a place as fairylike as a town
etched by Whistler, and some months of pensive and
abstracted life, full to overflowing with the joy and
eagerness of incessant cerebration; spent in a quiet
country-side, full of field-paths, and hedge-rows, and
shadowy woodland lanes—rich with red gables, surprises of woodbine and great sunflowers—where he
would walk meditatively in the sunsetting, seeing the
village lads and lassies pass, interested in their
homely life, and so resting his brain after the day's
labour; then in his study he would find the candles
already lighted, the kettle singing, his books and his
manuscripts ready for three excellent hours; upon
his face the night would breathe the rustling of
leaves and the rich odour of the stocks and tall
lilies, until he closed the window at midnight, after

casting one long sad and regretful look upon the gold mysteries of the heavens.

So his reverie ran, interrupted by the conversation in the next room. He heard his name mentioned frequently. The situation was embarrassing, for he could not open a door without being heard. At last he tramped boldly out, slamming the doors after him, leaving a note for Frank on the table in the passage. It ran as follows—" I am leaving town in a few days. I shall remove my things probably on Monday. Much obliged to you for your hospitality ; and now, good-bye." " That will look," he thought, " as if I had not overheard his remarks. How glad I shall be to get away ! Oh, for new scenes, new faces ! How pleasant it is to have money ! Heigh ho ! how pleasant it is to have money ! Whither shall I go ? Whither ? To Italy, and write my poem ? To Paris or Norway ? I feel as if I should never care to see this filthy Temple again." Even the old dining-hall, with its flights of steps and balustrades ; but he stayed to watch the long flight of the pigeons as they came on straightened wings from the gables. " What familiar birds they are ! Nothing is so like a woman as a pigeon ; perhaps that's the reason Norton does not like them. Norton ! I haven't seen him for ages—since . . ." He turned into Pump Court. The doors were wide open ; and there was luggage and some packing-cases on the landing. The floor-matting was rolled, and the screen which protected from draughts the high canonical chair in which Norton read and wrote was overthrown. John was packing his portmanteau, and on either side of him there was a Buddha and Indian warrior which he had lately purchased.

" What, leaving ? Giving up your rooms ?"

"Yes; I'm going down to Sussex. I do not think it is worth while keeping these rooms on."

Mike expressed his regret. No one understood John as Mike did. Herein lay the strength of Mike's nature; he won himself through all reserve, and soon John was telling him his state of soul: that he felt it would not be right for him to countenance with his presence any longer the atheism and immorality of the Temple. Lady Helen's death had come for a warning. "After the burning of my poems, after having sacrificed so much, it was indeed a pitiful thing to find myself one of that shocking revel which had culminated in the death of that woman."

"There he goes again," thought Mike, "running after his conscience like a dog after his tail—a performing dog, too; one that likes an audience." And to stimulate the mental antics in which he was so much interested, he said, "Do you believe she is in hell?"

"I refrain from judging her. She may have repented in the moment of death. God is her judge. But I shall never forget that morning; and I feel that my presence at your party imposes on me some measure of responsibility. As for you, Mike, I really think you ought to consider her fate as an omen. It was you . . ."

"For goodness sake, don't. It was Frank who invented the notion that she suicided herself because I had been flirting with her. I never heard of anything so ridiculous. I protest. You know the absurdly sentimental view he takes. It is grossly unfair."

Knowing well how to interest John, Mike defended himself passionately, as if he were really concerned to place his soul in a true light; and twenty minutes were agreeably spent in sampling, classifying, and judging of motives. Then the conversation turned

on the morality of women, and Mike judiciously
selected some instances from his stock of experiences
whereby John might judge of their animalism. Like
us all, John loved to talk sensuality ; but it was imperative that the discussion should be carried forward
with gravity and reserve.   Seated in his high canonical chair, wrapped in his dressing-gown, John would
bend forward listening, as if from the Bench or the
pulpit, awaking to a more intense interest when some
more than usually bitter vial of satire was emptied
upon the fair sex.   He had once amused Harding
very much by his admonishment of a Palais Royal
farce.

"It was not," he said, "so much the questionable-
ness of the play ; what shocked me most was the
horrible levity of the audience, the laughter with
which every indecent allusion was greeted."

The conversation had fallen, and Mike said—

"So you are going away?   Well, we shall all miss
you very much.   But you don't intend to bury yourself in the country; you'll come up to town sometimes."

"I feel I must not stay here ; the place has grown
unbearable."   A look of horror passed over John's
face.   "Hall has the rooms opposite.   His life is a
disgrace; he hurries through his writing, and rushes
out to beat up the Strand, as he puts it, for shop-
girls.   I could not live here any longer."

Mike could not but laugh a little ; and offended,
John rose and continued the packing of his Indian
gods.   Allusion was made to Byzantine art; and
Mike told the story of Frank's marriage; and John
laughed prodigiously at the account he gave of the
conversation overheard.   Regarding the quarrel John
was undecided.   He found himself forced to admit
that Mike's conduct deserved rebuke; but at the

same time, Frank's sentimental views were wholly distasteful to him. Then in reply to a question as to where he was going, Mike said he didn't know. He was invited to come and stay at Thornby Place.

"It is half-past three now. Do you think you could get your things packed in time to catch the six o'clock?"

"I think so. I can instruct Southwood; she will forward the rest of my things."

"Then be off at once; I have a lot to do. Hall is going to take my furniture off my hands. I have made rather a good bargain with him."

Nothing could suit Mike better. He had never stayed in a country house; and now as he hurried down the Temple, remembrances of Mount Rorke Castle rose in his mind—the parade of dresses on the summer lawns, and the picturesqueness of the shooting parties about the long, withering woods.

CHAPTER VI.

FOR some minutes longer the men lay resting in the heather, their eyes drinking the colour and varied lights and lines of the vast horizon. The downs rose like cliffs, and the dead level of the weald was freckled with brick towns; every hedgerow was visible as the markings on a chess-board; the distant lands were merged in blue vapour, and the windmill on its little hill seemed like a bit out of a young lady's sketch-book.

"How charming it is here!—how delightful! How sorrow seems to vanish, or to hang far away in one's life like a little cloud! It is only in moments of con-

templation like this when our wretched individuality
is lost in the benedictive influences of nature that true
happiness is found.   Ah! the wonderful philosophy
of the East, the wisdom of the ancient races!   Christianity is but a vulgarization of Buddhism, an adap-
tation, an arrangement for family consumption."

They were not a mile away from where John had
seen Kitty for a last time.   Now the mere recollection
of her jarred his joy in the evening, for he had long
since begun to understand that his love of her had
been a kind of accident, even as her death a strange
unaccountable divergation of his true nature.   He
had grown ashamed of his passion, and he now
thought that instead of yielding, that like Parsifal,
he should have looked down and seen a cross in the
sword's hilt, and the temptation should have passed.
That cruel death, never explained, so mysterious and
so involved in horror!   In what measure was he to
blame ?   In what light was he to view this strange
death as a symbol, as a sign?   And if she had not
been killed ? If he had married her? To escape from
these assaults of conscience he buried his mind in his
books and writings, not in his history of Christian
Latin.   His history of those writers appeared to him
sterile, and he congratulated himself that he had
outgrown love of such paradoxes .

Solemn, and with the great curves of palms, the
sky arched above them, and all the coombes filled
with all the mystery of evening shadow, and all about
the downs lay the sea—a rim of sea illimitable.

At the end of a long silence Mike spoke of his
poem.

"You must have written a good deal of it by this
time."

" No, I have written very little," and then yielding
to his desire to astonish, confessed he was working at

a trilogy on the life of Christ, and had already decided the main lines and incidents of the three plays. His idea was the disintegration of the legend, which had united under a godhead certain socialistic aspirations then prevalent in Judæa. In his first play, *John*, he introduces two reformers, one of whom is assassinated by John; the second perishes in a street broil, leaving the field free for the triumph of Jesus of Nazareth. In the second play, *Jesus*, he tells the love story of Jesus and the Magdalene. She throws over her protector, one of the Rabbi, and refuses her admirer, Judas, for Jesus. The Rabbi plots to destroy Jesus, and employs Judas. In the third play, *Peter*, he pictures the struggle of the new idea in pagan Rome, and it ends in Peter flying from Rome to escape crucifixion; but outside the city he sees Christ carrying His cross, and Christ says He is going to be crucified a second time, whereupon Peter returns to Rome.

As they descended the rough chalk road into the weald, John said, "I have sacrificed much for my religion. I think, therefore, I have a right to say that it is hard that my house should be selected for the manufacture of blasphemous trilogues."

Knowing that argument would profit him nothing, Mike allayed John's heaving conscience with promises not to write another line of the trilogy, and to devote himself entirely to his poem. At the end of a long silence, John said—

"Now the very name of Scohpenhauer revolts me. I accept nothing of his ideas. From that ridiculous pessimism I have drifted very far indeed. Pessimism is impossible. To live we must have an ideal, and pessimism offers none. So far it is inferior even to positivism."

"Pessimism offers no ideal! It offers the highest—

not to create life is the only good; the creation of life is the only evil; all else which man in his bestial stupidity calls good and evil is ephemeral and illusionary."

"Schopenhauer's arguments against suicide are not valid, that you admit, therefore it is impossible for the pessimist to justify his continued existence."

"Pardon me, the diffusion of the principle of sufficient reason can alone end this world, and we are justified in living in order that by example and precept we may dissuade others from the creation of life. The incomparable stupidity of life teaches us to love our parents—divine philosophy teaches us to forgive them."

That evening Mike played numerous games of backgammon with Mrs. Norton; talked till two in the morning to John of literature, and deplored the burning of the poems, and besought him to write them again, and to submit them, if needs be, to a bishop. He worked hard to obliterate the effect of his foolish confidences; for he was very happy in this large country house, full of unexpected impressions for him. On the wide staircases he stopped, tense with sensations of space, order, and ample life. He was impressed by the timely meals, conducted by well-trained servants; and he found it pleasant to pass from the house into the richly planted garden, and to see the coachman washing his carriage, the groom scraping out the horse's hoofs, the horse tied to the high wall, the cowman stumping about the rick-yard—indeed all the homely work always in progress.

Sometimes he did not come down to lunch, and continued his work till late in the afternoon. At five he had tea in the drawing-room with Mrs. Norton, and afterwards went out to gather flowers in the garden with her, or he walked around the house with John, listening to his plans for the architectural reformation of his residence.

Mike had now been a month at Thornby Place. He was enchanted with this countryside, and seeing it lent itself to his pleasure—in other words, that it was necessary to his state of mind—he strove, and with insidious inveiglements, to win it, to cajole it, to make it part and parcel of himself. But its people were reserved. Instinctively Mike attacked the line and the point of least resistance, and the point of least resistance lay about three miles distant. A young squire—a young man of large property and an unimpeachable position in the county—lived there in a handsome house with his three sisters. His life consisted in rabbit-shooting and riding out every morning to see his sheep upon the downs. He was the rare man who does not desire himself other than he is. But content, though an unmixed blessing to its possessor, is not an attractive quality, and Mr. Dallas stood sorely in need of a friend. He loved his sisters, but to spend every evening in their society was monotonous, and he felt, and they felt still more keenly, that a nice young man would create an interest that at present was wanting in country life. Mike had heard of this young squire and his sisters, and had long desired to meet him. But they had paid their yearly visit to Thornby Place, and he could not persuade John to go to Holly Park.

One day riding on the downs, Mike inquired the way to Henfield of a young man who passed him riding a bay horse. The question was answered curtly—so curtly that Mike thought the stranger could not be led into conversation. In this he was mistaken, and at the end of half a mile felt he had succeeded in interesting his companion. As they descended into the weald, Mike told him he was stopping at Thornby Place, and the young squire told him he was Mr. Dallas. When about to part, Mike asked to be directed to the nearest inn, complaining that he was dying of thirst, for he wished to give Mr. Dallas an excuse for asking him to his house. Mr. Dallas availed himself of the excuse; and Mike prayed that he might find the ladies at home. They were in the drawing-room. The piano was played, and amid tea and muffins, tennis was discussed, and allusion was made to man's inconstancy.

Mike left no uncertainty regarding his various qualities: he liked hunting as much as shooting, and having regard for the season of the year, he laid special stress upon his love for, and his prowess in, the game of tennis. A week later he received an invitation to tennis. Henceforth he rode over frequently to Holly Park. He was sometimes asked to stay the night, and an impression was gaining ground there that life was pleasanter with him than without him.

When he was not there the squire missed the morning ride and the game of billiards in the evening, and the companion to whom he could speak of his sheep and his lambs. Mike listened to the little troubles of each sister in the back garden, never failing to evince the profoundest sympathy. He was surprised to find that he enjoyed these conversations just as much as a metaphysical disquisition with John Norton. "I am not pretending," he often said to himself; "it is quite true;" and then he added philosophically, "were I not interested in them I should not succeed in interesting them."

The brother, the sisters, the servants, even the lapdog shared in the pleasure. The maidservants liked to meet his tall figure in the passages; the young ladies loved to look into his tender eyes when they came in from their walk and found him in the drawing-room. To touch Mike's skin was to touch his soul, and even the Yorkshire terrier was sensible of its gentleness, and soon preferred to doze under his hand than in any other place. He came into Dallas' room in the morning when he was taking his bath; he hung around the young ladies' rooms, speaking when the doors were ajar; then when the doors were open, they fled and wrapped themselves in dressing-gowns, and when they knew him better walked about with the bodies of their dresses off, speaking to him the while. He felt his power; and by insidious intimations, by looks, words, projects for pleasure, presents, practical jokes, books, and talks about books, he proceeded joyously in his corruption of the entire household.

Naturally Mike rode his host's horses, and he borrowed his spurs, breeches, boots, and hunting-whip. And when he began to realize what an excellent pretext hunting is for making friends, and staying in their houses, he bought a couple of horses, which he kept at Holly Park free of cost. He had long since put aside his poem and his trilogy, and now thought of nothing but shooting and riding. He could throw his energies into anything, were it writing a poem or playing chuck-farthing.

The first meet of the hounds was at Thornby Place, and in the vain hope of marrying her son, Mrs. Norton had invited the young girls of the entire countryside. Lady Edith Downsdale was especially included in her designs; but John instantly vetoed her hopes by asking Mike to take Lady Edith into lunch. She stood holding her habit; and feeling the necessity of being brilliant, Mike said, pointing to the hounds and horses—

"How strange it is that that is of no interest to the artist! It is only parade; whereas a bit of lane with a wind-blown hedge is a human emotion, and that is always interesting."

Soon after a fox was found in the plantation that rimmed the lawn, and seeing that Lady Edith was watching him, Mike risked a fall over some high wattles; and this was the only notice he took of her until late in the afternoon. All hope of hunting was ended. A fox had been "chopped" in cover, another had been miserably coursed and killed in a back garden. So he strove to make himself agreeable, riding with her along the hillsides, watching the huntsman trying each patch of gorse in the coombes. She seemed to him splendid and charming, and he wondered if he could love her—marry her, and never grow weary of her. But when the hounds found in a large wood beneath the hills, and streamed across the meadows, he forgot her, and making his horse go in and out he fought for a start. A hundred and fifty were cantering down a steep muddy lane; a horseman who had come across the field strove to open a strong farm-gate. "It is locked," he roared, "jump." The lane was steep and greasy, the gate was four feet and a half. Mike rode at it. The animal dropped his hind legs, Mike heard the gate rattle, and a little ejaculatory cry come from those he left behind. It was a close shave. Turning in his saddle he saw the immense crowd pressing about the gate, which could not be opened, and he knew very well that he would have the hounds to himself for many a mile.

He raced alone across the misty pasture lands, full of winter water and lingering leaf; the lofty downs like sea cliffs; appearing through great white masses of curling vapour. And all the episodes of that day —the great ox fences which his horse flew, going like a bird from field to field ; the awkward stile, the various brooks,—that one overgrown with scrub which his horse had refused. And when the day was done, as he rode through the gathering night, inquiring out the way down many a deep and flooded lane, happiness sang within him, and like a pure animal he enjoyed the sensation of life, and he intoxicated on the thoughts of the friends that would have been his, the women and the numberless pleasures and adventures he could have engaged in, were he not obliged to earn money, or were not led away from them " by his accursed literary tastes."

Should he marry one of the sisters ? Ridiculous ! But what was there to do ? To-day he was thirty ; in ten years he would be a middle-aged man ; and, alas ! for he felt in him manifold resources, sufficient were he to live for five hundred years. Must he marry Agnes ? He would if she were a peeress in her own right ! Or should he win a peerage for himself by some great poem, or by some great political treachery ? No, no ; he wanted nothing better than to live always strong and joyous in this corner of fair England ; and to be always loved by girls, and to be always talked of by them about their tea-tables. Oh, for a cup of tea and a slice of warm buttered toast !

A good hour's ride yawned between him and Holly Park, but by crossing the downs it might be reduced to three-quarters of an hour. He hesitated, fearing he might miss his way in the fog, but the tea-table lured him. He resolved to attempt it, and forced his horse up a slightly indicated path, which he hoped would led him to a certain barn. High above him a horseman, faint as the shadow of a bird, made his way cantering briskly. Mike strove to overtake him, but suddenly missed him: behind him the pathway was disappearing.

Fearing he might have to pass a night on the downs, he turned his horse's head; but the animal was obdurate, and a moment after he was lost. He said, "Great Scott! where am I? Where did this ploughed field come from? I must be near the dyke." Then thinking that he recognized the headland, he rode in a different direction, but was stopped by a paling and a chalk-pit, and, riding round it, he guessed the chalk-pit must be fifty feet deep. Strange white patches, fabulous hillocks, and distortions of ground loomed through the white darkness; and a valley opened on his right so steep that he was afraid to descend into it. Every minute was an hour, every mile was five.

"There's nothing for it but to lie under a furze-bush." With two pocket-handkerchiefs he tied his horse's fore-legs close together, and sat down and lit a cigar. The furze-patch was quite hollow underneath and almost dry.

"It is nearly full moon," he said; "were it not for that it would be pitch dark. Good Lord! thirteen hours of this; I wish I had never been born."

He had not, however, finished his first cigar before a horse's head and shoulders pushed through the mist. Mike sprang to his feet.

"Can you tell me the way off these infernal downs?" he cried. "Oh, I beg your pardon, Lady Edith."

"Oh, is that you, Mr. Fletcher? I have lost my way and my groom too. I am awfully frightened; I missed him of a sudden in the fog. What shall I do? Can you tell me the way?"

"Indeed I cannot; if I knew the way I should not be sitting under this furze-bush."

"What shall we do? I must get home."

"It is very terrible, Lady Edith, but I'm afraid you will not be able to get home till the fog lifts."

"But I must get home. I must! I must! What will they think? They'll be sending out to look for me. Won't you come with me, Mr. Fletcher, and help me to find the way?"

"I will, of course, do anything you like; but I warn you, Lady Edith, that riding about these downs in a fog is most dangerous; I as nearly as possible went over a chalk-pit fifty feet deep."

"Oh, Mr. Fletcher, I must get home; I cannot stay here all night; it is ridiculous."

They talked so for a few minutes. Then amid many protestations Lady Edith was induced to dismount. He forced her to drink, and to continue sipping from his hunting-flask, which was fortunately full of brandy; and when she said she was no longer cold, he put his arm about her, and they talked of their sensations on first seeing each other.

Three small stones, two embedded in the ground, the third, a large flint, lay close where the grass began, and the form of a bush was faint on the heavy white blanket in which the world was wrapped. A rabbit crept through the furze and frightened them; and they heard the horses browsing.

Mike declared he could say when she had begun to like him.

"You remember you were standing by the side-board holding your habit over your boots; I brought you a glass of champagne, and you looked at me. . ."

She told him of her troubles since she had left school. He related the story of his own precarious fortunes; and as they lay dreaming of each other, the sound of horse's hoofs came through the darkness.

"Oh, do cry out, perhaps they will be able to tell us the way."

"Do you want to leave me ?"

"No, no, but I must get home ; what will father think ?"

Mike shouted, and his shout was answered.

"Where are you ?' asked the unknown.

"Here," said Mike.

"Where is here ?"

"By the furze-bush."

"Where is the furze-bush ?"

It was difficult to explain, and the voice grew fainter. Then it seemed to come from a different side.

Mike shouted again and again, and at last a horseman loomed like a nightmare out of the dark. It was Parker, Lady Edith's groom.

"Oh, Parker, how did you miss me ? I have been awfully frightened ; I don't know what I should have done if I had not met Mr. Fletcher."

"I was coming round that barn, my lady ; you set off at a trot, my lady, and a cloud of fog came between us."

"Yes, yes ; but do you know the way home ?"

"I think, my lady, we are near the dyke ; but I wouldn't be certain."

"I nearly as possible rode into a chalk-pit," said Mike. "Unpleasant as it is, I think we had better remain where we are until it clears."

"Oh, no, no, we cannot remain here ; we might walk and lead the horses."

"Very well, you get on your horse ; I'll lead."

"No, no," she whispered, "give me your arm, and I'll walk."

They walked in the bitter, hopeless dark, stumbling over the rough ground, the groom following with the horses. But soon Lady Edith stopped, and leaning heavily on Mike, said—

"I can go no further ; I wish I were dead !"

"Dead ! No, no," he whispered ; "live for my sake, darling."

At that moment the gable of a barn appeared like an apparition. The cattle which were lying in the yard started from under the horses' feet, and stood staring in round-eyed surprise. The barn was half-full of hay, and in the dry pungent odour Mike and Lady Edith rested an hour. Sometimes a bullock filled the doorway with ungainly form and steaming nostrils ; sometimes the lips of the lovers met. In about half-an-hour the groom returned with the news that the fog was lifting, and discovering a cart-track, they followed it over the hills for many a mile.

"There is Horton Borstal," cried Parker, as they entered a deep cutting overgrown with bushes. "I know my way now, my lady ; we are seven miles from home."

When he bade Lady Edith good-bye, Mike's mind thrilled with a sense of singular satisfaction. Here was an adventure which seemed to him quite perfect ; it had been preceded by no wearisome preliminaries, and he was not likely ever to see her again.

Weeks and months passed, and the simple-minded country folk with whom he had taken up his abode seemed more thoroughly devoted to him ; the anchor of their belief seemed now deeply grounded, and in the peaceful bay of their affection his bark floated, safe from ship-wrecking current or storm. There was neither subterfuge nor duplicity in Mike ; he was always singularly candid on the subject of his sins and general worthlessness, and he was never more natural in word and deed than at Holly Park. If its inmates had been reasonable they would have cast him forth; but reason enters hardly at all in the practical conduct of human life, and our loves and friendships owe to it either origin or modification.

It was a house of copious meals and sleep. Mike stirred these sluggish livers, and they accepted him as a digestive; and they amused him, and he only dreamed vaguely of leaving them until he found his balance at the bank had fallen very low. Then he packed up his portmanteau and left them, and when he walked down the Strand he had forgotten them and all country pursuits, and wanted to talk of journalism; and he would have welcomed the obscurest paragraphist. Suddenly he saw Frank; and turning from a golden-haired actress who was smiling upon him he said—

"How do you do?" The men shook hands, and stood constrainedly talking for a few minutes; then Mike suggested lunch, and they turned into Lubini's. The proprietor, a dapper little man, more like a rich man's valet than a waiter, whose fat fingers sparkled with rings, sat sipping sherry and reading the racing intelligence to a lord who offered to toss him for half-crowns.

"Now then, Lubi," cried the lord, "which is it? Come on; just this once."

Lubi demurred. "You toss too well for me; last night you did win seven times running—damn!"

"Come on, Lubi; here it is flat on the table."

Mike longed to pull his money out of his pocket, but he had not been on terms with Lubi since he had called him a *Marchand de Soupe,* an insult which Lubi had not been able to forgive, and it was the restaurateur's women folk who welcomed him back to town after his long absence.

"What an air of dissipation, hilarity, and drink there is about the place!" said Mike. "Look!" and his eyes rested on two gross men—music-hall singers— who sat with their agent, sipping Chartreuse. "Three years ago," he said, " they were crying artichokes in the street, and the slum is still upon their faces."

No one else was in the long gallery save the waiters, who dozed far away in the mean twilight of the glass-roofing.

" How jolly it is," said Mike, "to order your own dinner! Let's have some oysters—three dozen. We'll have a Chateaubriand—what do you say? And an omelette soufflée—what do you think? And a bottle of champagne. Waiter, bring me the wine-list."

Frank had spoken to Mike because he felt lonely; the world had turned a harsh face on him. Lord Mount Rorke had married, and the paper was losing its circulation.

"And how is the paper going?"

" Pretty well; just the same as usual. Do you ever see it? What do you think of my articles?"

"Your continuation of my series, *Lions of the Season?* Very good; I only saw one or two. I have been living in the country, and have hardly seen a paper for the last year and a half. You can't imagine the life I have been leading. Nice kind people 'tis true; I love them, but they never open a book. That is all very nice for a time—for three months, for six, for a year—but after that you feel a sense of alienation stealing over you."

Mike saw that Frank had only met with failure; so he was tempted to brandish his successes. He gave a humorous description of his friends—how he had picked them up; how they had supplied him with horses to ride and guns to shoot with.

" And what about the young ladies?   Were they included in the hospitality ?"

" They included themselves.   How delicious love in a country house is !—and how different from other love it is, to follow a girl dressed for dinner into the drawing-room or library, and to take her by the waist, to feel a head leaning towards you and a mouth closing upon yours!   Above all, when the room is in darkness—better still in the firelight—the light of the fire on her neck. . . .   How good these oysters are ! Have some more champagne."

Then, in a sudden silence, a music-hall gent was heard to say that some one was a splendid woman, beautifully developed.

" Now then, Lubi, old man, I toss you for a sovereign," cried a lord, who looked like a sandwich-man in his ample driving-coat.

" You no more toss with me, I have done with you ; you too sharp for me."

" What ! are you going to cut me ? Are you going to warn me off your restaurant ?"

Roars of laughter followed, and the lions of song gazed in admiration on the lord.

" I may be hard up," cried the lord ; " but I'm damned if I ever look hard up ; do I, Lubi ?"

" Since you turn up head when you like, why should you look hard up ?"

" You want us to believe you are a 'mug,' Lubi, that's about it, but it won't do. ' Mugs' are rare nowadays.   I don't know where to go and look for them. . . .   I say, Lubi," and he whispered something in the restaurateur's ear, " if you know of any knocking about, bring them down to my place ; you shall stand in."

" Damn me ! You take me for a pump, do you? You get out !"

The genial lord roared the more, and assured Lubi he meant " mugs," and offered to toss him for a sovereign.

" How jolly this is!" said Mike. " I'm dying for a gamble ; I feel as if I could play as I never played before. I have all the cards in my mind's eye. By George! I wish I could get hold of a ' mug,' I'd fleece him to the tune of five hundred before he knew where he was. But look at that woman! She's not bad."

" A great coarse creature like that ! I never could understand you. . . . Have you heard of Lily Young lately?"

Mike's face fell.

" No," he said, " I have not. She is the only woman I ever loved. I would sooner see her than the green cloth. I really believe I love that girl. Somehow I cannot forget her."

" Well, come and see her to-day. Take your eyes off that disgusting harlot."

" No, not to-day," he replied, without removing his eyes. Five minutes after he said, " Very well, I will go. I must see her."

The waiter was called, the bill paid, a hansom hailed, and they were rolling westward. In the pleasure of this little expedition, Mike's rankling animosity was almost forgotten. He said—

" I love this drive west : I love to see London opening up, as it were, before the wheels of the hansom—Trafalgar Square, the Clubs, Pall Mall, St. James' Street, Piccadilly, the descent, and then the gracious ascent beneath the trees. You see how I anticipate it all."

" Do you remember that morning when Lady Helen committed suicide ? What did you think of my article ?"

" I didn't see it. I should have liked to have written about it ; but you said that I wouldn't write feelingly."

Mrs. Young hardly rose from her sofa ; but she welcomed them in plaintive accents. Lily showed less astonishment and pleasure at seeing him than Mike expected. She was talking to a lady, who was subsequently discovered to be the wife of a strange fat man, who, in his character of Orientalist, squatted upon the lowest seat in the room and wore a velvet turban on his head, a voluminous overcoat circulating about him.

" As I said to Lady Hazeldean last night—I hope Mr. Gladstone did not hear me, he was talking to Lady Engleton Dixon about divorce, I really hope he did not hear me—but I really couldn't help saying that I thought it would be·better if he believed less in the divorce of nations, even if I may not add that he might with advantage believe more in the divorce of persons not suited to each other."

When the conversation turned on Arabi, which it never failed to do in this house, the perfume-burners that had been presented to her and Mr. Young on their triumphal tour were pointed out.

" I telegraphed to Dilke," said Sir Joseph, " 'You must not hang that man.' " And when Mrs. Young accused him of not sufficient interest in Africa, he said—" My dear Mrs. Young, I am interested in Africa ! You forget what I have done for Africa ; how I have laboured for Africa. I shall not believe in the synthesis of humanity, nor will it be complete till we get the black notes."

" Mr. Young and Lord Granville used to have such long discussions about Buddhism, and it always used to end in Mr. Young sending a copy of your book to Lord Granville."

"A very great distinction for me—a very great distinction for me," murmured Buddha ; and allowing Mrs. Young to relieve him of his tea-cup, he said—"And now, Mrs. Young, I want to ask for your support and co-operation in a little scheme— a little scheme which I have been nourishing like a rose in my bosom for some years."

Sir Joseph raised his voice ; and it was not until he had imposed silence on his wife that he consented to unfold his little scheme.

Then the fat man explained that in a certain province in Cylone (a name of six syllables) there was a temple, and this temple had belonged in the sixth century to a tribe of Buddhists (a name of seven syllables), and this temple had in the eighth century been taken from the Buddhists by a tribe of Brahmins (a name of eight syllables).

"And not being Mr. Gladstone," said Sir Joseph, "I do not propose to depossess the Brahmins without compensation. I am merely desirous that the Brahmins should be bought out by the Indian Government at a cost of a hundred and fifty or two hundred thousand. If this were done the number of pilgrims to this holy shrine would be doubled, and the best results would follow."

"Oh, Mrs. Jellaby, where art thou?" thought Mike, and he boldly took advantage of the elaborate preparations that were being made for Sir Joseph to write his name on a fan, to move round the table and take a seat by Lily.

But Frank's patience was exhausted, and he rose to leave.

"People wonder at the genius of Shakespeare ! I must say the stupidity of the ordinary man surprises me far more," said Mike.

"I'm a poor man to-day," said Frank, "but I

would give £25 to have had Dickens with us—fancy walking up Piccadilly with him afterwards!"

"Now I must go," he said. "Lizzie is waiting for me. I'll see you to-morrow," he cried, and drove away.

"Just fancy having to look after her, having to attend to her wants, having to leave a friend and return home to dine with her in a small room! How devilish pleasant it is to be free!—to say, 'Where shall I dine?' and to be able to answer, 'Anywhere.' But it is too early to dine, and too late to play whist. Damn it! I don't know what to do with myself."

Mike watched the elegantly-dressed men who passed hurriedly to their clubs, or drove west to dinner-parties. Red clouds and dark clouds collected and rolled overhead, and in a chill wintry breeze the leaves of the tall trees shivered, fell, and were blown along the pavement with sharp harsh sound. London shrouded like a widow in long crape.

"What is there to do? Five o'clock! After that lunch I cannot dine before eight—three hours! Whom shall I go and see?"

A vision of women passed through his mind, but he turned from them all, and he said—

"I will go and see her."

He had met Miss Dudley in Brighton, in a house where he had been asked to tea. She was a small, elderly spinster with sharp features and gray curls. She had expected him to address to her a few common-place remarks for politeness' sake, and then to leave her for some attractive girl. But he had showed no wish to leave her, and when they met again he walked by her bath-chair the entire length of the Cliff. Miss Dudley was a cripple. She had fallen from some rocks when a child playing on the beach,

and had injured herself irremediably. She lived with
her maid in a small lodging, and being often confined
to her room for days, nearly every visitor was welcome. Mike liked this pallid and forgotten little
woman. He found in her a strange sweetness—a
wistfulness. There was poetry in her loneliness and
her ruined health. Strength, health, and beauty had
been crushed by a chance fall. But the accident
had not affected the mind, unless perhaps it had
raised it into more intense sympathy with life. And
in all his various passions and neglected correspon-
dence he never forgot for long to answer her letters,
nor to allow a month to pass without seeing her.
And now he bought for her a great packet of roses
and a novel; and with some misgiving he chose
Zola's *Page d'Amour.*

" I think this is all right. She'll be delighted with
it, if she'll read it."

She would have read anything he gave, and seen
no harm since it came from him. The ailing caged
bird cannot but rapture in the thrilling of the wild
bird that comes to it with the freedom of the sky
and fields in its wings and song. She listened to all
his stories, even to his stories of pigeon-shooting.
She knew not how to reproach him. Her eyes fixed
upon him, her gentle hand laid on the rail of her
chair, she listened while he told her of the friends he
had made, and his life in the country; its seascape
and downlands, the furze where he had shot the rabbits, the lane where he had jumped the gate. Her
pleasures had passed in thought—his in action; the
world was for him—this room for her.

There is the long chair in which she lies nearly
always; there is the cushion on which the tired head
is leaned, a small beautifully-shaped head, and the
sharp features are distinct on the dark velvet, for the

lamp is on the mantelpiece, and the light falls full on the profile. The curtains are drawn, and the eyes animate with gratitude when Mike enters with his roses, and after asking kindly questions he takes a vase, and filling it with water, places the flowers therein, and sets it on the table beside her. There is her fire—(few indeed are the days in summer when she is without it)—the singing kettle suggests the homely tea, and the saucepan on the hearth the invalid. There is her bookcase, set with poetry and religion, and in one corner are the yellow-backed French novels that Mike has given her. They are the touches the most conclusive of reality in her life; and she often smiled, thinking how her friends will strive to explain how they came into her life when she was gone.

" How good of you to come and see me ! Tell me about yourself, what you have been doing. I want to hear you talk."

" Well, I've brought you this book; it is a lovely book—you can read it—I think you can read it, otherwise I should not have given it to you."

He remained with her till seven, talking to her about hunting, shooting, literature, and card-playing.

" Now I must go," he said, glancing at the clock.

" Oh, so soon," exclaimed Miss Dudley, waking from her dream ; " must you go ?"

" I'm afraid I must ; I haven't dined yet."

" And what are you going to do after dinner ? You are going to play cards."

" How did you guess that ?"

" I can't say," she said, laughing, " I think I can often guess your thoughts."

And during the long drive to Piccadilly, and as he eat his sole and drank his Pomard, he dreamed of the hands he should hold, and of the risks he should run when the cards were bad. His brain glowed with subtle combinations and surprises, and he longed to measure his strength against redoubtable antagonists. The two great whist players, Longley and Lovegrove, were there. He always felt jealous of Lovegrove's play. Lovegrove played an admirable game, always making the most of his cards. But there was none of that dash, and almost miraculous flashes of imagination and decision which characterized Mike, and Mike felt that if he had the money on, and with Longley for a partner, he could play as he had never played before; and ignoring a young man whom he might have rooked at ecarté, and avoiding a rich old gentleman who loved his game of piquet, and on whom Mike was used to rely in the old days for his Sunday dinner (he used to say the old gentleman gave the best dinners in London; they always ran into a tenner), he sat down at the whist-table. His partner played wretchedly, and though he had Longley and Lovegrove against him, he could not refrain from betting ten pounds on every rubber. He played till the club closed, he played till he had reduced his balance at the bank to nineteen pounds.

Haunted by the five of clubs, which he should have and did not play on one occasion, he walked till he came to the Haymarket. Then he stopped. What could he do? All the life of idleness and luxury which he had so long enjoyed faded like a dream, and the spectre of cheap lodgings and daily journalism rose painfully distinct. He pitied the street-sweepers, and wondered if it were possible for him to slip down into the gutter. "When I have paid my hotel bill, I shan't have a tenner." He thought of Mrs. Byril, but the idea did not please him, and he remembered Frank had told him he had a cottage on the river. He would go there. He might put up for a night or two at Hall's.

"I will start a series of articles to-morrow. What

shall it be?" An unfortunate still stood at the corner of the street. "'Letters to a Light o' Love!' Frank must advance me something upon them. . . Those stupid women! if they were not so witless they could rise to any height. If I had only been a woman! . . If I had been a woman I should have liked to have been Ninon de Lenclos."

———————

CHAPTER VIII.

WHEN Mike had paid his hotel bill, very few pounds were left for the card-room, and judging it was not an hour in which he might tempt fortune, he "rooked" a young man remorselessly. Having thus replenished his pockets he turned to the whist-table for amusement. Luck was against him; he played, defying luck, and left the club owing eighty pounds, five of which he had borrowed from Longley.

Next morning as he dozed, he wondered if he had played the ten of diamonds instead of the seven of clubs, if it would have materially altered his fortune; and from cards his thoughts wandered, till they took root in the articles he was to write for the *Pilgrim*. He was in Hall's spare bed-room—a large, square room, empty of all furniture except a camp bedstead. His portmanteau lay wide open in the middle of the floor, and a gaunt fireplace yawned amid some yellow marbles.

" 'Darling, like a rose you hold the whole world between your lips, and you shed its leaves in little kisses.' That will do for the opening sentences." Then as words slipped from him he considered the component parts of his subject.

" The first letter is of course introductory, and I

must establish certain facts, truths which have become distorted and falsified, or lost sight of. Addressing an ideal courtesan, I say, ' You must understand that the opening sentence of this letter does not include any part of the old reproach which has been levelled against you since man began to love you, and that was when he ceased to be an ape and became man.

" ' If you were ever sphinx-like and bloodthirsty, which I very much doubt, you have changed flesh and skin, even the marrow of your bones. In these modern days you are a kind-hearted little woman who, to pursue an ancient metaphor, sheds the world rosewise in little kisses; but if you did not so shed it, the world would shed itself in tears. Your smiles and laughter are the last lights that play around the white hairs of an aged duke ; your winsome tendernesses are the dreams of a young man who writes " pars " about you on Friday, and dines with you on Sunday ; you are an ideal in many lives which without you would certainly be ideal-less.' Deuced good that ; I wish I had a pencil to make a note ; but I shall remember it. Then will come my historical paragraph. I shall show that it is only by confounding courtesans with queens, and love with ambition, that any sort of case can be made out against the former. Third paragraph—' Courtesans are a factor in the great problem of the circulation of wealth, etc.' It will be said that the money thus spent is unproductive. . . So much the better ! For if it were given to the poor it would merely enable them to bring more children into the world, thereby increasing immensely the general misery of the race. Schopenhauer will not be left out in the cold after all. Quote Lecky,—' The courtesan is the guardian angel of our hearths and homes, the protector of our wives and sisters.' "

" Will you have a bath this morning, sir ?" cried the laundress, through the door.

" Yes, and get me a chop for breakfast."

" I shall tell her (the courtesan, not the laundress) how she may organize the various forces latent in her, and culminate in a power which shall contain in essence the united responsibilities of church, music-hall, and picture gallery." Mike turned over on his back and roared with laughter. " Frank will be delighted. It will make the fortune of the paper. Then I shall attack my subject in detail. Dress, house, education, friends, female and male. Then the money question. She must make a provision for the future. Charming chapter there is to be written on the old age of the courtesan—charities—ostentatious charities—charitable bazaars, reception into the Roman Catholic faith."

" Shall I bring in your hot water, sir ?" screamed the laundress.

" Yes, yes. . . . . Shall my courtesan go on the stage? No, she shall be a pure courtesan, she shall remain unsullied of any labour. She might appear once on the boards ;—no, no, she must remain a pure courtesan. Charming subject ! It will make a book. Charming opportunity for wit, satire, fancy. I shall write the introductory letter after breakfast."

Frank was in shoaling water, and could not pay his contributors; but Mike could get blood out of a turnip, and Frank advanced him ten pounds on the proposed articles. Frank counted on these articles to whip up the circulation, and Mike promised to let him have four within the week, and left the cottage at Henley, where Frank was living, full of dreams of work. And every morning before he got out of bed he considered and reconsidered his subject, finding always more than one idea, and many a witty fancy ; and every day after breakfast the work undone hung

like a sword between Hall and him as they sat
talking of their friends, of art, of women, of things
that did not interest them. They hung around each
other, loth yet desirous to part ; they followed each
other through the three rooms, buttoning their braces
and shirt collars. And when conversation had worn
itself out, Mike accepted any pretext to descend into
the court. He had to fetch ink or cigarettes.

But he was always detained, if not by friends, by
the beauty of the gardens or the river. Never did
the old dining-hall and the staircases, balustraded
—on whose gray stone a leaf, the first of many,
rustles—seem more intense and pregnant with that
mystic mournfulness which is the Thames, and
which is London. The dull sphinx-like water rolling
through the multitude of bricks, seemed to mark
on this wistful autumn day a more melancholy enchantment, and looking out on the great waste of
brick delicately blended with smoke and mist, and
seeing the hay-boats sailing picturesquely, and the
tugs making for Blackfriars, long lines of coal-barges
in their wake, laden so deep that the water slopped
over the gunwales, he thought of the spring morning
when he had waited there for Lily. How she persisted in his mind! Why had he not asked her to
marry him instead of striving to make her his
mistress? She was too sweet to be cast off like the
others ; she would have accepted him if he had asked
her. He had sacrificed marriage for self, and what
had self given him?

Mike was surprised at these thoughts, and pleased,
for they proved a certain residue of goodness in him ;
at all events, called into his consideration a side of
his nature which he was not wearisomely familiar
with. Then he dismissed these thoughts as he might
have the letter of a determined creditor. He could

still bid them go. And having easily rid himself of them, he noticed the porters in their white aprons, and the flight of pigeons, the sacred birds of the Temple, coming down from the roofs. And he loved now more than ever Fleet Street, and the various offices where he might idle, and the various luncheon-bars to which he might adjourn with one of the staff, perhaps with the editor of one of the newspapers. The October sunlight was warm and soft, greeting his face agreeably as he lounged, stopping before every shop in which there were books or prints. Ludgate Circus was always a favourite with him, partly because he loved St. Paul's, partly because women assembled there; and now in the mist, delicate and pure, rose above the town the lovely dome.

"None but the barbarians of the Thames," thought Mike, "none other would have allowed that most shameful bridge."

Mike hated Simpson's. He could not abide the stolid city folk, who devour fifty saddles of mutton in an evening. He liked better the Cock Tavern, quiet, snug, and intimate. Wedged with a couple of chums in a comfortable corner, he shouted—

"Henry, get me a chop and a pint of bitter."

There he was sure to meet a young barrister ready to talk to him, and they returned together, swinging their sticks, happy in their bachelordom, proud of the old inns and courts. Often they stayed to look on the church, the church of the Knight Templars, those terrible and mysterious knights who, with crossed legs for sign of mission, and with long swords and kite-shaped shields, lie upon the pavement of the church.

One wet night a deep cloying darkness had wiped out every architectural outline; the doors of the church were ajar, and the pathetic stories of the windows became dreamily alive. The young men entered, seeing the painted arches and clustered columns; and in the pomp of the pipes, and in shadow starred by the candles, the lone organist sat playing a fugue by Bach.

"It is," said Mike, "like turning the pages of some precious missal, adorned with gold thread and be- dazzled with rare jewels. It is like a poem by Edgar Allan Poe." Quelled, and in strange awe they lis- tened, and when the music ceased, unable at once to return to the simple prose of their chambers, they lingered, commenting on the mock taste of the architecture of the dining-hall, and laughing at the inflated inscription over the doorway.

"It is worse," said Mike, "than the Middle Temple Hall—far worse; but I like this old colonnade, there is something so suggestive in this old inscription in bad Latin.

> 'Vetustissima Templariorum porticu
> Igne consumptâ an 1679
> Nova hoc sumptibus medii
> Templie tructa an 1681
> Gulielmo Whiteloche arm
> Thesauör.'"

Once or twice a week Hall dined at the Cock for the purpose of meeting his friends, whom he invited after dinner to his rooms to smoke and drink till midnight. His welcome was so cordial that all were glad to come. The hospitality was that which is met in all chambers in the Temple. Coffee was made with difficulty, delay, and uncertain result; a bottle of port was sometimes produced; of whiskey and water there was always plenty. Every one brought his own tobacco; and in decrepit chairs beneath dangerously-laden bookcases some six or seven barristers enjoyed themselves in conversation, smoke, and drink. Mike recognized on entering how characteristically Temple was this society, how different from the heterogeneous visitors of Temple Gardens in the heyday of Frank's fortune.

James Norris was a small, thin man, dark and with regular features, clean shaven like a priest or an actor, vaguely resembling both, inclining towards the hieratic rather than to the histrionic type. He dressed always in black, and the closely buttoned jacket revealed the spareness of his body. He was met often in the evening, going to dine at the Cock; but was rarely seen walking about the Temple in the day-time. It was impossible to meet any one more suasive and agreeable; his suavity was penetrating as his small dark eyes. He lived in Elm Court, and his rooms impressed you with a sense of cleanliness and comfort. The furniture was all in solid mahogany; there were no knick-knacks or any lightness, and almost the only æsthetic intentions were a few sober engravings— portraits of men in wigs and breast-plates. He took pleasure in these and also in some first editions, containing the original plates, which, when you knew him well, he produced from the bookcase and descanted on their value and rarity.

Mr. Norris had always an excellent cigar to offer you, and he pressed you to taste of his old port, and his Chartreuse; there was whiskey for you too, if you cared to take it, and allusion was made to its age. But it was neither an influence nor a characteristic of his rooms; the port wine was. If there was fruit on the sideboard, there was also pounded sugar; and it is such detail as the pounded sugar that announces an inveterate bachelorhood. Some men are born bachelors. And when a man is born a bachelor, the signs unmistakable are hardly apparent at thirty: it is not until the fortieth year is approached that the fateful markings become recognizable. James Norris was forty-two and was therefore a full-fledged bachelor. He was a bachelor in the complete equipment of his chambers. He was bachelor in his arm-chair and his stock of wine; his hospitality was that of a bachelor, for a man who feels instinctively that he will never own a " house and home," constructs the materiality of his life in chambers upon a fuller basis than the man who feels instinctively that he will, sooner or later, exchange the perch-like existence of his chambers for the nest-like completeness of a home in South Kensington.

James Norris was of an excellent county family in Essex. He had a brother in the army, a brother in the Civil Service, and a brother in the Diplomatic Service. He has also a brother who composes somewhat unsuccessful waltz tunes, who borrows money, and James thinks that his brother causes him some anxiety of mind. The eldest brother, John Norris, lives at the family place, Halton Grange, where he stays when he goes on the Eastern circuit. James is far too securely a gentleman to speak much of Halton Grange; nevertheless, the flavour of landed estate transpires in the course of conversation with him. He returns from circuit, having finished up with a partridge drive, etc.

James Norris was a sensualist. His sensuality was recognizable in the close set eyes and in the sharp prominent chin (he resembled vaguely the portrait of Baudelaire in Les Fleurs du Mal); he never spoke of his amours, but occasionally he would drop an observation, especially if he were talking to Mike Fletcher, that afforded a sudden glimpse of a soul touched if not tainted with erotism. But James Norris was above all things prudent, and knew how to keep vice well in hand.

Like another, he had had his love story, or that which in the life of such a man might pass for a love story. He had flirted a great deal when he was thirty, with a married woman. She had not troubled, she had only slightly eddied, stirred with a few ripples the placidity of a placid stream of life. In hours of lassitude it pleased him to strive to think that she had ruined his life. Man is ever ready to think that his failure comes from without rather than from within. He wrote to her every week a long letter, and spent a large part of the long vacation in her house in Yorkshire, telling her that he had never loved any one but her.

James Norris was an able lawyer, and he was an able lawyer for three reasons. First, because he was a clear-headed man of the world, who had not allowed his intelligence to rust ;—it formed part of the routine of his life to read some pages of a standard author before going to bed; he studied all the notorious articles that appeared in the reviews, attempting the assimilation of the ideas which seemed to him best in our time. Secondly, he was industrious, and if he led an independent life, dining frequently in a tavern instead of touting for briefs in society, and so harmed himself, such misadventure was counter-balanced by his industry and his prudence. Thirdly, his sweetness and geniality made him a favourite with the bench. He had much insight into human nature, he studied it, and could detect almost at once the two leading spirits on a jury; and he was always aware of the idiosyncrasies of the judge he was pleading before, and knew how to respect and to flatter them.

Charles Stokes was the oldest man who frequented Hall's chambers, and his venerable appearance was an anomaly in a company formed principally of men under forty. In truth, Charles Stokes was not more than forty-six or seven, but he explained that living everywhere, and doing everything, had aged him beyond his years. In mind, however, he was the youngest there, and his manner was often distressingly juvenile. He wore old clothes which looked as if they had not been brushed for some weeks, and his linen was of dubious cleanliness, and about his rumpled collar there floated a half-tied black necktie. Mike, who hated all things that reminded him of the casualness of this human frame, never was at ease in his presence, and his eye turned in disgust from sight of the poor old gentleman's trembling and ossified fingers. His beard was long and almost white; he snuffed, and smoked a clay pipe, and sat in the arm-chair which stood in the corner beneath the screen which John Norton had left to Hall.

He was always addressed as Mr. Stokes; Hall kept him well supplied with whiskey-and-water. He was listened to on account of his age—that is to say, on account of his apparent age, and on account of his gentleness. Harding had described him as one who talked learned nonsense in sweetly-measured intonations. But although Harding ridiculed him, he often led him into conversation, listening with obvious interest, for Mr. Stokes had drifted through many modes and manners of life, and had in so doing acquired some vague knowledge.

He had written a book on the ancient religions of India, which he called the *Cradleland of Arts and Creeds*, and Harding, ever on the alert to pick a brain, however poor it might be, enticed him into discussion in which frequent allusion was made to Vishnu and Siva.

Yes, drifted is the word that best expresses Mr. Stokes' passage through life—he had drifted. He was one of the many millions who live without a fixed intention, without even knowing what they desire;

and he had drifted because in him strength and weakness stood at equipoise; no defect was heavy enough for anchor, nor was there any quality large enough for sufficient sail ; he had drifted from country to country, from profession to profession, whither winds and waves might bear him.

" Of course I'm a failure," was a phrase that Mr. Stokes repeated with a mild, gentle humour, without any trace of bitterness. He spoke of himself with the naïve candour of a docile school-boy, who has taken up several subjects for examination and been ploughed in them all. For Mr. Stokes had been to Oxford, and left it without taking a degree. Then he had gone into the army and had proved himself a thoroughly inefficient soldier, and more than any man before or after, had succeeded in rousing the ire of both adjutant and colonel. It was impossible to teach him any drill; what he was taught to-day he forgot to-morrow ; when the general came down to inspect, the confusion he created in the barrack-yard had proved so complex, that for a second it had taxed the knowledge of the drill-sergeant to get the men straight again.

Mr. Stokes was late at all times and all occasions : he was late for drill, he was late for mess, he was late for church ; and when sent for he was always found in his room, either learning a part or writing a play. His one passion was theatricals ; and wherever the regiment was stationed, he very soon discovered those who were disposed to get up a performance of a farce.

When he left the army he joined the Indian bar, and there he applied himself in his own absent-minded fashion to the study of Sanscrit, neglecting Hindustani, which would have been of use to him in his profession. Through India, China, and America he had drifted. In New York he had edited a newspaper; in San Francisco he had lectured, and he returned home with an English nobleman who had engaged him as private secretary.

When he passed out of the nobleman's service he took chambers in the Temple, and devoted his abundant leisure to writing his memoirs, and the pleasantest part of his life began. The Temple suited him perfectly, its Bohemianism was congenial to him, the library was convenient, and as no man likes to wholly cut himself adrift from his profession, the vicinity of the law courts, and a modicum of legal conversation in the evening sufficed to maintain in his absent-minded head the illusion that he was practising at the bar. His chambers were bare and dreary, unadorned with spoils from India or China. Mr. Stokes retained nothing; he had passed through life like a bird; he did not possess a copy even of his *Cradleland of Arts and Creeds*. He had gathered nothing, but had lost much, especially his relations. He had lost all except a small property in Kent; he appeared to be quite alone in the world.

Mr. Stokes talked rarely of his love affairs, and his allusions were so partial that nothing exact could be determined about him. It was, however, noticed that he wore a gold bracelet indissolubly fastened upon his right wrist, and it was supposed that an Indian princess had given him this, and that a goldsmith had soldered it upon him in her presence, as she lay on her death-bed. It was noticed that a young girl came to see him at intervals, sometimes alone, sometimes accompanied by her aunt. Mr. Stokes made no secret of this young person, and he spoke of her as his adopted daughter. Mr. Stokes dined at a theatrical club. All men liked him; he was genial and harmless.

Mr. Joseph Silk was the son of a London clergy-

man. He was a tall, spare young man, who was
often met about the Temple, striding towards his
offices or the library.   He was comically careful not
to say anything that might offend, and nervously
concerned to retreat from all persons and things
which did not seem to him to offer possibilities of
future help.   His assumed geniality and good-fellow-
ship hung about him awkwardly, like the clothes of
a broad-chested, thick-thighed man would about
miserable limbs.   For some time Silk had been
seriously thinking of cutting himself adrift from all
acquaintanceship with Hall. He had, until now,
borne with his acquaintanceship because Hall was
connected with a society journal that wrote peril-
ously near the law of libel ; several times the paper
had been threatened with actions, but had somehow,
much to Silk's chagrin, managed to escape.   All the
actionable paragraphs had been discussed with Silk ;
on each occasion Hall had come down to his office
for advice, and he felt sure that he would be employed
in the case when it did come off.   But unfortunately
it showed no signs of accomplishment.   Silk read the
paper every week for the paragraph that was to
bring him fame ; he would have given almost anything to be employed " in a good advertising case."
But he had noticed that instead of becoming more
aggressive and personal, that week by week the newspaper was moderating its tone.   In the last issue
several paragraphs had caught his eye, which could
not be described otherwise than as complimentary ;
there were also several new pages of advertisements ;
and these robbed him of all hope of an action.   He
counted the pages, " twelve pages of advertisements
—nothing further of a questionable character will go
into that paper," thought he, and forthwith fell to
considering Hall's invitation to " come in that evening,

if he had nothing better to do." He had decided
that he would not go, but at the last moment had
gone, and now, as he sat drinking whiskey-and-water,
he glanced round the company, thinking it might
injure him if it became known that he spent his
evenings there, he inwardly resolved he would never
again be seen in Hall's rooms.

Silk had been called to the bar about seven years.
The first years he considered he had wasted, but
during the last four he applied himself to his profession. He had determined "to make a success of
life," that was how he put it to himself. He had,
during the last four years, done a good deal of
" devilling"; he had attended at the Old Bailey watching for "soups" with untiring patience. But lately,
within the last couple of years, he had made up his
mind that waiting for "soups" at the Old Bailey
was not the way to fame or fortune. His first idea
of a path out of his present circumstances was through
Hall and the newspaper; but he had lately bethought
himself of an easier and wider way, one more fruitful
of chances and beset with prizes. This broad and
easy road to success which he had lately begun to see,
wound through his father's drawing-room. London
clergymen have, as a rule, large salaries and abundant
leisure, and young Silk determined to turn his father's
leisure to account. The Reverend Silk required no
pressing. "Show me what line to take, and I will
take it," said he; and young Silk, knowing well the
various firms of solicitors that were dispensing such
briefs as he could take, instructed his father when
and where he should exercise his tea-table agree-
abilities, and forthwith the reverend gentleman commenced his social wrigglings. There were teas and
dinners, and calls, and lying without end. Over the
wine young Silk cajoled the senior member of the

firm, and in the drawing-room, sitting by the wife, he alluded to his father's philanthropic duties, which he relieved with such sniggering and pruriency as he though the occasion demanded.

About six months ago, Mr. Joseph Silk had accidentally learnt, in the treasurer's offices, that the second floor in No. 5, Paper Buildings was un-occupied. He had thought of changing his chambers, but a second floor in Paper Buildings was beyond his means. But two or three days after, as he was walking from his area in King's Bench Walk to the library, he suddenly remembered that the celebrated advocate, Sir Arthur Haldane, lived on the first floor in Paper Buildings. Now at his father's house, or in one of the houses his father frequented, he might meet Sir Arthur; indeed, a meeting could easily be arranged. Here Mr. Silk's sallow face almost flushed with a little colour, and his heart beat as his little scheme pressed upon his mind. Dreading an obstacle, he feared to allow the thought to formulate; but after a moment he let it slip, and it said—"Now if I were to take the second floor, I should often meet Sir Arthur on the doorstep and staircase. What an immense advantage it would be to me when Stoggard and Higgins learnt that I was on terms of friendship with Sir Arthur. I know as a positive fact that Stoggard and Higgins would give anything to get Sir Arthur for some of their work. . . But the rent is very heavy in Paper Buildings. I must speak to father about it."

A few weeks after, Mr. Joseph transferred his furniture to No. 2, Paper Buildings; and not long after he had the pleasure of meeting him at dinner.

Mr. Silk's love affairs were neither numerous nor interesting. He had spent little of his time with women, and little of his money upon women, and his

amativeness had led him into no wilder exploit than
the seduction of his laundress's daughter, by whom he
had had a child. Indeed, it had once been whispered
that the mother, with the child in her arms, had
knocked at King's Bench Walk and had insisted on
being admitted. Having not the slightest knowledge
or perception of female nature, he had extricated himself with difficulty from the scandal by which he was
menaced, and was severely mulcted before the girl
was induced to leave London. About every three
months she wrote to him, and these letters were
read with horror and burnt in trembling haste; for
Mr. Joseph Silk was now meditating for matrimonial
and legal purposes one of the daughters of one of
the solicitors he had met in Paper Buildings, and
being an exceedingly nervous, ignorant, and unsym-
pathetic man in all that did not concern his profession, was vastly disturbed at every echo of his
indiscretion.

Harding, in reply to a question as to what he
thought of him, Silk, said—

"What do I think of Silk? Cotton back" . . .
and every one laughed, feeling the intrinsic truth
of the judgment.

Mr. George Cooper was Mr. Joseph Silk's friend.
Cooper consulted Silk on every point. Whenever he
saw a light in Silk's chambers he thrilled a little with
anticipation of the pleasant hour before him, and
they sat together discussing the abilities of various
eminent judges and barristers. Silk told humorous
anecdotes of the judges; Cooper was exercised concerning their morality, and enlarged anxiously on
the responsibility of placing a man on the Bench
without having full knowledge of his private life.
Silk listened, puffing at his pipe, and to avoid committing himself to an opinion, asked Cooper to have
another glass of port. Before they parted allusion

was made to the law book that Cooper was writing—
Cooper was always bringing out new editions of other
people's books, and continually exposed the bad law
they wrote in his conversation. He had waited his
turn like another for "soups" at the Bailey, and like
another had grown weary of waiting; besides the
meditative cast of his mind enticed him towards
chamber practice and away from public pleading
before judge and jury. Silk sought "a big advertising case"; he desired the excitement of court, and,
though he never refused any work, he dreaded the
lonely hours necessary for the perfect drawing up of
a long indictment. Cooper was very much impressed
with Silk's abilities; he thought him too hard and
mechanical, not sufficiently interested in the science
of morals; but these defects of character were forgotten in his homage to his friend's worldly shrewdness.
For Cooper was unendowed with worldly shrewdness,
and, like all dreamers, was attracted by a mind which
controlled while he might only attempt to understand; and Cooper's aspirations towards an ideal
tickled Silk's mind as it prepared its snares. Cooper
often invited Silk to dine with him at the National
Liberal Club; Silk sometimes asked Cooper to dine
with him at the Union. Silk and Cooper were considered alike, and there were many points in which
their appearances coincided. Cooper was the shorter
man of the two, but both were tall, thin, narrow, and
sallow-complexioned; both were essentially clean,
respectable, and middle-class.

Cooper was the son of a Low Church bishop who
had gained his mitre by temperance oratory, and
what his Grace was in the cathedral, Cooper was in
the suburban drawing-rooms, where radical politics
and the woman's cause were discussed. When he
had a brief he brought it to the library to show it;
he almost lived in the library. He arrived the

moment it was opened, and brought a packet of sandwiches so as not to waste time going out to lunch. His chambers were furnished without taste, but the works of Comte and Spencer showed that he had attempted to think; and the works of several socialistic writers showed that he had attempted to solve the problem of human want. On the table were several novels by Balzac, which conversation with Harding had led him to purchase and to read. He likewise possessed a few volumes of modern poetry, but he freely confessed that he preferred Pope, Dryden, and Johnson; and it was impossible to bring him to understand that De Quincey was more subtle and suggestive than the author of London.

Generally our souls are made of one conspicuous modern mental aspect; but below this aspect we are woven and coloured by the spirit of some preceding century, our chance inheritance, and Cooper was a sort of product of the pedantry of Johnson and the utilitarian mysticism of Comte. Perhaps the idea nearest to Cooper's heart was " the woman's cause." The misery and ignominy of human life had affected him, and he dreamed of the world's regeneration through women; and though well aware that Comte and Spencer advocate the application of experience in all our many mental embarrassments, he failed to reconsider his beliefs in female virtue, although frequently pressed to do so by Mike. Some personal animosity had grown out of their desire to convince each other. Cooper had once even meditated Mike's conversion, and Mike never missed an opportunity of telling some story which he deemed destructive of Cooper's faith. His faith was to him what a microscope is to a scientist, and it enabled him to discover the finest characteristics in the souls of bar girls, chorus girls, and prostitutes; and even when he fell, and they fell, his belief in their virtue and the nobility of their womanly instincts remained unshaken.

Mike had just finished a most racy story concerning his first introduction to a certain countess. Cooper had listened in silence, but when Mike turned at the end of his tale and asked him what he thought of his conduct, Cooper rose from his chair.

" I think you behaved like a blackguard."

In a moment Mike was aware that he had put himself in the wrong—that story about the countess could not be told except to his destruction in any language except his own, and that he must therefore forbear to strike Cooper and swallow the insult.

" You ass, get out; I can't quarrel with you on such a subject."

The embarrassment was increased by Cooper calling to Silk and asking if he were coming with him. The prudent Silk felt that to stay was to signify his approval of Mike's conduct in the case of the indiscreet countess. To leave 'with Cooper was to write himself down a prig, expose himself to the sarcasm of several past masters in the art of gibing, and to make in addition several powerful enemies. But the instinct not to compromise himself in any issue did not desert him, and rushing after Cooper he attempted the peace-maker. He knew the attempt would mean no more than some hustling in the doorway, and some ineffectual protestation, and he returned a few minutes after to join in the ridicule heaped upon the unfortunate Cooper and to inwardly vow that this was his last evening in Bohemia.

By the piano, smoking a clay pipe, there sat a large, rough, strong man. His beard was bristly and flame-colored, his face was crimson and pimply; lion-like locks hung in profusion about the collar of his shabby jacket. His linen was torn, and thin; crumpled was the necktie, and nearly untied, and the trousers were worn and frayed, and the boots heavy. He looked as if he could have carried a trunk excellently well, but as that thought struck you your eyes fell upon his hands which were the long, feminine-shaped hands generally found in those of naturally artistic temperament, nearly always in those who practice two or more of the arts. Sands affected all the arts. Enumerate: He played snatches of Bach on the violin, on the piano, and on the organ; he composed fragments for all those three instruments. He painted little landscapes after (a long way after) the manner of Corot, of whom he could talk until the small hours in the morning if an occasional drink and cigar were forthcoming. He modelled little statuettes in wax, cupids and nymphs, and he designed covers for books. He could do all these things a little, and not stupidly, although inefficiently. He had been a volunteer, and therefore wrote on military subjects, and had on certain occasions been permitted to criticize our naval defences and point out the vices and shortcomings in our military system in the leading evening papers. He generally was seen with one under his arm going towards Charing Cross or Fleet Street. He never strayed further west than Charing Cross, unless he was going to a " picture show," and there was no reason why he should pass Ludgate Circus, for further east there were neither newspapers nor restaurants. He was quite without vanity and therefore without ambition, Buddha was never more so, not even after attaining the Nirvana. A picture show in Bond Street, a half-crown dinner at Simpson's, or the Rainbow, coffee and cigars after, was all that he desired; give him that, and he was a pleasant companion who would remain with you until you turned him out, or in charity, for he was often homeless, allowed him to sleep on your sofa.

Sands was not a member of the Temple, but Hall's rooms were ever a refuge to the weary—there they might rest, and there was there ever for them a drink and a mouthful of food. And there Sands had met the decayed barrister who held the rooms opposite; which, although he had long ceased to occupy, and had no use for, he still wished to own, if he could do so without expense; this might be done by letting rooms, and reserving one for himself.

The unwary barrister, believing in the solvency of whomever he met at Hall's, entrusted his chambers to Sands, without demanding the rent in advance. A roof to sleep under had been the chief difficulty in Sands' life. He thought not at all of a change of clothes, and clean linen troubled him only slightly. Now almost every want seemed provided for. Coals he could get from Hall, also occasional half-crowns; these sufficed to pay for his breakfast; a dinner he could generally "cadge," and if he failed to do so, he had long ago learnt to go without. It was hard not to admire his gentleness, his patience and for-bearance. If you refused to lend him money he showed no faintest trace of anger. Hall's friends were therefore delighted that the chambers opposite were let on conditions so favourable to Sands; they anticipated with roars of laughter the scene that would happen at the close of the year, and looked forward to seeing, at least during the interim, their friend in clean clothes, and reading "his copy" in the best journals. But the luxury of having a fixed place to sleep in, stimulated, not industry, but vicious laziness of the most ineradicable kind. Henceforth Sands abandoned all effort to help himself. Uncombed, unwashed, in dirty clothes he lay in an arm-chair through all the morning, rising from time to time to mess some paint into the appearance of some incoherent landscape, or to rasp out some bars of Beethoven on his violin.

" Never did I imagine any one so idle; he is fairly putrid with idleness," said Hall after a short visit. " Would you believe it, he has only ninepence for sole shield between him and starvation. The editor of the *Moon* has just telegraphed for the notice he should have written of the Academy, and the brute is just sending a ' wire '—' nothing possible this week.' Did any one ever hear of such a thing? To-night he won't dine and he could write the notice in an hour."

Besides having contributed to almost every paper in London, from the *Times* downwards, Sands had held positions as editor and sub-editor of numerous journals. But he had lost each one in turn, and was beginning to understand that he was fated to die of poverty, and was beginning to grow tired of the useless struggle. No one was better organized to earn his living than Peter Sands, and no one failed more lamentably. Had fortune provided him with a dinner at Simpson's, a cigar and a cup of coffee, he would have lived as successfully as another. But our civilization is hard upon those who are only conversationalists, it does not seem to have taken them into account in its scheme, and, in truth, Peter could not do much more than to æstheticise agreeably.

Paul L'Estrange admitted freely that he was not fitted for a lawyer; but even before he explained that he considered himself one of those beings who had slipped into a hole that did not fit them, it was probable that you had already begun to consider the circumstances that had brought him to choose the law as a profession; for his vague intelligence "where nothing was and all things seemed," lay mirrored in his mild eyes like a landscape in a pool.   Over such a partial and a meditative mind as L'Estrange's, the Temple may exercise a destructive fascination; and since the first day, when a boy he had walked through the closes gathering round the church, and had heard of the knights, had seen the old dining-hall with its many inscriptions, going back even to 1400, he had never ceased to dream of the Temple—that relic of the past, saved with all its traditions out of the ruin of time; and the memory of his cousin's chambers, and the association and mutuality of the life of the Temple, the picturesqueness of the wigs and gowns passing, and the uncommonness of it all had taken root and grown, overshadowing other ideals, and when the time came for him to choose a profession, no choice was open to him but the law, for the law resided in the Temple.

Soon after his father died, the family property was sold and the family scattered; some went to Australia, some to Canada; but L'Estrange had inherited a hundred a year from a grandaunt, and he lived on that, and what he made by writing in the newspapers, for of course no one had thought of entrusting him with a brief; and what he made by journalism varied from a hundred and fifty to two hundred and fifty a year.   Whenever a new scare arose he was busy among blue-books in the library.

L'Estrange loved to dine at the Cock Tavern with a party of men from the inn and to invite them to his chambers to take coffee afterwards.   And when they had retired, and only one remained he would say, " What a nice fellow so-and-so is; you do meet a nice lot of fellows in the Temple, don't you?"   It seemed almost sufficient that a man should belong to the Temple for L'Estrange to find him admirable.

The dinners in hall were especially delightful. Between the courses he looked in admiration on the portraits and old oak carvings, and the armorial bearings, and would tell how one bencher had been debarred from election as treasurer because he had, on three occasions, attended dinner without partaking of any food. Such an insult to the kitchen could not be forgiven. L'Estrange was full of such stories, and he relished their historical flavour as a gourmet an unusually successful piece of cooking. He regarded the Temple and its associations with love.

When he had friends to dinner in his rooms the dinner was always brought from the hall ; he ordered it himself in the large spacious kitchen, which he duly admired, and prying about amid the various meats, he chose with care, and when told that what he desired could not be obtained that day, he continued his search notwithstanding. He related that on one occasion he discovered a greengage pie, after many assurances that there was no such thing in the kitchen. If he was with a friend he laid his hand on his shoulder and pointing out an inscription, he said, " Now one thing I notice about the Temple is, that never is an occasion missed of putting up an inscription ; and note the legal character of the inscriptions, how carefully it is explained, that, for instance, the cloisters, although they are for the use of the Inner as well as the Middle Temple, yet it was the Middle Temple that paid to have them put up, and therefore owns the property." L'Estrange always spoke of the gardens as " our gardens," of the church as " our church." He was an authority on all that related to the Temple, and he delighted in a friend in whom he might confide ; and to walk about the courts with Hall or Sands, stopping now and then to note some curious piece of sculpture or date, and forthwith to relate an anecdote that brought back some of the fragrance and colour of old time, and to tell how he intended to work such curious facts into the book he was writing on the Temple, was the essence and the soul of this dreamy man's little life.

Saturday night is the night of dalliance in the Temple, and not unfrequently on Sunday morning, leaving a lady love, L'Estrange would go to church —top hat, umbrella, and prayer-book—and having a sense of humour, he was amused by the incongruity.

"I have left the accursed thing behind me," he once said to Mr. Collier, and by such facetiousness had seriously annoyed the immense and most staid Mr. Collier.

A gaunt, hollow-eyed man was he, worn to a thread by diabetes ; and to keep the disease in check, strictly dieted.   His appearance was so suggestive of illness that whenever he was present the conversation always turned on what he might eat and what he must refrain from touching.   A large, gray-skinned man, handsome, somewhat like a figure of Melancholy cut out of a block of limestone.   Since he had left Oxford, where he had taken a double first, he had failed at the bar, in literature, in love.   It was said that he had once written an absurd letter asking a lady, who hoped to marry a duke, to go to South America with him.   This letter had been his only adventure.

He was like a bookcase, a store of silent learning, with this difference, from the bookcase much may be extracted, from Mr. Edmund Collier nothing.   Of a dry well, a London fog, an abandoned quarry, the desert of Sahara, the North Pole, did Mr. Collier remind you ; of all dull and lugubrious things he seemed the type.   Nature had not afflicted him with passions nor any original thought, he therefore lived an exemplary existence, his mind fortified with common-place opinions, doctrines, and general views.

" I wonder if he is alive," Mike had once said.

" *Hé, hé, tout au plus,*" Harding had replied, sardonically.

Collier was now learning Sanscrit and writing an article for the *Quarterly.* L'Estrange used, as he said, " to dig at him," and after many exhausting efforts brought up interesting facts to the effect that he had just finished his treatise on the Greek participle, and was about to launch a volume of verses mainly addressed to children.

Collier had once possessed considerable property, but he had invested some in a newspaper of which he was editor, and he had squandered much in vague speculation. From the account he gave of his losses it was difficult to decide whether he had been moved by mercenary or charitable temptations. Now only the merest competence remained. He lived in a small garret where no solicitor had penetrated, studying uninteresting literatures, dimly interested in all that the world did not care for. He lived in the gloom of present failure, embittered by the memory of past successes, wearied with long illness, and therefore constrained to live like a hermit, never appearing anywhere except in Hall's rooms.

Even Mr. Horace Baird, the recluse of the Temple, was sometimes met in Hall's chambers. When he lifted his hat, the white locks growing amid the black, magnificent masses of hair caught the eye, and set the mind thinking on the brevity of youth, or wondering what ill-fortune had thus done the work of time. A passing glance told you that he was unsuccessful in his profession and unfortunate in his life, and if you spoke to him, an affected gaiety of manner confirmed the truth of the visual expression. Near him sat the patriarchal barrister who had travelled in the colonies, had had political appointments, and in vague hopes of further political appointments professed advanced views, which he endeavoured to redeem with flavourless humour. There were also the two young men who shared chambers and took in pupils. Fine tales their laundress told of the state of their sitting-room in the morning, the furniture thrown about, the tablecloth drenched in whiskey, the basin on the floor in case of accidents. There was the young man whose hobby was dress and chorus girls. There was the young man whose hobby was pet birds ; he talked about the beautiful South American bird he had just bought, and he asked you to come and see it taking its bath in the morning. Several persons were writing law books, such as *Chitty on Contracts.*

The Temple, like a fatherland, never loses its influence over its children. He who has lived in the Temple will return to the Temple. All things are surrendered for the Temple. All distances are traversed to reach the Temple. The Temple is never forgotten. The briefless barrister, who left in despair and became Attorney-General of New South Wales, grows homesick, surrenders his position, and returns. The young squire wearies in his beautiful country house, and his heart is fixed in the dingy chambers, which he cannot relinquish, and for which wealth cannot compensate him. Even the poor clerks do not forget the Temple, and on Saturday afternoons they prowl about their old offices, and often give up lucrative employments. They are drawn by the Temple as by a magnet, and must live again in the shadow of the old inns. The laundresses' daughters pass into wealthy domesticities, but sooner or later they return to drudge again in the Temple.

"How awfully jolly; I do enjoy an evening like this," said Mike, when the guests had departed.

At that moment a faint footstep was heard on the landing; Hall rushed to see who was there, and returned with two women. They explained that they wanted a drink. Mike pressed them to make themselves at home, and Hall opened another bottle.

"How comfortable you bachelors are here by yourselves," said one.

"I should think we are just; no fear of either of us being such fools as to break up our home by getting married," replied Mike.

Sometimes Mike and Hall returned early from the restaurant, and wrote from eight to eleven; then went out for a cup of coffee and a prowl, or to beat up the Strand for women. They stayed out smoking and talking at the corners till the streets were empty. Sometimes they sent a couple of harlots to rouse a learned old gentleman who lived in Brick Court, and with bated breath listened from the floor beneath to the dialogue above.

But to continue this life, which he enjoyed so intensely that he had even lost his desire to gamble, Mike was forced to borrow. Knowing how such things are bruited about, Mike preferred to go to a woman than to any of his men friends. Mrs. Byril lent him twenty pounds, wherefore he thought it necessary to lecture Hall for one whole evening on the immorality of ever accepting money from women; and he remained for weeks in an idleness, smoking and drinking in restaurants and bar-rooms, deaf to Frank's many pleadings for "copy." At last he roused a little, and feeling he could do nothing in

London, proposed to come and stay with Frank in his cottage at Marlow, and there write the letters.

It was a bright October afternoon, Frank had gone to the station, and Lizzie, to appease the baby, had unbuttoned her dress. The little servant-girl who assisted with the house-work was busy in the kitchen; for the fatted calf had been killed—that is to say, a pair of soles, a steak, and a partridge were in course of preparation. Lizzie thought of the partridge. She had omitted soup from the dinner so that she might herself see to the fish; the steak, unless something quite unforeseen occurred, Annie would be able to manage, but the partridge! Lizzie determined she would find an excuse for leaving the room; Frank would not like it, but anything would be better than that the bird should appear in a raw or cindery condition, which would certainly be the case if she did not see to it. The jam-pudding was boiling and would be taken out of the pot at a fixed time. And with baby upon her breast, she watched Sally scrape and clean the fish and beat the steak; then, hearing the front door open, she buttoned her dress, put baby in his cot, and went to meet her visitor. Mike said he had never seen her looking so well; but in truth he thought she had grown fat and coarse; and in half an hour he had realized all the detail of their misfortune. He guessed that she had helped to cook the dinner, that the wine had come from the public-house, that they had given up their room to him, and were sleeping in some small cupboard-like place at the end of the passage.

Of the many various unpleasantnesses of married life which had crowded into his consciousness since he had been in the cottage, this impressed him the most. He went to sleep thinking of it, and when he sat down to write next morning (a little study had been arranged for him), it was the first thought that stirred in him.

" How fearfully unpleasant!—and after having been married for nearly two years! I could not do it. If I were married—even if I were to marry Lily, I should insist on having separate rooms. Even with separate rooms marriage is intolerable. How much better to see her sometimes, sigh for her from afar, and so preserve one's ideal. Married! One day I should be sure to surprise her washing herself; and I know of no more degrading spectacle than that of a woman washing herself over a basin. Degas painted it once. I'd give anything to have that picture."

But he could not identify Lily as forming part of that picture; his imagination did not help him, and he could only see her staid and gracious, outside all the gross materialism of life. He felt that Lily would never lose her dignity and loveliness, which in her were one, and in his mind she ever stood like a fair statue out of reach of the mud and the contumely of the common street; and ashamed, an unsuccessful iconoclast, he could not do otherwise than kneel and adore her.

And when at the end of a week he received an invitation to a ball where he thought she would be, he could only obey, and go with tremulous heart. She was engaged in a quadrille that passed to and fro beneath blue tapestry curtains, and he noticed the spray of lilies of the valley in her bodice, so emblematic did they seem of her. Beneath the blue curtain she stood talking to her partner after the dance; and he did not go to speak to her, but remained looking. They only danced together twice; and that evening was realized by him in a strangely intense and durable perception of faint scent and fluent rhythm. The sense of her motion, of her frailness, lingered in his soul ever afterwards. And he remembered ever afterwards the moments he spent with her in a distant corner—the palm, the gold of the screen, the movement of her white skirt as she sat down. All was, as it were, bitten upon his soul—exquisite etchings! Even the pauses in the conversation were remembered; pauses full of mute affection; pauses full of thought unexpressed, falling in sharp chasms of silence. In such hours and in such pauses is the essence of our lives, the rest is adjunct and decoration. He watched, fearing each man that looked through the doorways might claim her for the next dance. His thought swept through his soul edgeways. Did he love her? Would he love her always? And he was conscious of the contrast his speech presented, to the tumult that raged and shrieked within him. Yet he couldn't speak the word, and he cursed his little cowardice.

The ball came and went—a little year with its four seasons; and when in the hall he stood by her, helping her with her cloak (silk and gray fur, folding the delicate line of the neck), and became aware that even those last moments did not hold the word his soul was whispering, he cursed his cowardice, and, weary of himself, he turned down the dark street, feeling that he had lost his life.

"Now all is ended," he thought, "I'm like a convict who attempted escape and has been brought back and yoked again in the sweaty and manacled gang; and I must continue in and bear with this life of gross sensuality and dirty journalism, 'which I have borne and yet must bear'—a wearisome repetition of what has been done and re-done a thousand times, 'till death-like sleep shall steal on me,' and I may hear some horrible lodging-house keeper ' breathe o'er my dying brain a last monotony.' And in various degradations my intellect will suffer, will decay ; but with her refining and elevating influence, I might be a great writer. It is certain that the kernel of Art is aspiration for higher things; at all events, I should have led a cleanly life. If I were married to her I could not write this book. It certainly is a disgraceful book ; and yet it amuses me."

His thoughts paused, then an idea came, and with his pen he pursued it and the quickly rising flight which followed for a couple of hours.

" Why should I not write and ask her to marry me ?" He smiled at the thought, but the thought was stronger than he, and he went to bed thinking of her, and he rose thinking of her; and the desire to write and tell her that he loved her and wanted her for wife persisted ; he shook it off a dozen times, but it grew more and more poignant, until it settled on his heart, a lancinating pain which neither work nor pleasure could remove. Daily he grew feebler, losing at each effort some power of resistance, and one day he took up the pen to write the irrevocable. But the reality of the ink and paper frightened him. " Will you be my wife ?" seemed to him silly. Even in this crisis self-esteem lay uppermost in his mind ; and he wrote many letters before he felt certain he had guarded himself against ridicule. At last he folded up a sheet upon which he had written—"Dearest Lily, you are the only woman I may love, will you allow me to love you forever?" He put this into an envelope and directed it; nothing remained but to post it. The clock told him he could catch the post if he started away at once, but he drew back, frightened at the reality of the post-office, and decided to sleep over his letter.

The night was full of Lily—fair, chaste, dreams, whence he rose as from a bath clothed in the samite of pure delight.   While dressing he felt sure that marriage—at least marriage with Lily must be but the realization of such dreams, and that it would be folly not to post his letter.   Still, it might be as well to hear the opinion of one who had taken the important step, and after breakfast he drew Frank into conversation about Lizzie.

"I am quite happy," he said. "Lizzie is a good wife, and I love her better to-day than the day I married her; but the price I paid for her was too high.   Mount Rorke has behaved shamefully, and so has everybody but you.   I never see any of the old lot now.   Snowdown came once to dine about a year ago, but I never go anywhere where Lizzie is not asked.   Mount Rorke has only written once since my marriage, and then it was to say he never wished to see me again.   The next I heard was the announcement of his marriage."

"So he has married again," said Mike, looking at Frank, and then he thought—"So you who came from the top shall go to the bottom! Shall he who came from the bottom go to the top?"

"I have not heard yet of a child.   I have tried to find out if one is expected; but what does it matter?—Mount Rorke wouldn't give me a penny piece to save me from starvation, and I should have time to starve a good many times before he goes off the hooks.   I don't mind telling you I'm about as hard up as a man possibly can be.   I owe three quarters' rent for my rooms in Temple Gardens, nearly two hundred pounds.   The Inn is pressing me, and I can't get three hundred for my furniture, and I'm sure I paid more than fifteen hundred for what there is there."

"Why don't you sell a share in the paper?"

"I have sold a small part of it, a very small part of it, a fifth, and there is a fellow called Thigh—

you know the fellow, he has edited every stupid weekly that has appeared and disappeared for the last ten years—well, he has got hold of a mug, and by all accounts a real mug, one of the right sort, a Mr. Beacham Brown. Mr. Brown wants a paper and has commissioned Thigh to buy him one. Thigh wants me to sell a half share in the *Pilgrim* for a thousand, but I shall have to give Thigh back four hundred; and I shall—that is to say, I shall if I agree to Thigh's terms—become assistant editor at a salary of six pounds a week; two pounds a week of which I shall have to hand over to Thigh, who comes in as editor at a salary of ten pounds a week. All the staff will be engaged on similar conditions. Thigh is 'working' Beacham Brown beautifully—he won't have a sixpence to bless himself with when Thigh has done with him."

"And are you going to accept Thigh's terms?"

"Not if I can possibly help it. If your articles send up the circulation and my new advertising agent can do the West End tradesmen for a few more advertisements, I shall stand off and wait for better terms. My new advertising agent is a wonder, the finest in Christendom. The other day a Bond Street jeweller who advertises with us came into my office. He said, 'Sir, I have come to ask you if you circulate thirty thousand copies a week.' 'Well,' I said, 'perhaps not quite.' 'Then, sir,' he replied, 'you will please return me my money; I gave your agent my advertisement upon his implicit assurance that you circulated thirty thousand a week.' I said there must be some mistake; Mr. Tomlinson happens to be in the office, if you'll allow me I'll ask him to step down-stairs. I touched the bell, and told the boy to ask Mr. Tomlinson to step into the office. 'Mr. Tomlinson,' I said, 'Mr. Page says that he gave you his advertisement on your implicit assurance that we circulated thirty thousand copies weekly. Did you tell him that?' Quite unabashed, Tomlinson answered, 'I told Mr. Page that we had more than thirty thousand readers a week. We send to ten line regiments and five cavalry regiments—each regiment consists of, let us say, eight hundred. We send to every club in London, and each club has on an average a thousand members. Why, sir,' exclaimed Tomlinson, turning angrily on the jeweller, 'I might have said that we had a hundred thousand readers and I should have still been under the mark!' The jeweller paid for his advertisement and went away crestfallen. Such a man as Tomlinson is the very bone and muscle of a society journal."

" And the nerves too," said Mike.

" Better than the contributors who want to write about the relation between art and morals."

The young men laughed mightily.

" And what will you do," said Mike, " if you don't settle with Thigh?"

" Perhaps my man will be able to pick up another advertisement or two; perhaps your articles may send up the circulation. One thing is certain, things can't go on as they are; at this rate I shall not be able to carry the paper on another six months."

The conversation fell, and Mike remembered the letter in his side pocket; it lay just over his heart. Frank's monetary difficulties had affected his matrimonial aspirations. " For if the paper 'burst's up' how shall I live, much less support a wife? Live! I shall always be able to live, but to support a wife is quite another matter. Perhaps Lily has some money. If she had five hundred a year I would marry her. But I don't know if she has a penny. She must have some, a few thousands—enough to pay the first expenses. To get a house and get into

the house would cost a thousand." A cloud passed
over his face. The householder, the payer of rates
and taxes which the thought evoked, jarred and
caricatured the ideal, the ideal Mike Fletcher, which
in more or less consistent form was always present
in his mind. He who had always received, would
have to make presents. The engagement ring would
cost five-and-twenty pounds, and where was he to
get the money? That he would have to buy at once;
and his entire fortune did not for the moment
amount to ten pounds. Her money, if she had any,
would pay for the honeymoon; and it was only right
that a woman should pay for her honeymoon. They
would go to Italy. She was Italy! At least she
was his idea of Italy. Italy! he had never been
there; he had always intended to keep Italy for his
wedding tour. He was virgin of Italy. So much
virginity he had at all events kept for his wife. She
was the emblem and symbol of Italy.

Venice rose into his eyes. He is in a gondola
with her; the water is dark with architrave and pil-
lar; and a half moon floats in a boundless sky. But
remembering that this is the Venice of a hundred
"chromos," his imagination filled the well-known
water way with sunlight and maskers, creating the
carnival upon the Grand Canal. Laughing and
mocking Loves; young nobles in blue hose, sword
on thigh, as in Shakespeare's plays; young brides in
tumultuous satin, with collars of translucent pearls;
garlands reflected in the water; scarves thrown about
the ample bosoms of patrician matrons. Then the
brides, the nobles, the pearls, the loves, and the
matrons disappear in a shower of confetti. Wearying
of Venice he strove to see Florence, "the city of
lilies;" but the phrase only suggested flower-sellers.
He intoxicated upon his love, she who to him was
now Italy. He imagined confidences, sudden sights

of her face more exquisite than the Botticelli women in the echoing picture galleries, more enigmatic than the eyes of a Leonardo; and in these days of desire, he lived through the torment of impersonal love, drawn for the first time out of himself. All beautiful scenes of love from books, pictures, and life floated in his mind. He especially remembered a sight of lovers which he had once caught on an hotel staircase. A young couple, evidently just returned from the theatre, had entered their room; the woman was young, tall and aristocratic; she was dressed in some soft material, probably a dress of cream-coloured lace in numberless flounces; he remembered that her hair was abundant and shadowed her face. The effect of firelight played over the hangings of the bed; she stood by the bed and raised the fur cloak from her shoulders. The man was tall and thin, and the light caught the points of the short sharp beard. The scene had bitten itself into Mike's mind, and it reappeared at intervals perfect as a print, for he sometimes envied the calm and healthfulness of honourable love.

"Great Scott! twelve o'clock!" Smiling, conscious of the incongruity he set to work, and in about three hours had finished a long letter, in which he usefully advised "light o' loves" on the advantages of foreign travel.

."I wonder," he thought, " how I can write in such a strain while I'm in love with her. What beastliness! I hate the whole thing. I desire a new life; I have tried vice long enough and am weary of it; I'm not happy, and if I were to gain the whole world it would be dust and ashes without her. Then why not take that step which would bring her to me?" He faced his cowardice angrily, and resolved to post the letter. But he stopped before he had walked fifty yards, for his doubts followed him, buzzing and stinging like bees. Striving to rid himself of them, and weary of considering his own embarrassed condition, he listened gladly to Lizzie, who deplored Mount Rorke's cruelty and her husband's continuous ill luck.

"I told him his family would never receive me; I didn't want to marry him; for days I couldn't make up my mind; he can't say I persuaded him into it."

"But you are happy now; don't you like being married?"

"Oh, yes, I should be happy enough if things only went better with us. He is so terribly unlucky. No one works harder than Frank; he often sits up till three o'clock in the morning writing. He tries everything, but nothing seems to succeed with him. There's this paper. I don't believe he has ever had a penny out of it. Tell me, Mr. Fletcher, do you think it will ever succeed?"

"Newspapers generally fail for want of a concerted plan of appeal to a certain section of society kept steadily in view; they are nearly always vague and undetermined; but I believe when four clever pens are brought together, and write continuously, and with set purpose and idea, that they can, that they must and invariably do create a property worth at least twenty thousand pounds."

"Frank has gone to the station to meet Thigh. I distrust that man dreadfully; I hope he won't rob my poor husband. Frank told me to get a couple of pheasants for dinner. Which way are you going? To the post-office? Do you want a stamp?"

"No, thank you, my letter is stamped." He held the letter in the box unable to loose his fingers, embarrassed in the consideration whether marriage would permit him to develop his artistic nature as he intended. Lizzie was looking at him, and it was with difficulty that he concealed from her the fact that he had not dropped his letter in the box.

When they returned to the cottage they found

Thigh and Frank were turning over the pages of the
last number of the *Pilgrim*.

"Just let's go through the paper," said Frank.
"One, two, three—twelve columns of paragraphs!
and I'll bet that in every one of those columns there
is a piece of news artistic, political, or social, which
no other paper has got. Here are three articles, one
written by our friend here, one by me, and one by a
man whose name I am not at liberty to mention;
but I may tell you he has written some well-known
books, and is a constant contributor to the *Fort-
nightly;* here is a column of gossip from Paris excellently well done ; here is a short story . . . What
do you think the paper wants?"

Thigh was a very small and very neatly-dressed
man. His manner was quiet and reserved, and he
caressed a large fair moustache with his left hand,
on which a diamond ring sparkled.

"I think it wants smartening up all round," he
said. "You want to make it smarter; people will
have things bright nowadays."

"Bright!" said Frank, "I don't know where you
are going for brightness nowadays. Just look at the
other papers—here is the *Club*—did you ever see
such a rag? Here is the *Spy*—I don't think you
could tell if you were reading a number of last year
or this week if you didn't look at the date! I've
given them up for news. I look to see if they have
got a new advertisement; if they have, I send Tomlinson and see if I can get one too."

Thigh made some judicious observations, and the
conversation was continued during dinner. Frank
and Mike vying with each other to show their deference to Thigh's literary opinions—Lizzie eager to
know what he thought of her dinner.

Thigh said the turbot was excellent, that the cut-
lets were very nice, that the birds were splendid;

the jam pudding was voted delicious. And they leaned back in their chairs, their eyes filled with the torpor of digestion. Frank brought out a bottle of old port, the last of a large supply which he had had from Mount Rorke's wine merchant. The pleasure of the wine was in their stomachs, and under its influence they talked of Tennyson, Leonardo da Vinci, Corot, and the *Ingoldsby Legends*. The servant had brought in the lamp, cigars were lighted, the clock struck nine. As yet not a word had been spoken of the business, and seeing that Mike was deep in conversation with Lizzie, Frank moved his chair towards Thigh, and said—

"Well, what about buying half of the paper?"

"I'm quite ready to buy half the paper on the conditions I've already offered you."

"But they won't do. If I have to go smash, I may as well go smash for a large sum as a small one. To clear myself of debts I must have five hundred pounds."

"Well, you'll get six hundred; you'll receive a thousand and you'll give me back four hundred."

"Yes, but I did not tell you that I have sold a small share in the paper to an old school-fellow of mine. When I have paid him I shall have only two hundred, and that won't be of the slightest use to me."

"Oh, you have sold part of the paper already, have you? How do you know your friend will consent to be bought out? That complicates matters."

"My friend only did it to oblige me; he is only too anxious to be bought out. He is in a fearful funk lest he should be compromised in a libel action."

"Oh, then I think it can be managed. Were I in your place I should try and get rid of him for nothing. I can't offer you better terms; it wouldn't pay me to do so; I might as well start a new paper."

"Yes, but tell me how can I get rid of him for nothing?"

Thigh looked at Frank inquiringly, and apparently satisfied he drew his chair nearer, stroked his moustache, and said, speaking under his breath—

"Have you collected what money is owing to the paper lately? Have you many outstanding debts?"

"We have got some."

"Well, don't collect any money that is owing, but make out a long statement of the paper's liabilities; don't say a word about the outstanding debts, and tell your friend that he is responsible as part owner of the paper for this money. When you have sufficiently frightened him, suggest that he should sign over his share to you, you being a man of straw whom it would be useless to proceed against. Or you might get your printer to press you for money—"

"That won't be difficult."

"Offer him a bill, and then mix the two accounts up together in it."

At this moment Mike was speaking to Lizzie of love. She told him there was no real happiness except in married life, assured him that though they might be beggars to-day, she would not give up her husband for all the wealth of the three kingdoms.

Very anxious to inquire out the truth about married life, Mike pressed Lizzie upon several points; the old ache awoke about his heart, and again he resolved to regenerate his life, and love Lily and none but her. He looked round the room, considering how he could get away. Frank was talking business. He would not disturb him. No doubt Thigh was concocting some swindle, but he (Mike) knew nothing of business; he had a knack of turning the king at ecarté, but was nowhere once bills and the cooking of accounts were introduced. Should he post the letter? That was the question, and it played in his ears like an electric bell. Here was the letter; he could feel it through his coat, lying over his heart, and there it had lain since he had written it.

Frank and Thigh continued talking; Lizzie went to the baby, and Mike walked into the night, and looked at the stars. He walked along the white high road—to him a road of dreams, towards the white town—to him a town of chimeras, and leaning over the moon-lit river, shaking himself free from the hallucination within and without him, he said—

" On one hand I shall belong to one woman. Her house shall be my house, her friends shall be my friends; the others, the beautiful, fascinating others, will cease to dream of me, I shall no longer be their ideal. On the other hand I shall gain the nicest woman, and surely it must be right to take, though it be for life, the nicest woman in the world. She will supply what is wanting in my character; together we shall attain a goal; alone I shall attain none. In twenty years I shall be a foolish old bachelor whom no one cares for. I have stated both cases—on which side does the balance turn?"

The balance still stood at equipoise; a formless moon soared through a white cloud wrack, and broken gold lay in the rising tide. The sonorous steps of the policeman on the bridge startled him, and obeying the impulse of the moment, he gave the officer the letter, asking him to post it. He waited for some minutes, as if stupefied, pursuing the consequences of his act even into distant years. No, he would not send the letter just yet. But the officer had disappeared in some bye streets, and followed by the spirits of future loves, Mike ran till he reached the post-office, where he waited in nervous apprehension. Presently steps were heard in the stillness, and getting between him and the terrible slot Mike determined to fight for his letter if it were refused him.

" I met you just now on the bridge and asked you to post a letter ; give it back to me, if you please. I've changed my mind."

The officer looked at him narrowly, but he took the proffered shilling, and returned the letter.

" That was the narrowest squeak I've had yet," thought Mike.

When he returned to the cottage he found Frank and Thigh still together.

" Mr. Beacham Brown," said Thigh, " is now half-proprietor of the *Pilgrim*. The papers are signed. I came down quite prepared. I believe in settling things right off. When Mrs. Escott comes in, we will drink to the new *Pilgrim*, or if you like it better, to the old *Pilgrim*, who starts afresh with a new staff and scrip, and a well filled scrip too," he added, laughing vacuously.

" I hope," said Mike, " that Holloway is not the shrine he is journeying towards."

" I hope your book won't bring us there."

" Why, I didn't know you were going to continue—"

" Oh, yes," said Thigh ; " that is to say if we can come to an arrangement about the purchase," and Thigh lapsed into a stony silence, as was his practice when conducting a bargain.

" By God !" Mike thought, " I wish we were playing at écarté or poker. I'm no good at business."

" Well," he said at last, " what terms do you propose to offer me ?"

Thigh woke up.

" I never bargain," he said. " I'll give you Beacham Brown's cheque for a hundred and fifty if you will give me a receipt for three hundred," and he looked inquiry out of his small, pale blue eyes, and

Mike noticed the diamond ring on the hand that caressed his moustache.

"No," said Mike, "that isn't fair. You don't write a line of the book. There is not even the excuse of commission, for the book is now appearing."

"Escott would not have paid you anything like that amount. I think I'm treating you very liberally. Indeed I don't mind telling you that I should not offer you anything like such terms if Beacham Brown were not anxious to have the book; he read your last article in the train, and came back raving about it."

Bright pleasure passed across Mike's face; he thought Thigh had slipped in the avowal, and he girt himself for resolute resistance and cautious attack. But Thigh was the superior strategist. Mike was led from the subject, and imperceptibly encouraged to speak of other things, and without interruption he span paradoxes and scattered jokes for ten minutes. Then the conversation dropped, and annoyed, Mike fixed his eyes on Thigh, who sat in unmovable silence.

"Well," said Mike, "what do you intend to do?"

"About what?" said Thigh, with a half-waking stare.

"About this book of mine. You know very well that if I take it to another shop you'll find it difficult to get anything like as good a serial. I know pretty well what talent is walking about Fleet Street."

Thigh said nothing, only raised his eyes as if Mike's words were full of suggestion, and again beguiled, Mike rambled into various criticisms of contemporary journalism. Friends were laughed at, and the papers they edited were stigmatized as rags that lived upon the ingenuity of the lies of advertising agents. When the conversation again dropped,

Thigh showed no inclination of returning to the book, but, as before, sat in stony silence, and out of temper with himself, Mike had to ask him again what the terms were.

"I cannot offer you better terms than I have already done."

"Very well; I'll take one hundred and fifty for the serial rights."

"No, for the entire rights."

"No, I'll be damned, I don't care what happens!"

Then Frank joined in the discussion. Every one withdrew the offer he had made, and all possibility of agreement seemed at an end. Somehow it was suggested that Thigh should toss Mike whether he should pay him two hundred or a hundred and fifty. The men exchanged questioning looks, and at that moment Lizzie entered with a pack of cards, and Thigh said—

"I'll play you at écarté—the best out of seven games."

Mike realized at once the situation, and he hoped Frank would not betray him. He saw that Thigh had been drinking. "God has given him into my hands," he thought; and it was agreed that they should play the best out of seven games for twenty-five pounds, and that the loser should have the right to call for a return match. Mike knew nothing of his opponent's play, but he did not for a moment suspect him of superior skill. Such a thing could hardly be, and he decided he would allow him to win the first games, watching carefully the while, so that he might study his combinations and plans, and learn in what measure he might pack and " bridge " the cards. There is much in a shuffle, and already Mike believed him to be no more than an ordinary club player, capable of winning a few sovereigns from

a young man fresh from the university; and although
the cards Mike held did not warrant such a course,
he played without proposing, and when he lost the
trick he scanned his opponent's face, and seeing it
brighten, he knew the ruse had succeeded.   But luck
seemed to run inexplicably against him, and he was
defeated.   In the return match he met with similar
luck, and rose from the table, having lost fifty
pounds.   Mike wrote a second I O U for twenty-
five pounds, to be paid out of the hundred and fifty
pounds to which he had agreed in writing to accept
for the book before sitting down to play.   Then
he protested vehemently against his luck, and so
well did he act his part, that even if Thigh had not
drunk another glass of whiskey-and-water he would
not have perceived that Mike was simulating an
excitement which he did not feel.

"I'll play you for a hundred pounds—the best out
of seven games; damn the cards!   I can beat you
no matter how they run!"

"Very well, I don't mind, anything to oblige a
friend."

Lizzie besought Mike not to play again, and she
nearly upset the apple-cart by angrily telling Thigh
she did not wish her house to be turned into a
gambling-hell.   Thigh rose from the table, but Frank
apologized for his wife, and begged of him to sit
down.   The incident was not without a good effect,
for it removed Thigh's suspicions, if he had any, and
convinced him that he was "in for a real good thing."
He laid on the table a cheque, signed Beacham
Brown, for a hundred pounds; Mike produced his
nearly completed manuscript.   Thigh looked over
the MS., judging its length.

"It is all here?"

"No, there's one chapter to come; that's good
enough for you."

"Oh yes, it will do.   You'll have to finish it, for you'll want to write for the paper."

This time the cards were perfectly packed, and Mike turned the king.

"Cards?"

"No, play."

Frank and Lizzie leaned breathless over the table, their faces white in the light of the unshaded lamp. Mike won the whole five tricks.   But luck was dead against him, and in a few minutes the score stood at three games all.   Then outrageously, for there was no help for it, as he never would have dared if his opponent had been quite sober, he packed and bridged the cards.   He turned the king.

"Cards?"

"No, play."

Mike won the fourth game, and put Mr. Beacham Brown's cheque in his pocket.

"I'll play you again," said Thigh.

Mike accepted, and before eleven o'clock Thigh had paid three hundred pounds for the manuscript and lost all his available spare cash.   He glanced narrowly at Mike, paused as he put on his hat and coat, and Frank wished Lizzie would leave the room, feeling sure that violent words were inevitable.   But at that moment Mike's shoulders and knuckles seemed more than usually prominent, and Mr. Beacham Brown's agent slunk away into the darkness.

"You did turn the king pretty often," said Frank, when the door closed.   "I'm glad there was no row."

"Row!   I'd have broken his dirty neck.   Not content with swindling poor Beacham Brown, he tries it on with the contributors.   I wish I had been able to get him to go on.   I would willingly have fleeced him of every penny he has in the world."

Lizzie bade them good-night, and the servant brought in a letter for Mike, a letter which she explained had been incorrectly addressed, and had just come from the hotel. Frank took up a newspaper which Thigh had left on the table. He turned it over, glancing hastily through it. Then something caught his eye, and the expression of his face changed. And what caused him pain could be no more than a few words, for the paper fell instantly from his hands and he sat quite still, staring into space. But neither the sound of the paper falling, nor yet the frozen rigidity of his attitude drew Mike's thoughts from the letter he was reading. He glanced hastily through it, then he read it attentively, lingering over every word. He seemed to suck sweetness out of every one; it was the deep, sensual absorption of a fly in a pot of treacle. His eyes were dim with pleasure long drawn out; they saw nothing, and it was some moments before the pallor and pain of Frank's face dispelled the melliferous Edens in which his soul moved.

"What is the matter, old chap? Are you ill?"

Frank did not answer.

"Are you ill? Shall I get you a drink?"

"No, no," he said. "I assure you it is nothing; no, it is nothing." He struggled for a moment for shame's sake to keep his secret, but it was more than he could bear. "Ah!" he said, "it is all over; I'm done for—read."

He stooped to pick up the paper. Mike took the paper from him and read—

"Thursday—Lady Mount Rorke, of a son."

Whilst one man hears his doom pronounced, another sees a golden fortune fallen in his hand, and the letter Mike had just read was from a firm of solicitors, informing him that Lady Seeley had left him her entire fortune, three thousand a year in various securities, and a property in Berkshire; house, pictures, plate—in a word, everything she possessed. The bitterness of his friend's ill-fortune contrasting with the sweetness of his own good fortune, struck his heart, and he said, with genuine sorrow in his voice—

" I'm awfully sorry, old chap."

" There's no use being sorry for me, I'm done for ; I shall never be Lord Mount Rorke now. That child, that wife, are paupers ; that castle, that park, that river, all—everything that I was led to believe would be mine one day, has passed from me irrevocably. It is terribly cruel—it seems too cruel to be true ; all those old places—you know them—all has passed from me. I never believed Mount Rorke would have an heir, he is nearly seventy ; it is too cruel."

Tears swam in his eyes, and covering his face in his hands he burst into a storm of heavy sobbing.

Mike was sincere, but there is something not wholly disagreeable to us in hearing of the misfortunes even of our best friends, and Mike felt the old thought forced into his mind that he who had come from the top had gone to the bottom, and that he who came from the bottom was going—had gone to the top. Taking care, however, that none of the triumph ebullient within him should rise into his voice, he said—

" I am really sorry for you, Frank. You mustn't despair ; perhaps the child won't live, and perhaps the paper will succeed. It must succeed. It shall succeed."

" Succeed ! nothing succeeds with me. I and my wife and child are beggars on the face of the earth. It matters little to me whether the paper succeeds or fails. Thigh has got pretty nearly all of it. When my debts are paid I shall not have enough to set myself up in rooms."

At the end of a painful silence, Mike said—

"We've had our quarrels, but you've been a damned good friend to me; it is my turn now to stand to you. To begin with, here is the three hundred that I won from Thigh. I don't want it. I assure you I don't. Then there are your rooms in Temple Gardens, I'll take them off your hands. I'll pay all the arrears of rent, and give you the price you paid for your furniture."

"What damned nonsense! how can you do that? Take three hundred pounds from you—the price of your book. You have nothing else in the world!"

"Yes, I have; it is all right, old chap; you can have the money. The fact is," he said, "Lady Seeley has left me her whole fortune; the letter I just received is from the solicitors. They say three thousand a year in various securities, and a property in Berkshire. So you see I can afford to be generous. I shall feel much hurt if you don't accept. Indeed, it is the least I can do; I owe it to you."

The men looked at each other, their eyes luminous with intense and quickening emotions. Fortune had been so derisive that Mike feared Frank would break into foolish anger, and that only a quarrel and worse hatred might result from his offer of assistance.

"It was in my box you met her; I remember the night quite well. You were with Harding."[1] The men exchanged an inquiring look. "She wanted me to go home and have supper with her; she was in love with me then; I might have been her lover. But I refused, and I went into the bar and spoke to Lizzie; when she went off on duty I went and sat with you and Harding. Not long after I saw you at Reading, in the hotel overlooking the river. I was with Lizzie."[2]

---

[1] See *Spring Days.*   [2] See *Spring Days.*

"You can't accuse me of having cut you out. You could have got her, and—"

"I didn't want her; I was in love with Lizzie, and I am still. And strange as it may appear to you, I regret nothing, at least nothing that concerns Lizzie."

Mike wondered if this were true. His fingers fidgetted with the cheques. "Won't you take them?"

Frank took them. It was impossible to continue the conversation. Frank made a remark, and the young men bade each other good-night.

As Mike went up the staircase to his room, his exultation swelled, and in one of those hallucinations of the brain consequent upon nerve excitement, and in which we are conscious of our insanity, he wondered the trivial fabric of the cottage did not fall, and his soul seemed to pierce the depth and mystery imprisoned in the stars. He undressed slowly, looking at himself in the glass, pausing when he drew off his waistcoat, unbuttoning his braces with deliberation.

"I can make nothing of it; there never was any one like me. . . . I could do anything, I might have been Napoleon or Cæsar."

As he folded his coat he put his hand into the breast pocket and produced the unposted letter.

"That letter will drive me mad! Shall I burn it? What do I want with a wife? I've plenty of money now."

He held the letter to the flame of the candle. But he could not burn it.

"This is too damned idiotic!" he thought, as he laid it on the table and prepared to get into bed; "I'm not going to carry that letter about all my life. I must either post it or destroy it."

Then the darkness became as if charged with a

personality sweet and intense; it seemed to emanate from the letter which lay on the table, and to materialize strangely and inexplicably. It was the fragrance of brown hair, and the light of youthful eyes; and in this perfume, and this light, he realized her entire person; every delicate defect of thinness. She hung over him in all her girlishness, and he clasped her waist with his hands.

"How sweet she is! There is none like her."

Then wearying of the strained delight he remembered Belthorpe Park, now his. Trees and gardens waved in his mind; downs and river lands floated, and he half imagined Lily there smiling upon them; and when he turned to the wall, resolute in his search for sleep, the perfume he knew her by, the savour of the skin, where the first faint curls begin, haunted in his hallucinations, and intruded beneath the bed-clothes. One dream was so exquisite in its tenderness, so illusive was the enchanted image that lay upon his brain, that fearing to lose it, he strove to fix his dream with words, but no word pictured her eyes, or the ineffable love they expressed, and yet the sensation of both was for the moment quite real in his mind. They were sitting in a little shady room; she was his wife, and she hung over him, sitting on his knee. Her eyes were especially distinct and beautiful, and her arms—those thin arms which he knew so well—and that waist were clothed in a puritanic frock of some blue material. His happiness thrilled him, and he lay staring into the darkness till the darkness withered, and the lines of the room appeared —the wardrobe, the washing-stand, and then the letter. He rose from his bed. In all-pervading grayness the world lay; not a whiff of smoke ascended, not a bird had yet begun, and the river, like a sheet of zinc, swirled between its low banks.

"God! it is worse than the moonlight!" thought Mike, and went back to bed. But he could not rest, and when he went again to the window there was a faint flush in the sky's cheek; and then a bar of rose pierced the heavy ridge of clouds that hung above the woodland.

"An omen! I will post her letter in the sun-rise." And conscious of the folly, but unable to subdue that desire of romance so inveterate in him, he considered how he might leave the house. He remembered, and with pleasure, that he could not pass down the staircase without disturbing the dog, and he thought of the prolonged barking that would begin the moment he touched the chain on the front door. He would have to get out of the window; but the window was twenty feet from the ground. "A rope! I have no rope. How absurd!" he thought, and, rejoicing in the absurdity, he drew a sheet from the bed and made it fast. Going to Lily through a window seemed to relieve marriage of some of its shame.

"Life wouldn't be complete without her. Yes, that's just it; that sums it up completely; curious I did not think of that before. It would have saved such a lot. Yes, life would not be complete without her. The problem is solved," and he dropped the letter as easily as if it had been a note asking for seats in the theatre. "I'm married," he said. "Good heavens! how strange it seems. I shall have to give her a ring, and buy furniture. I had forgotten! . . . . No difficulty about that now. We shall go to my place in Berkshire."

He could not go back to bed, and he walked down to the river, his fine figure swinging beautifully distinct in his light clothing. The dawn wind thrilled in his chest, for he had only a light coat over the tasselled silk night-shirt; and the dew drenched his feet as he swung along the pathway to the river. The old willow was full of small birds; they sat ruffling their feathers, and when Mike sprang into the boat they flew through the gray light, taking refuge in some osier beds. And as he looked down stream he saw the night clouds dispersing in the wind. He pulled, making the boat shoot through the water for about a mile, then touched by the beauty of the landscape, paused to view it. Cattle lay in the long, moist meadows, harmonizing in their semi-unconsciousness with the large gray earth; mist hung in the sedges, floated evanescent upon the surface of the water, within reach of his oars, floated and went out in the sunshine. But on the verge of an oak wood, amid tangled and tawny masses of fern and grass, a hound stopped and looked up. Then the huntsman appeared galloping along the upland, and turning in the saddle, he blew a joyful blast.

Mike sat still, his heart close shut, the beauty of the scene in its quick and core. Then yielding utterly he drove the boat ashore, and calling to the nearest, to one who had stopped and was tightening his horse's girths, he offered to buy his horse. A hundred pounds was asked. "It is not worth it," he thought; "but I must spend my four thousand a year." The desire to do what others think of doing but don't do was always active in Mike. He gave his name and address; and, fearing to miss dealing on such advantageous terms, the owner consented to allow Mike to try the horse then and there. But the hounds had got on the scent of a fox. The horn was heard in the seared wood, again in the crimson morning, and the hounds streamed across the meadows.

"I must try him over some fences. Take my boat and row up to Ash Cottage; I'll meet you there."

"I'll do nothing of the sort!" roared the man in top boots.

" Then walk across the fields," cried Mike ; and he rode at the hedge and rail, coming down heavily, but before the owner could reach him he had mounted and was away.

Some hours later, as he approached the cottage, he saw Frank and a man in top boots engaged in deep converse.

"Get off my horse instantly !" exclaimed the latter.

" The horse is mine," said Mike, who unfortunately could not control his laughter.

" Your horse ! Certainly not ! Get off my horse, or I'll pull you off."

Mike jumped off.

" Since you will have it so, I'll not dispute with you. There is your horse ; not a bad sort of animal —capital sport."

" Now pay me my hundred pounds !" said the owner, between his clenched teeth.

" You said just now that you hadn't sold me the horse. There is your horse, and here is the name of my solicitors, if you want to go to law with me."

" Law with you ! I'll give you law !" and letting go the horse, that immediately began to browse, he rushed at Mike, his whip in the air.

Mike fought, his long legs wide apart, his long arms going like lightning, straight from the shoulder, scattering blood over necktie and collar ; and presently the man withdrew, cursing Mike for an Irish horse-stealer.

" I never heard of such a thing !" said Frank. " You got on his horse and rode away, leaving him standing on the outside of the cover."

" Yes," shouted Mike, delighted with his exploit ; " I felt I must go after the hounds."

" Yes, but to go away with the man's horse !"

" My dear fellow, why not ? Those are the things

that other fellows think of doing but don't do. An excitement like that is worth anything."

While waiting for Lily's answer, Mike finished the last chapter of his book, and handed the manuscript to Frank. Between the sentences he had speculated on the state of soul his letter would produce in her, and had imagined various answers. "Darling, how good of you! I did not know you loved me so well." She would write, "Your letter surprised me, but then you always surprise me. I can promise you nothing; but you may come and see me next Thursday." She would write at once, of that there could be no doubt; such letters were always answered at once. He watched the postman and the clock; every double knock made tumult in his heart; and in his stimulated perceptions he saw the well-remembered writing as if it lay under his eyes. And the many communications he received during those days whetted the edge of his thirst, and aggravated the fever that floated in his brain.

And towards the end of the week, at the end of a long night of suffering, he went to London. And for the first time, forgetful of himself, without a thought of the light he would appear in, he told the cabman where to drive. His heart failed him when he heard that Miss Young had been ordered abroad by the doctor. And as he walked away a morbid sense instilled in him that Lily would never be his bride. Fear for her life persisted, and corrupted all his joy. He could not listen to Lady Seeley's solicitors, and he could not meditate upon the new life which Helen had given him. He had inherited sixty thousand pounds in various securities, yielding three thousand a year; the estate in Berkshire brought in fifteen hundred a year; and a sum of twelve hundred pounds lay in the bank for immediate uses.

" Dear, sweet Helen—she was the best of the lot—none were as sweet as she. Well, after all, it isn't so strange when one thinks of it—she hadn't a relation in the world. I must see her grave. I'll put a beautiful marble tomb over her; and when I'm in Berkshire I'll go there every day with flowers."

Then a shocking thought appeared in his mind. Accustomed to analyze all sentiments, he asked his soul if he would give up all she had given him to have her back in life ; and he took courage and joy when the answer came that he would. And delighted at finding himself capable of such goodness, he walked in a happier mood. His mind hung all day between these two women—while he paid the rent that was owing there in Temple Gardens ; while he valued the furniture and fixtures. He valued them casually, and in a liberal spirit, and wrote to Frank offering him seven hundred pounds for the place as it stood. " It is not worth it," he thought, " but I'd like to put the poor fellow on his legs."

Where should he dine ? He wanted distraction, and unable to think of any better relief, he turned into Lubi's for a merry dinner. The little gilt gallery was in disorder, Sally Slater having spent the afternoon there. Her marquis was with her ; her many admirers clustered about the cigarette-strewn table, anxious to lose no word of her strange conversation. One drunkard insisted on telling anecdotes about the duke, and asking the marquis to drink with him.

" I tell you I remember the circumstances perfectly —the duke wore a gray overcoat," said drunkard No. 1.

" Get out ! I tell you to get out !" cried drunkard No. 2. " Brave Battlemoor, I say ; long live Battlemoor ! Have a drink ?—I want Battlemoor to drink with me."

" For God's sake have a drink with him," said Sally,
" and then perhaps he'll take another box for my
benefit."

" What, another?"

" Only a guinea one this time ; there's the ticket—
fork out.   And now I must be off."

The shout echoed with the porter's whistle, and half
a dozen cabs came racing for these excellent customers.

To the Trocadero they went.   Mike, Sally, Marquis
and the drunkards lingered in the bar behind the
auditorium, and brandies-and-sodas were supplied to
them over a sloppy mahogany counter.   A woman
screamed on the stage in green silk, and between the
heads of those standing in the entrance to the stalls,
her open mouth and an arm in black swede were seen
occasionally.

Tired of drunkenness and slang Mike went into
the stalls.   The boxes were bright with courtesans ;
the young men whispered invitations to drink, and the
chairman, puffing at a huge cigar, used his little
hammer and announced " Miss Sally Slater will
appear next."   Battlemoor roared approval, and then
in a short skirt and black stockings Sally rushed to
the footlights and took her audience, as it were, by
the throat.

> " Oh, you men, what would you do without us?
>   You kiss us, you cuddle and play,
>   You win our hearts away.
> Oh, you men, there's something so nice about us."

The " Oh, you men," was given with a shake of
the fist and the waggle of the bustle, in which there
was genius, and Mike could not but applaud.   Suddenly he became conscious that a pair of opera
glasses were bracketed upon him.   Looking up he
saw Kitty Carew sitting with a young nobleman, and

he saw the white line of her teeth, for she was laughing. She waved him to come to her.

"You dear old sweet," she said, "where have you been all this time?. Come, kiss me at once." And she bent her head towards him.

"And now Newtimber, good-bye; I want to be with Mike. But you'll not forget me, you'll come and see me one of these days?" And she spoke so winningly that the boy hardly perceived that he was dismissed. Mike and Kitty exchanged an inquiring look.

"Ah! do you remember,"she said,"when I was at the Avenue, and you used to come behind? . . . You remember the dear old marquis? When I was ill he used to come and read to me. He used to say I was the only friend he had. The dear marquis—and he is gone now. I went to his grave yesterday, and I strewed the tomb with chrysanthemums, and every spring he has the first lilac of my garden."

"And who is your lover?"

"I assure you I haven't got one. Harding was the last, but he is becoming a bore; he philosophizes. I dare say he's very clever, but people don't kiss each other because they are clever. I don't think I ever was in love. . . But tell me, how do'you think I am looking? Does this dress suit me? Do I look any older?"

Mike vowed he had never seen her so charming.

"Very well, if you think so, I'll tell you what we'll do. As soon as Coburn has sung his song, we go; my brougham is waiting . . . You'll come home and have supper with me."

A remembrance of Lily came over him, but in quick battle he crushed it out of mind and murmured, "That'll be very nice; you know I always wanted to love you."

At that moment they were interrupted by cheers and yells. Muchross had just entered at the head of

his gang ; his lieutenants, Snowdown and Dicky the
driver, stood beside him. They stood under the
gallery bowing to the courtesans in the boxes, and
singing—

> " Two lovely black eyes,
> Oh ! what a surprise,
> Two lovely black eyes."

" I wish we could avoid those fellows," said Kitty ;
" they'll only bother me with questions. Come, let's
be off, they'll be up here in a moment." But they
were intercepted by Muchross and his friends in a
saloon where Sally and Battlemoor were drinking
with various singers waiting their turns.

" Where are you going ? You aren't going off like
that ?" cried Muchross, catching her by her sleeve.

" Yes, I am ; I am going home."

" Let me see you home," whispered Dicky.

" Thanks, Mike is seeing me home."

" You are in love," cried Muchross, " I shan't leave
you."

" You are in drink, I'll leave you in charge if you
don't loose my sleeve."

" This joker," cried Sally, " will take a ticket if
something wins a Lincoln, and he doesn't know
which." She stood in the doorway, her arms a-
kimbo. " People are very busy here," she snarled,
when a woman tried to pass.

" I beg your pardon," said the ex-chorus girl.

" And a good thing too," said Sally. " You are one
of the busy ones, just got your salary for shoving, I
suppose." There was no competing with Sally's
tongue, and the girl passed without replying.

This queen of song was attired in a flowery gown
of pale green, and she wore a large hat lavishly
trimmed with wild flowers ; she moved slowly, conscious of her importance and fame.

But at that moment a man in a check suit said, doffing his cap, " Very pleased to see you here, Miss Slater."

Sally looked him over. " Well, I can't help that."

" I was at your benefit. Mr. Jackson was there, and he introduced me to you after the performance."

" No, I'm sure he didn't "

" I beg your pardon, Miss Slater. Don't you remember when Peggy Praed got on the table and made a speech ?"

" No, I don't ; you saw *me* on the stage and you paid your money for that. What more do you want ?"

" I assure you—"

" Well, that's all right, now's your chance to lend me a fiver."

" I'll lend you a fiver or a tenner, if you like, Miss Slater."

" You could not do it if you tried, and now the roast pork's off."

The witticism was received with a roar from her admirers, and satisfied with her victory, she said— " And now, you girls, you come and have drinks with me. What will you have, Kitty, what will you have ? give it a name."

Kitty protested, but was forced to sit down. The courtesans joined the comic vocalists waiting to do their " turns." Lord Muchross and Lord Snowdown ordered magnums and soon the hall was almost deserted. A girl was, however, dancing prettily on the stage, and Mike stood to watch her. Her hose were black, and in limp pink silk skirts she kicked her slim legs surprisingly to and fro. After each dance she ran into the wings, reappearing in a fresh costume, returning at length in wide sailor's trousers of blue silk, her bosom partially covered in white cambric. As the band played the first notes of the hornpipe, she withdrew a few hair-pins and forthwith an abundant darkness fell to her dancing knees, almost to her tiny dancing feet, heavy as a wave, shadowy as sleeping water. As some rich weed in the warm sea pulsing, as some fair cloud in radiant atmosphere, her hair floated, every parted tress an impalpable film of gold in the crude limelight turned upon her; and when she danced towards the footlights, the bright softness of the threads clung almost amorously about her white wrists—faint cobwebs hanging from white flowers were not more faint, fair and soft; wonderful was the hair of this dancing girl, suggesting all fabled enchantments, all visions of delicate perfume and all the poetry of evanescent colour.

She was followed by the joyous Peggy Praed (sweet minx), the soul and voice of the small back streets. Screwing up her winsome, comical face, drawling a word here, accentuating a word there, she evoked, in an illusive moment, the washing day, the quarrel with the mother-in-law (who wanted to sleep in the house), tea-time, and the trip to the seaside, with all its concomitant adventures amid bugs and landladies. With an accent, with a gesture, she recalled in a moment a phase of life, creating pictures vivid as they were transitory, but endowing each with the charm of the best and most highly finished works of the Dutch masters. Lords, courtesans and fellow artists crowded to listen, and profiting by the opportunity, Kitty touched Mike on the shoulder with her fan.

"Now we had better go."

"I'm driving to-morrow. Come down to Brighton with us," said Dicky the driver. "Shall I keep places for you?"

Rising, Kitty laid her hand upon his mouth to silence him and whispered, "Yes; we'll come, and good night."

In the soft darkness of the brougham, gently swung together, the passing gaslights revealing the blueness of the cushions, a diamond stud flashing intermittently, they lay, their souls sunk deep in the intimacy of a companionship akin to that of a nest—they, the inheritors of the pleasure of the night and the gladness of the morrow.

Next morning Kitty had to adjure Mike to say no more; if he did she should go mad. Dressing was delirium. Breakfast had to be skipped, and it was only by bribing a cabman to gallop to Westminster that they caught the coach. Even so they would have missed it had not Mike sprung at risk of limb from the hansom and sped on the toes of his patent leather shoes down the street, his gray cover coat flying.

"What a toff he is," thought Kitty, full of the pride of her love. Bessie, whom dear Laura had successfully chaperoned into well-kept estate, sat with Dicky on the box; Laura sat with Harding in the back seat; Muchross and Snowdown sat opposite them. The middle of the coach was taken up by what Muchross said were a couple of bar-girls and their mashers.

On rolled the coach over Westminster Bridge, through Lambeth, in picturesqueness and power, a sympathetic survival of aristocratic days. The aristocracy and power so vital in the coach was soon communicated to those upon it. And now when Jem Gregory, the celebrated whip, with one leg swinging over the side, tootled, the passers-by seemed littler than ever, the hansoms at the corner seemed smaller, and the folk standing at their poor doors seemed meaner. As they passed through those hungry streets ragged urchins came alongside, throwing themselves over and over, beseeching coppers from Muchross, and he threw a few, urging them to further prostrations. Tootle, Jim, tootle; whether they starve or whether they feed, we have no thought. The clatter of the hoofs of the bays resounds through those poor back-rooms, full of human misery; the notes of our horn are perhaps sounding now in dying ears. Tootle, Jim, tootle; what care we for that pale mother and her babe, or that toiling coster whose barrow is too heavy for him. If there is to be revolution, it will not be in our time; we are the end of the world. Laura is with us to-day, Bessie sits on the box, Kitty is with our Don Juan; we know there is gold in our pockets, we see our courtesans by us, our gallant bays are bearing us away to pleasure. Tootle, Jim, my boy, tootle; the great Muchross is shouting derision at the poor perspiring coster. " Pull up, you devil, pull up," he cries, and shouts to the ragged urchins and scatters halfpence that they may tumble once more in the dirt. See the great Muchross, the clean shaven face of the libertine priest, the small sardonic eyes. Hurrah for the great Muchross! Long may he live, the singer of " What cheer, Ria?" the type and epitome of the white necktie and the brandy-and-soda.

Gaily trotted the four bays, and as Clapham was approached brick tenements disappeared in Portland stone and iron railings. A girl was seen swinging; the white flannels of tennis players passed to and fro, and a lady stood by a tall vase watering red geraniums. Harding told Mike that the shaven lawns and the greenhouses explained the lives of the inhabitants, and represented their ideas; and Laura's account of the money she had betted was followed by an anecdote concerning a long ramble in a wood, with a man who had walked her about all day without even so much as once asking her if she had a mouth on her.

" Talking of mouths," said Mike, as they pulled up to change horses, " we had to start without breakfast. I wonder if one could get a biscuit and a glass of milk."

"Glass of milk!" screamed Muchross, "no milk allowed on this coach."

"Well, I don't think I could drink a brandy-and-soda at this time in the morning."

"At what time could you drink one then? Why, it is nearly eleven o'clock! What will you have, Kitty? A brandy?"

"No, I think I'll take a glass of beer."

The beauty of the landscape passed unperceived. But the road was full of pleasing reminiscences. As they passed through Croydon dear old Laura pointed out an hotel where she used to go every Sunday with the dear Earl, and in the afternoons they played cribbage in the sitting-room overlooking the street. And some miles further on the sweetness of the past burst unanimously from all when Dicky pointed out with his whip the house where Bessie had gone for her honeymoon, and where they all used to spend from Saturday till Monday. The incident of Bill Longside's death was pathetically alluded to. He had died of D. T. "Impossible," said Laura, "to keep him from it. Milly, poor little woman, had stuck to him almost to the last. He had had his last drink there. Muchross and Dicky had carried him out."

The day was filled with fair remembrances of summer, and the earth was golden and red ; and the sky was folded in lawny clouds, which the breeze was lifting, revealing beautiful spaces of blue. All the abundant hedgerows were red with the leaf of the wild cherry, and the oak woods wore masses of sere and russet leafage. Spreading beeches swept right down to the road, shining in beautiful death ; once a pheasant rose and flew through the polished trunks towards the yellow underwood. Sprays trembled on naked rods, ferns and grasses fell about the gurgling watercourses, a motley undergrowth ; and

in the fields long teams were ploughing, the man
labouring at the plough, the boy with the horses;
and their smock-frocks and galligaskins recalled an
ancient England which time has not touched, and
which lives in them.   And the farm-houses of gables
and weary brick, sometimes well-dismantled and
showing the heavy beam, accentuated these visions
of past days. Yes, indeed, the brick villages, the
old gray farm-houses, and the wind-mill were very
beautiful in the endless yellow draperies which this
autumn country wore so romantically.   One spot
lingered in Mike's memory, so representative did it
seem of that country.   The road swept round a
beech wood that clothed a knoll, descending into the
open country by a tall redding hedge to a sudden
river, and cows were seen drinking and wading in the
shallows, and this last impression of the earth's
loveliness smote the poet's heart to joy which was
near to grief.

At Three Bridges they had lunch, in an old-fashioned
hotel called the George.   Muchross cut the sirloin,
filling the plates so full of juicy meat that the ladies
protested.   Snowdown paid for champagne, and in
conjunction with the wine, the indelicate stories
which he narrated made some small invasion upon
the reserve of the bar-girls; for their admirers did
not dare forbid them the wine, and could not prevent them from smiling.   After lunch the gang was
photographed in the garden, and Muchross gave the
village flautist half a " quid," making him promise
to drink their healths till he was " blind."

" I never like to leave a place without having done
some good," he shouted, as he scrambled into his
seat.

This sentiment was applauded until the sensual
torpor of digestion intervened.   The clamour of the
coach lapsed into a hush of voices.   The women

leaned back, drawing their rugs about their knees, for it was turning chilly, arms were passed round yielding waists, hands lay in digestive poses, and eyes were bathed in deep animal indolences.

Conversation had almost ceased. The bar-girls had not whispered one single word for more than an hour; Muchross had not shouted for at least twenty minutes; the only interruption that had occurred was an unexpected stopping of the coach, for the off-leader was pulling Dicky so hard that he had to ask Jem to take the ribbons, and now he snoozed in the great whip's place, seriously incommoding Snowdown with his great weight. Suddenly awaking to a sense of his responsibility Muchross roared—

"What about the milk cans?"

"You'd better be quick," answered Jem, "we shall be there in five minutes."

One of the customs of the road was a half crown lottery, the winning member to be decided by the number of milk cans outside a certain farm-house.

"Ease off a bit, Jem," bawled Muchross. "Damn you! give us time to get the numbers out."

"It ain't my fault if you fall asleep."

"The last stage was five miles this side of Cuck-field, you ought to know the road by this time. How many are we?"

"Eight," shouted Dicky, blowing the blatant horn. "You're on, Jem, aren't you? Number two or three will get it; at this time of the year milk is scarce. Pass on the hat quick; quick, you devil, pass it on. What have you got, Kitty?"

"Just like my luck," cried Muchross, "I've got eight."

"And I've seven," said Snowdown; "never have I won yet. In the autumn I get sevens and eights, in the summer ones and twos. Damn!"

"I've got five," said Kitty, "and Mike has got

two ; always the lucky one. A lady leaves him four thousand a year and he comes down here and rooks us."

The coach swept up a gentle ascent, and Much-ross shouted—

" Two milk cans ! Hand him over the quid and chuck him out !"

The downs rose, barring the sky ; and they passed along the dead level of the weald, leaving Henfield on their right ; and when a great piece of Gothic masonry appeared between some trees, Mike told Kitty how it had been once John Norton's intention to build a monastery.

" He would have founded a monastery had he lived two centuries ago," said Harding ; " but this is an age of concessions, and instead he puts up a few gargoyles. Time modifies but does not eradicate, and the modern King Cophetua marries not the beggar, but the bar-maid."

The conversation fell in silence, full of conster-nation ; and all wondered if the two ladies in front had understood, and they were really bar-maids. Be this as it may, they maintained their unalterable reserve ; and with suppressed laughter, Mike per-suaded Dicky, who had resumed the ribbons, to turn into the lodge-gates.

" Who is this Johnny ?" shouted Muchross. " If he won't stand a drink, we don't want none of his blooming architecture."

" And I wouldn't touch a man with a large pole, who didn't like women," said Laura. At which em-phatic but naïve expression of opinion, the whole coach roared ;—even the bar-girls smiled.

" Architecture ! It is a regular putty castle," said Kitty, as they turned out of an avenue of elms and came in view of the house.

Not a trace of the original Italian house remained. The loggia had been replaced by a couple of Gothic towers. Over the central hall he had placed a light lantern roof, and the billiard-room had been converted into a chapel. A cold and corpse-like sky was flying; the shadows falling filled the autumn path with sensations of deep melancholy. But the painted legend of St. George overthrowing the dragon, which John had placed in commemoration of his victories over himself, in the central hall, glowed full of colour and story; and in the melodious moan of the organ, and in the resonant chord which closes the awful warning of the *Dies Iræ*, he realized the soul of his friend. Castle, window, and friend were now one in his brain, and seized with dim, undefinable weariness of his companions, and an irritating longing to see John, Mike said—

"I must go and see him."

"We can't wait here while you are paying visits; who doesn't like getting drunk or singing, 'What cheer, Ria?' Let's give him a song." Then the whole coach roared; even the bar-girls joined in.

> "What cheer, Ria?
> Ria's on the job;
> What cheer, Ria?
> Speculate a bob."

As soon as he could make himself heard, Mike said—

"You need not wait for me. We are only five minutes from Brighton. I'll ride over in an hour's time. Do you wait for me at the 'Ship,' Kitty."

"I don't think this at all nice of you."

Mike waved his hand; and as he stood on the steps of this Gothic mansion, listening to the chant, watching the revellers disappearing in the gray and yellow gloom of the park, he said—

" The man here is the one who has seized what is best in life ; he alone has loved. I should have founded with him a new religious order. I should walk with him at the head of the choir. Bah! life is too pitifully short. I should like to taste of every pleasure —of every emotion ; and what have I tasted ? Nothing. I have done nothing. I have wheedled a few women who wanted to be wheedled, that is all."

CHAPTER IX.

"AND how are you, old chap ? I am delighted to see you."

" I'm equally glad to see you. You have made alterations in the place . . . I came down from London with a lot of Johnnies and tarts—Kitty Carew, Laura Stanley and her sister. I got Dicky the driver to turn in here. You were playing the *Dies Iræ*. I never was more impressed in my life. You should have seen the coach beneath the great window . . . St. George overcoming the Johnnies . . . the tumult of the organ . . . and I couldn't stand singing 'Two Lovely Black Eyes.' I sickened of them—the whole thing—and I felt I must see you."

"And are they outside ?"

" No ; they have gone off."

Relieved of fear of intrusion, John laughed loudly, and commented humorously on the spectacle of the Brighton coach filled with revellers drawn up beneath his window. Then, to discuss the window— the quality of the glass—he turned out the lamps ; the hall filled with the legend, and their hearts full of it, and delighting in the sensation of each other, they walked up and down the echoing hall. John remembered a certain fugue by Bach, and motioning to the page to blow, he seated himself at the key-board. The celestial shield and crest still remained in little colour. Mike saw John's hands moving over the keyboard, and his soul went out in worship of that soul, divided from the world's pleasure, self-sufficing, alone; seeking God only in his home of organ fugue and legended pane. He understood the nobleness and purity which was now about him—it seemed impossible to him to return to Kitty.

Swift and complete reaction had come upon him, and choked with the moral sulphur of the last twenty-four hours, he craved the breath of purity. He must talk of Plato's *Republic*, of Wagner's operas, of Schopenhauer; even Lily was not now so imperative as these, and next day, after lunch, when the question of his departure was alluded to, Mike felt it was impossible to leave John; but persecuted with scruples of disloyalty to Kitty, he resisted his friend's invitation to stay. He urged he had no clothes. John offered to send the coachman into Brighton for what he wanted.

"But perhaps you have no money," John said, inadvertently, and a look of apprehension passed into his face.

"Oh, I have plenty of money—'tisn't that. I haven't told you that a friend of mine, a lady, has left me nearly five thousand a year. I don't think you ever saw her—Lady Seeley."

John burst into uncontrollable laughter. "That is the best thing I ever heard in all my life. I don't think I ever heard anything that amused me more. The grotesqueness of the whole thing." Seeing that Mike was annoyed he hastened to explain his mirth. "The inexplicableness of human action always amuses me ; the inexplicable is romance, at least that is the only way I can understand romance. When you reduce life to a logical sequence you destroy all poetry, and, I think, all reality. We do things constantly, and no one can say why we do them. Frederick the Great coming in, after reviewing his troops, to play the flute, that to me is intensely romantic. A lady, whom you probably treated exceedingly badly, leaving you her property, that too is, to me."

Admonished by his conscience, John's hilarity clouded into a sort of semi-humorous gravity, and he advised Mike on the necessity of reforming his life.

" I am very sorry, for there is no one whose society is as attractive to me as yours; there is no one in whom I find so many of my ideas, and yet there is no one from whom I am so widely separated; at times you are sublime, and then you turn round and roll in the nastiest dirt you can find.'"

Mike loved a lecture from John, and he exerted himself to draw his friend into new confidences.

Looking at each other in admiration, they regretted the other's weaknesses. Mike deplored John's conscience, which had forced him to burn his poems; John deplored Mike's unsteady mind, which veered and yielded to every passion. And in the hall they talked of the great musician and the great king, or John played the beautiful hymns of the Russian Church, in whose pathetic charm he declared Chopin had found his inspiration ; they spoke of the *Grail* and the *Romance of the Swan*, or, wandering into the library, they read aloud the ever-flowering eloquence of De Quincey, the marmorial loveliness of Landor, the nurselike tenderness of Tennyson.

Through all these æstheticisms Lily Young shone, her light waxing to fulness day by day. Mike had written to Frank, beseeching him to forward any letters that might arrive.   He expected an answer from Lily within the week, and not until its close did he begin to grow fearful.   Then rapidly his fear increased, and unable to bear with so much desire in the presence of John Norton, he rushed to London, and thence to Marlow.   He railed against his own weakness in going to Marlow, for if a letter had arrived it would have been forwarded to him.

"Why deceive myself with false hopes?   If the letter had miscarried, it would have been returned through the post-office.   I wrote my address plain enough."   Then he railed against Lily.   "The little vixen!   She will show that letter; she will pass it round; perhaps at this moment she is laughing at me!   What a fool I was to write it!   However, all's well that ends well, and I am not going to be married—I have escaped after all."

The train jogged like his thoughts, and the land-scape fled in fleeting visions like his dreams.   He laid his face in his hands, and could not disguise the truth that he desired her above all things, for she was the sweetest he had seen.

"There are," he said, talking to Frank and Lizzie, "two kinds of love—the first is a strictly personal appetite, which merely seeks its own assuagement; the second draws you out of yourself, and is far more terrible.   I have found both these loves, but in different women."

"Did no woman ever inspire both loves in you?" said Lizzie.

"I thought one woman had."

"Oh, tell us about her."

Mike changed the conversation, and he talked of the newspaper until it was time to go to the station. He was now certain that Lily had rejected him.   His grief soaked through him like a wet, dreary day.

Sometimes, indeed, he seemed to brighten, but there is often a deeper sadness in a smile than in a flood of tears, and he was more than ever sad when he thought of the life he had desired, and had lost ; which he had seen almost within his reach, and which had now disappeared for ever. He had thought of this life as a green isle, where there were flowers and a shrine. Isle, flowers, and shrine had for ever vanished, and nothing remained but the round monotony of the desert ocean. Then throwing off his grief with a laugh, he eagerly anticipated the impressions of the visit he meditated to Belthorpe Park, and his soul went out to meet this new adventure. He thought of the embarrassment of the servants receiving their new master ; of the attitude of the country people towards him ; and deciding that he had better arrive before dinner, just as if he were a visitor, he sent a telegram saying that the groom was to meet him at the station, and that dinner was to be prepared.

Lady Seeley's solicitors had told him that according to her ladyship's will Belthorpe was to be kept up exactly as it had been in her life-time, and the servants had received notice that, in pursuance of her ladyship's expressed wish, Mr. Fletcher would make no changes, and that they were free to remain on if they thought proper. Mike approved of this arrangement—it saved him from a task of finding new servants, a task which he would have bungled sadly, and which he would have had to attempt, for he had decided to enjoy all the pleasures of a country place, and to act the country gentleman until he wearied of the part. Life is but a farce, and the more different parts you play in that farce the more you enjoy. Here was a new farce—he the Bohemian, going down to an old ancestral home to play the part of the Squire of the parish. It could not but prove rich in amusing situations, and he was determined to play it. What a sell it would be for Lily, for perhaps she had refused him because she thought he was poor. Contemptuous thoughts about women rose in his mind, but they died in thronging sensations of vanity —he, at least, had not found women mercenary. Lily was the first! Then putting thoughts of her utterly aside, he surrendered himself to the happy consideration of his own good fortune! "A new farce! Yes; that was the way to look upon it. I wonder what the servants will think! I wonder what they'll think of me! . . . Harrison, the butler, was with her in Green Street. Her maid, Fairfield, was with her when I saw her last—nearly three years ago. Fairfield knew I was her lover, and she has told the others. But what does it matter? I don't care a damn what they think. Besides servants are far more jealous of our honour than we are ourselves; they'll trump up some story about cousinship, or that I had saved her ladyship's life—not a bad notion that last; I had better stick to it myself."

As he sought a plausible tale, his thoughts detached themselves, and it struck him that the gentleman sitting opposite was his next door neighbour. He imagined his visit; the invitation to dine; the inevitable daughters in the drawing-room. How would he be received by the country folks?

"That depends," he thought, "entirely on the number of unmarried girls there are in the neighbourhood. The morals and manners of an English county are determined by its female population. If the number of females is large, manners are familiar, and morals are lax; if the number is small, manners are reserved, and morals severe."

He was in a carriage with two unmistakably county squires, and their conversation—certain references to a meet of the hounds and a local bazaar—left no doubt that they were his neighbours. Indeed, Lady

Seeley was once alluded to, and Mike was agitated with violent desires to introduce himself as the owner of Belthorpe Park. Several times he opened his lips, but their talk suddenly turned into matters so foreign that he abandoned the notion of revealing his identity, and five minutes after he congratulated himself he had not done so.

The next station was Wantage Street; and as he looked to see that the guard had put out his portmanteau, a smart footman approached and touching his cockaded hat said, " Mr. Fletcher." Mike thrilled with pride. His servant—his first servant.

" I've brought the dog-cart, sir; I thought it would be the quickest; it will take us a good hour, the roads are very heavy, sir."

Mike noticed the coronet worked in red upon the yellow horse-cloth, for the lamps cast a bright glow over the mare's quarters; and wishing to exhibit himself in all his new fortune before his fellow-passengers, who were getting into a humbler conveyance, he took the reins from the groom; and when he turned into the wrong street, he cursed under his breath, fancying all had noticed his misadventure. When they were clear of the town, touching the mare with the whip he said—

" Not a bad animal, this."

" Beautiful trotter, sir. Her ladyship bought her only last spring; gave seventy guineas for her."

After a slight pause, Mike said, " Very sad, her ladyship's death, and quite unexpected, I suppose. She wasn't ill above a couple of days."

" Not what you might call ill, sir; but her ladyship had been ailing for a long time past. The doctors ordered her abroad last winter, sir, but I don't think it did her much good. She came back looking very poorly."

" Now tell me which is the way? do I turn to the right or left?"

" To the right, sir."

" How far are we from Belthorpe Park now?"

" About three miles, sir."

" You were saying that her ladyship looked very poorly for some time before she died. Tell me how she looked. What do you think was the matter?"

" Well, sir, her ladyship seemed very much depressed. I heard Miss Fairfield, her ladyship's maid, say that she used to find her ladyship constantly in tears; her nerves seemed to have given way."

" I suppose I broke her heart," thought Mike; " but I'm not to blame; I couldn't go on loving any woman for ever, not if she were Venus herself." And questioning the groom regarding the servants then at Belthorpe, he learnt with certain satisfaction that Fairfield had left immediately after her ladyship's death. The groom had never heard of Harrison (he had only been a year and a half in her ladyship's service).

" This is Belthorpe Park, sir—these are the lodge gates."

Mike was disappointed in the lodge. The park he could not distinguish. Mist hung like a white fleece. There were patches of ferns; hawthorns loomed suddenly into sight; high trees raised their bare branches to the brilliancy of the moon.

" Not half bad," thought Mike, " quite a gentleman's place."

" Rather rough land in parts—plenty of rabbits," he remarked to the groom; and he won the man's sympathies by various questions concerning the best method of getting hunters into condition. The rooks talked gently in the branches of some elms, around which the drive turned through rough undulating

ground. Plantations became numerous; tall, spire-
like firs appeared, their shadows floating through the
interspaces; and, amid straight walks and dwarf
yews, in the fulness of the moonlight, there shone a
white house, with large French windows and a tower
at the further end. A white peacock asleep on a
windowsill startled Mike, and he thought of the
ghost of his dead mistress.

Nor could he account for his trepidation as he
waited for the front door to open, and Hunt seemed
to him aggressively large and pompous, and he would
have preferred an assumption on the part of the
servant's part that he knew the relative positions of
the library and drawing-room. But Hunt was resolved on explanation, and as they went up-stairs he
pointed out the room where Lady Seeley died, and
spoke of the late Earl. "You want the sack, and
you shall get it, my friend," thought Mike, and he
glanced hurriedly at the beautiful pieces of furniture
about the branching staircase and the gallery leading
into the various corridors. At dinner he ate without noticing the choiceness of the cooking, and he
drank several glasses of champagne before he remarked the excellence of the wine.

"We have not many dozen left, sir; I heard that
his lordship laid it down in '75."

Hunt watched him with cat-like patience and
hound-like sagacity, and seeing he had forgotten his
cigar-case, he instantly produced a box; Mike helped
himself without daring to ask where the cigars came
from, nor did he comment on their fragrance. He
smoked in discomfort; the presence of the servant
irritated him, and he walked into the library and shut
the door. The carved panelling, in the style of the
late Italian renaissance, was dark and shadowy, and
the eyes of the portraits looked upon the intruder.
Men in armour, holding scrolls; men in rich doub-

lets, their hands on their swords ; women in elaborate
dresses of a hundred tucks, and hooped out prodigiously.   He was especially struck by one, a lady.
in green, who played with long white hands on a
spinet.   But the massive and numerous oak book-
cases, strictly wired with strong brass wire, and the
tall oak fireplace, surmounted with a portrait of a
man in a red coat holding a letter, whetted the edge
of his depression, and Mike looked round with a
pain of loneliness upon his face.   Speaking aloud for
relief, he said—

"No doubt it is all very fine, everything is up to
the mark, but there's no denying that it is—well,
it is dull.   Had I known it was going to be like this
I'd have brought somebody down with me—a nice
woman.   Kitty would be delightful here.   But no;
I would not bring her here for ten times the money
the place is worth ; to do so would be an insult on
Helen's memory. . . . Poor dear Helen !   I wish I
had seen her before she died ; and to think that she
has left me all—a beautiful house, plate, horses, car-
riages, wine ; nothing is wanting ; everything I have
is hers, even this cigar."   He threw the end of his
cigar into the fireplace.

"How strange, what an extraordinary transformation.   And all this is mine, even her ancestors !   How
angry that old fellow looks at me—me, the son of an
Irish peasant !   Yes, my father was that—well, not
exactly that, he was a grazier.   But why fear the facts,
he was a peasant ; and my mother was a French maid
—well, a governess—well, a nursery governess, *une
bonne ;* she was dismissed from her situation for carry-
ing on (it seems awful to speak of one's mother so ;
but it is the fact) . . . Respect !   I love my mother well
enough, but I'm not going to delude myself because
I had a mother.   Mother didn't like our cabin by
the roadside ; father treated her badly ; she ran away,

taking me with her. She was lucky enough to meet
with a rich manufacturer, who kept her fairly well
—I believe he used to allow her a thousand francs a
month—and I used to call him uncle. When mother
died he sent me back to my father in Ireland. That's
my history. There's not much blue blood in me. . .
I believe if one went back. . . Bah, if one went back!
Why deceive myself? I was born a peasant, and I
know it. . . Yet no one looks more like a gentleman ;
reversion to some original ancestor, I suppose. Not
one of these earls looks more like a gentleman than
I. But I don't suppose my looks would in any
measure reconcile them to the fact of my possession
of their property.

"Ah, you old fools—periwigs, armour, and scrolls
—you old fools, you laboured only to make a gentleman of an Irish peasant. Yes, you laboured in
vain, my noble lords—you, old gentleman yonder,
you with the telescope—an admiral, no doubt—you
sailed the seas in vain ; and you over there, you
mediæval-looking cuss, you carried your armour
through the battles of Cressy and Poictiers in vain ;
and you, noble lady in the high bodice, you whose
fingers play with the flaxen curls of that boy—he
was the heir of this place two hundred years ago—
I say, you bore him in vain, your labour was in
vain ; and you, old fogey that you are, you in the red
coat, you holding the letter in your gouty fingers,
a commercial-looking letter, you laboured in trade
to rehabilitate the falling fortunes of the family, and
I say you too laboured in vain. Without labour,
without ache, I possess the result of all your centuries
of labour.

"There, that sordid, wizen old lady, a miser to
judge by her appearance, she is eyeing me mali-
ciously now, but I say all her eyeing is in vain ; she

pinched and scraped and starved herself for me. Yes, I possess all your savings, and if you were fifty years younger you would not begrudge them to me."

Laughing at his folly, Mike said, "How close together lie the sane and the insane; any one who had overheard me would have pronounced me mad as a March hare, and yet few are saner." He walked twice across the room. "But I'm mad for the moment, and I like to be mad. Have I not all things—talent, wealth, love? I asked for life, and I was given life. I have drunk the cup—no, not to the dregs, there is plenty more wine in the cup for me; the cup is full, I have not tasted it yet. Lily! yes, I must get her; a fool I have been; my letter miscarried, else she would have written. Refuse me! who would refuse me? Yes, I was born to drink the cup of life as few have drunk it; I shall drink it even like a Roman emperor . . . But they drank it to madness and crime! Yet even so; I shall drink of life even to crime.

"The peasant and the card-sharper shall go high, this impetus shall carry me very high; and Frank Escott, that mean cad, shall go to the gutter; but he is already there, and I am here! I knew it would be so; I felt my destiny, I felt it here—in my brain. I felt it even when he scorned me in boyhood days. I believe that in those days he expected me to touch my cap to him. But those days are over, new days have begun. When to-morrow's sun rises it will shine on what is mine, down-land, meadow-land, park-land, and wood-land. Strange is the joy of possession; I did not know of its existence. The stately house too is mine, and I would see it. But that infernal servant, I suppose, is in bed. I would not have him find me. I shall get rid of him. I can hear him saying in his pantry, '·He! I wouldn't give much for him; I found him last night spying about, examining his fine things, for all the world like a beggar to whom you had given an old suit of clothes.'"

Mike took his bed-room candle, and having regard for surprises on the part of the servants, he roamed about the passages, looking at the Chippendale furniture on the landings and the pictures and engravings that lined the walls. Fearing bells, he did not attempt to enter any of the rooms, and it was with some difficulty that he found his way back to the library. Throwing himself into the arm-chair he wondered if he should grow accustomed to spend his evenings in this loneliness. He thought of whom he should invite there—·Harding, Thompson, John Norton; certainly he would ask John. He couldn't ask Frank without his wife, and Lizzie would prejudice him in the eyes of the county people. Then, as his thoughts detached themselves, he exclaimed against the sepulchral solemnity of the library. The house was soundless. At the window he heard the soft moonlight-dreaming of the rocks; and when he threw open the window the white peacock roosting there flew away and paraded on the pale sward like a Watteau lady.

Next morning, rousing in the indolence of a bed hung with curtains of Indian pattern, Mike said to the footman who brought in his hot water—

"Tell the coachman that I shall go out riding after breakfast."

"What horse will you ride, sir?"

"I don't know what horses you have in the stable."

"Well, sir, you can ride either her ladyship's hunter or the mare that brought you from the station in the dog-cart."

"Very well. I'll ride her ladyship's hunter. (My hunter, damn the fellow," he said, under his breath.) "And tell the bailiff I shall want him; let him come round on his horse. I shall go over the farms with him."

The morning was chilly. He stood before the fire while the butler brought in eggs, kidneys, devilled legs of fowl, and coffee. The beauty of the coffee-pot caught his eye, and he admired the plate that made such rich effect on the old Chippendale sideboard. The peacocks on the window-sills knocking with their strong beaks for bread, pleased him; they recalled evenings passed with Helen; she had often spoken of her love for these birds. He went to the window with bread for the peacocks and the landscape came into his eyes: the clump of leafless trees on the left, rugged and untidy with rooks' nests; the hollow, dipping plain, melancholy of aspect now, misty, gray and brown beneath a lowering sky, dipping and then rising in a long, wide shape, and ringing the sky with a brown line. The terrace with its straight walks, balustrades, urns, and closely cropped yews was a romantic note, severe, even harsh.

One day, wandering from room to room, he found himself in Helen's bed-room. "There is the bed she died in, there is the wardrobe." Mike opened the wardrobe. He turned the dresses over, seeking for those he knew; but he had not seen her for three years, and there were new dresses, and he had forgotten the old. Suddenly he came upon one of soft, blue material, and he remembered she wore that dress the first time she sat on his knees. Feeling the need of an expressive action he buried his face in the pale blue dress, seeking in its softness and odour commemoration of her who lay beneath the pavement. How desolate was the room. He would not linger. This room must be forever closed, left to the silence, the mildew, the dust, and the moth. None must enter here but he, it must be sacred from other feet. Once a year, on her anniversary, he would come to mourn her, and not on the anniversary of her death, but on that of their first kiss. He had forgotten the exact day and feared he had not preserved all her letters. Perhaps she had preserved his.

Moved with such an idea he passed out of her bedroom, and calling for *his* keys, went into her boudoir and opened her escritoire, and very soon he found his letters; almost the first he read, ran as follows—

" MY DEAR HELEN,

"I am much obliged to you for your kind invitation. I should like very much to come and stay with you, if I may come as your friend. You must not think from this that I have fallen in love with some one else; I have not. I have never seen any one I shall love better than you; I love you to-day as well as ever I did; my feelings ragarding you have changed in nothing, yet I cannot come as your lover. I am ashamed of myself, I hate myself, but it is not my fault.

" I have been your lover for more than a year, and I could not be any one's lover—no, not if she were Venus herself—for a longer time.

" My heart is full of regret. I am losing the best and sweetest mistress ever man had. No one is able to appreciate your worth better than I. Try to understand me; do not throw this letter aside in a rage. You are a clever woman; you are, I know, capable of understanding it. And if you will understand, you will not regret; that I swear, for you will gain the best and most loyal friend. I am as good a friend as I am

a worthless lover. Try to understand, Helen, I am
not wholly to blame.

"I love you—I esteem you far more to-day than
I did when I first knew you. Do not let our love
end upon a miserable quarrel—the commonplace
quarrel of those who do not know how to love."

He turned the letter over. He was the letter; that
letter was his shameful human nature, and worse, it
was the human nature of the whole wide world. On
the same point, or on some other point, every human
being was as base as he. Such baseness is the in-
alienable birth-stain of human life. His poem was
no pretty imagining, but the eternal, implacable
truth. It were better that human life should cease.
Until this moment he had only half understood its
awful, its terrifying truth. . . . It were better that
man ceased to pollute the earth. His history is but
the record of crime: his existence is but a disgraceful episode in the life of one of the meanest of the
planets.

We cannot desire what we possess, and so we progress from illusion to illusion. But when we cease
to distinguish between ourself and others, when our
thoughts are no longer set on the consideration of
our own embarrassed condition, when we see into the
heart of things, which is one, then disappointment
and suffering cease to have any meaning, and we attain that true serenity and peace which we sometimes
see reflected in a seraph's face by Raphael.

As Mike's thoughts floated in the boundless atmosphere of Schopenhauer's poem, of the denial of the
will to live, he felt creeping upon him, like sleep upon
tired eyelids, all the sweet and suasive fascination of
death. "How little," he thought, "does any man
know of any other man's soul. Who among my
friends would believe that I, in all my intense joys

and desire of life, am perhaps, at heart, the saddest man, and perhaps sigh for·death more ardently, and am tempted more than any other to cull the dark fruit which hangs so temptingly over the wall of the garden of life more ardently than any one."

A few days after, his neighbour, Lord Spennymoor, called, and his visit was followed by an invitation to dinner. The invitation was accepted. Mike was on his best behaviour. During dinner he displayed as much reserve as his nature allowed him to, but afterwards, yielding to the solicitations of the women, he abandoned himself, and when twelve o'clock struck they were still gathered round him, listening to him with rapt expression, as if in hearing of delightful music. Awaking suddenly to a sense of the hour and his indiscretion, he bade Lord Spennymoor, who had sat talking all night with his brother in a far corner, good-night.

When the sound of the wheels of his trap died away, when the ladies had retired, Lord Spennymoor returned to the smoking-room, and at the end of a long silence asked his brother, who sat smoking opposite him, what he thought of Fletcher.

" He is one of those men who attract women, who attract nine people out of ten. . . . Call it magnetism, electro-biology, give it what name you will. The natural sciences——"

" Never mind the natural sciences. Do you think that either of my girls—Victoria, for instance—was attracted by him? I don't believe for a moment his story of having saved Lady Seeley from drowning in Italy, but I'm bound to say he told it very well. I can see the girls sitting round him listening. Poor Mrs. Dickens, her eyes were——"

" I shan't ask her here again. . . . But tell me, do you think he'll marry?"

" It would be very hard to say what will become of him. He may suddenly weary of women and become a woman-hater, or perhaps he may develop into a sort of Baron Hulot. He spoke about his writings—he may become ambitious and spend his life writing epics . . . He may go mad! He seemed interested in politics, he may go into Parliament; I fancy he would do very well in Parliament. A sudden loathing of civilization may come upon him and send him to Africa or the Arctic Regions. A man's end is always infinitely more in accordance with his true character than any conclusion we could invent. No writer, even if he have genius, is so extravagantly logical as nature."

During the winter months Mike was extensively occupied with the construction of the mausoleum in red granite, which he was raising in memory of Helen; and this interest remained paramount. He took many journeys to London on its account, and studied all the architecture on the subject, and with great books on his knees, he sat in the library making drawings or composing epitaphs and memorial poems.

Belthorpe Park was often full of visitors, and when walking with them on the terraces, his thoughts ran on Mount Rorke Castle, his own success, and Frank's failure; and when he awoke in the sweet, luxurious rooms, in the houses where he was staying, his brain filled with febrile sensations of triumph, and fitful belief that he was above any caprice of destiny.

It pleased him to write letters with Belthorpe Park printed on the top of the first page, and he wrote many for this reason. Quick with affectionate remembrances he thought of friends he had not thought of for years, and the sadnesses of these separations touched him deeply; and the mutability of things moved him in his very entrails, and he thought that perhaps no one had felt these things as he felt them. He remembered the women who had passed out of his life, and looking out on his English park, soaking with rain and dim with mist, he remembered those whom he had loved, and the peak whence he viewed the desert district of his amours—Lily Young. She haunted in his life.

He saw himself a knight in the tourney, and her eyes fixed on him, while he calmed his fiery dexter and tilted for her; he saw her in the silk comfort of the brougham, by his side, their bodies rocked gently together; he saw her in the South when reading Mrs. Byril's descriptions of rocky coast and olive fields.

The English park lay deep in snow, and the familiar word roses then took magical significance, and the imagined southern air was full of Lily.

" There's a sweet girl here, and I'm sure you would like her; she is so slender, so blithe and winsome, and so wayward. She has been sent abroad for her health, and is forbidden to go out after sunset, but will not obey. I am afraid she is dying of consumption . . . She has taken a great fancy to me. There is no one in our hotel but a few old maids, who discuss the peerage, and she runs after me to talk about men. I fancy she must have carried on pretty well with some one, for she loves talking about *him*, and is full of mysterious allusions."

The romance of the sudden introduction of this girl into the landscape took him by the throat. He saw himself walking with this dying girl in the beauty of blue mountains toppling into blue skies, and reflected in bluer seas; he sat with her beneath the palm trees; palms spread their fan-like leaves upon sky and sea, and in the rich green of their leaves

oranges grew to deep, and lemons to paler, gold;
and he dreamed that the knowledge that the object
of his love being transitory, would make his love
perfect and pure. Now in his solitude, with no object to break it, this desire for love in death haunted
in his mind. It rose unbidden, like a melody, stealing forth and surprising him in unexpected moments.
Often he asked himself why he did not pack up his
portmanteau and rush away; and he was only de-
terred by the apparent senselessness of the thought.
" What slaves we are of habit! Why more stupid
to go than to remain?"

Soon after, he received another letter from Mrs.
Byril. He glanced through it eagerly, for some
mention of the girl. Whatever there was of sweetness and goodness in Mike's nature was reflected in
his eyes (soft violet eyes, in which tenderness dwelt),
whatever there was of evil was written in the lips and
chin (puckered lips and goat-like chin), the long neck
and tiny head accentuating the resemblaace.

Now his being was concentrated in the eyes as a
landscape is sometimes in a piece of sky. He read:
" She told me that she had been once to see her
lover in the Temple." It was then Lily. He turned
to Mrs. Byril's first letter, and saw Lily in every line
of the description. Should he go to her? Of course
. . . When? At once! Should it not prove to be
Lily? . . . He did not care . . . He must go, and
in half an hour he touched the swiftly trotting mare
with the whip and glanced at his watch. " I shalt
just do it." The hedges passed behind, and the
wintry prospects were unfolded and folded away.
But as he approached the station a rumble and then
a rattle came out of the valley, and though he lashed
the mare into a gallop, he arrived only in time to
see a vanishing cloud of steam.

The next train did not reach London till long after the mail had left Charing Cross.

It froze hard during the night, and next morning his feet chilled in his thin shoes, as he walked to and fro, seeking a carriage holding a conversational-looking person. At Dover the wind was hard as the ice-bound steps which he descended, and the sea rolled in dolefully about the tall cliffs, melting far away into the bleak grayness of the sky. But more doleful than the bleak sea was sullen Picardy. Mike could not sleep, and his eyes fed upon the bleak black of swampy plains, utterly mournful, strangely different from green and gladsome England. And two margins of this doleful land remained impressed upon his mind, the first, a low grange, discoloured, crouching on the plain, and curtained by seven lamentable poplars, and Mike thought of the human beings that came from it, to see only a void landscape, and to labour in bleak fields. He remembered also a marsh with osier beds and pools of water ; and in the largest of these there was a black and broken boat. Thin sterile hills stretched their starved forms in the distance, and in the raw wintry light this landscape seemed like a page of the primitive world, and the strange creature striving with an oar recalled our ancestors.

Paris was steeped in great darkness and starlight, and the cab made slow and painful way through the frost-bound streets. The amble and the sliding of the horse was exasperating, the drive unendurable with uncertainty and cold, and Mike hammered his frozen feet on the curving floor of the vehicle. Street succeeded street, all growing meaner as they neared the Gare de Lyons. Fearing he should miss the express, he called to the impassive driver to hasten the vehicle. Three minutes remained to take his ticket and choose a carriage, and hoping for sleep and dreams of Lily, he rolled himself up in a rug for which he had paid sixty guineas, and fell asleep.

Ten hours after, he was roused by the guard, and stretching his stiffened limbs, he looked out, and in the vague morning saw towzled and dilapidated travellers, slipping upon the thin ice that covered the platform, striving to reach long, rough tables, spread with coffee, fruit and wine. Mike drank some coffee, and thinking of Mrs. Byril's roses, wondered when they should get into the sunshine.

As the train moved out of the platform the twilight vanished into daylight, the sky flushed, and he saw a scant land, ragged and torn with twisted plants, cacti and others, gashed and red, and savage as a negress's lips. So he saw the South through the breath-misted windows. He lay back; he dozed a little, and awoke an hour after to feel soft air upon the face, and to see a bush laden with blossom literally singing the spring. Thenceforth at every mile the land grew into more frequent bloom. The gray-green olive tree appeared, a crooked, twisted tree—habitual phase of the red land—and between its foliage gray, green brick façades, burnt and reburnt by the sun. The roofs of the houses grew flatter and campanile, and the domes rose, silvery or blue, in the dazzling day. A mountain shepherd, furnished with water-gourd, a seven-foot staff, and a gigantic pipe, lingered in the country railway-station. This shepherd's skin was like coffee, and he wore hair hanging far over his shoulders, and his beard reached to his waist.

Nice! A town of cheap fashion, a town of glass and stucco. The pungent odour of the eucalyptus trees, the light breeze stirred not the foliage, sheared into mathematical lines. It was like yards of baize dwindling in perspective; and between the tall trunks great plate-glass windows gleamed, filled with *l'article de Londres.*

He drove to the hotel from which Mrs. Byril had written, and learnt that she had left yesterday and that Mrs. and Miss Young were not staying there. They had no such name on the books. Looking on the sea and mountains he wondered himself what it all meant.

Having bathed and changed his clothes, he sallied forth in a cab to call at every hotel in the town, and after three hours' fruitless search, returned in despair. Never before had life seemed so sad ; never had fate seemed so cruel—he had come a thousand miles to regenerate his life, and an accident, the accident of a departure, hastened perhaps only by a day, had thrown him back on the past ; he had imagined a beautiful future made of love, goodness, and truth, and he found himself thrown back upon the sterile shore of a past of which he was weary, and of whose fruits he had eaten even to satiety. After much effort he had made sure that nothing mattered but Lily, neither wealth nor liberty, nor even his genius. In surrendering all he would have gained all—peace of mind, unending love and goodness. Goodness ! that which he had never known, that which he now knew was worth more than gratification of flesh and pride of spirit.

The night was full of tumult and dreams—dreams of palms, and seas, and endless love, and in the morning he walked into the realities of his imaginings.

Passing through an archway, he found himself in the gaud of the flower-market. There a hundred umbrellas, yellow, red, mauve and magenta, lemon yellow, cadmium yellow, gold, a multi-coloured mass, spread their extended bellies to a sky blue as the blouses.

The brown fingers of the peasant women are tying and pressing all the miraculous bloom of the earth into the fair fingers of Saxon girls—great packages of roses, pink lilies, clematis, stephanotis, and honeysuckle. A gentle breeze is blowing, rocking the umbrellas, wafting the odour of the roses and honeysuckle, bringing hither an odour of the lapping tide, rocking the immense umbrellas. One huge and ungainly sunshade creaks, swaying its preposterous rotundity. Beneath it the brown woman slices her pumpkin. Mike scanned every thin face for Lily, and as he stood wedged against a flower-stand, a girl passed him. She turned. It was Lily.

"Lily, is it possible? I was looking for you everywhere."

"Looking for me! When did you arrive in Nice? How did you know I was here?"

"Mrs. Byril wrote. She described a girl, and I knew from her description it must be you. And I came on at once."

"You came on at once to find me?"

"Yes; I love you more than ever. I can think only of you . . . But when I arrived I found Mrs. Byril had left, and I had no means of finding your address."

"You foolish boy; you mean to say you rushed away on the chance that I was the girl described in Mrs. Byril's letter!. . . . A thousand miles! and never even waited to ask the name or the address! Well, I suppose I must believe that you are in love. But you have not heard . . . They say I'm dying. I have only one lung left. Do you think I'm looking very ill?"

"You are looking more lovely than ever. My love shall give you health; we shall go—where shall we go? To Italy? You are my Italy. But I'm forgetting—why did you not answer my letter? It was cruel of you. Deceive me no more, play with me no longer; if you will not have me, say so, and I will end myself, for I cannot live without you."

"But I do not understand, I haven't had any letter; what letter?"

"I wrote asking you to marry me."

They walked out of the flower market on to the *Promenade des Anglais*, and Mike told her about his letters, concealing nothing of his struggle. The sea lay quite blue and still, lapping gently on the spare beach; the horizon floated on the sea, almost submerged, and the mountains, every edge razor-like, hard, and metallic, were veiled in a deep, transparent blue; and the villas, painted white, pink and green, with open loggias and balconies completed the operatic aspect.

"My mother will not hear of it; she would sooner see me dead than married to you."

"Why?"

"She knows you are an atheist for one thing."

"But she does not know that I have six thousand a-year."

"Six thousand a-year! and who was the fairy that threw such fortune into your lap? I thought you had nothing."

Vanity took him by the throat, but he wrenched himself free, and answered evasively that a distant cousin had left him a large sum of money, including an estate in Berkshire.

"Well, I'm very glad for your sake, but it will not influence mother's opinion of you."

"Then you will run away with me? Say you will."

"That is the best—for I'm not strong enough to dispute with mother. I dare say it is very cowardly of me, but I would avoid scenes; I've had enough of them. . . . We'll go away together, where shall we go? To Italy?"

" Yes, to Italy—my Italy. And do you love me? Have you forgiven me my conduct the day when you came to see me?"

" Yes, I love you ; I have forgiven you."

" And when shall we go?"

" When you like. I should like to go over that sea; I should like to go, Mike, with you, far away! Where, Mike?—Heaven?"

" We should find Heaven dull; but when shall we go across that sea, or when shall we go from here— now?"

" Now !"

" Why not?"

" Because here are my people coming to meet me. Now say nothing to my mother about marriage or she will never leave my side. I'm more ill than you think I am—I should have no strength to struggle with her."

Not again that day did Mike succeed in speaking alone with Lily, and the next day she and her mother and Major Downside, her uncle, went to spend the day with some friends who had a villa in the environs of the town. The day after he met mother and daughter out walking in the morning. In the afternoon Lily was obliged to keep her room. Should she die, should the irreparable happen! Mike crushed the instinct, that made him see a poem in the death of his beloved ; and he determined to believe that he should possess her, love her and only her ; he saw himself a new Mike, a perfect and true husband-lover. Never was man more weary of vice, more desirous of reformation.

He had studied the train service until he could not pretend to himself there remained any crumb of

excuse for further consideration of it. He wandered
about the corridors, a miserable man. On Sunday
she came down-stairs and drove to church with her
mother. Mike followed, and full of schemes for
flight, holding a note ready to slip into her hand, he
wondered if such pallor as hers were for this side of
life. In the note it was written that he would wait
all day for her in the sitting-room, and about five,
as he sat holding the tattered newspaper, his thoughts
far away in Naples, Algiers and Egypt, he heard a
voice calling—

"Mike! Mike! Mother is lying down; I think we
can get away now, if there's a train before half-past
five."

Mike did not need to consult the time table. He
said, "At last, at last, darling, come! . . . Yes, there
is a train for the Italian frontier at a few minutes
past five. We shall have just time to catch it.
Come!"

But in the gardens they met the Major, who would
not hear of his niece being out after sunset and sent
her back. Mike overtook Lily on the staircase.

"I can endure this no longer," he said, "you must
come with me to-night when every one is in bed.
There is a train at two."

"I cannot; I have to pass through my mother's
room. She would be sure to awake."

"Great Scott! what shall we do? My head is
whirling. You must give your mother a sleeping
potion, will you? She drinks something before she
goes to bed?"

"Yes, but——"

"There must be no buts. It is a case of life and
death. You do not want to die, as many girls die.
To many a girl marriage is life. I will get something quite harmless, and quite tasteless."

She waited for him in the sitting-room. He returned in a few minutes with a small bottle, which he pressed into her hand. "And now, *au revoir;* in a few hours you will be mine for ever."

After leaving her he dined; after dinner went to a gambling hell, where he lost a good deal of money and would have lost more, had the necessity of keeping at least £200 for his wedding tour not been so imperative. He wandered about the streets talking to and sometimes strolling about with the prostitutes, listening to their lamentable stories—"anything," he thought, "to distract my mind." He was to meet Lily on the staircase at one o'clock, and now it was half-past twelve, and giving the poor creature whose chatter had beguiled the last half-hour a louis, he returned hurriedly to his hotel.

The lift had ceased working, and he ascended the great staircase, three steps at a time. On the second floor he stopped to reconnoitre. The *gardien* lay fast asleep on a bench; he could not do better than sit on the stairs and wait; if the man awoke he would have to be bribed. Lily's number was 45, a dozen doors down the passage. At one o'clock the *gardien* awoke. Mike entered into conversation with him, gave him a couple of francs, bade him good-night, and went partly up the next flight of stairs. Listening for every sound, expecting every moment to hear a door open, he waited till the clocks struck the half-hour. Then he became as if insane, and he deemed it would not be enough if she were to disappoint him to set the hotel on fire and throw himself from the roof. Something must happen, if he were to remain sane, and determined to dare all, he decided he would seek her in her room and bear her away. He knew he would have to pass through Mrs. Young's room. What should he do if she awoke, and taking him for a robber, raised the alarm?

Putting aside such surmises he turned the handle of

her door as quietly as he could. The lock gave forth hardly any sound, the door passed noiselessly over the carpet. He hesitated, but only for a moment, and drawing off his shoes he prepared to cross the room. A night-light was burning, and it revealed the fat outline of a huge body huddled in the bed-clothes. He would have to pass close to Mrs. Young. He glided by, passing swiftly towards the further room, praying that the door would open without a sound. It was ajar, and opened without a sound. "What luck!" he thought, and a moment after he stood in Lily's room. She lay upon the bed, as if she had fallen there, dressed in a long travelling-cloak, her hat crushed on one side.

"Lily, Lily!" he whispered, "'tis I, awake! speak, tell me you are not dead." She moved a little beneath his touch, then wetting a towel in the water-jug he applied it to her forehead and lips, and slowly she revived.

"Where are we?" she asked. "Mike, darling, are we in Italy? . . . I have been ill, have I not? They say I'm going to die, but I'm not; I'm going to live for you, my darling."

Then she recovered recollection of what had happened, and whispered that she had failed to give her mother the opiate, but had nevertheless determined to keep her promise to him. She had dressed herself and was just ready to go, but a sudden weakness had come over her. She remembered staggering a few steps and nothing more.

"But if you have not given your mother the opiate, she may awake at any moment. Are you strong enough, my darling, to come with me? Come!"

"Yes, yes, I'm strong enough . . . Give me some more water, and kiss me, dear."

The lovers wrapped themselves in each other's arms. But hearing some one moving in the adjoining room, the girl looked in horror and supplication in Mike's eyes. Stooping, he disappeared beneath a small table; and drew his legs beneath the cloth. The sounds in the next room continued, and he recognized them as proceeding from some one searching for clothes. Then Lily's door was opened and Mrs. Young said—

"Lily, there is some one in your room; I'm sure Mr. Fletcher is here."

"Oh, mother, how can you say such a thing; indeed he is not."

"He is; I am not mistaken. This is disgraceful; he must be under that bed."

"Mother, you can look."

"I shall do nothing of the kind. I shall fetch your uncle."

When he heard Mrs. Young retreating with fast steps, Mike emerged from his hiding.

"What shall I do?"

"You can't leave without being seen. Uncle sleeps opposite."

"I'll hide in your mother's room; and while they are looking for me here, I will slip out."

"How clever you are, darling! Go there. Do you hear, uncle is answering her? To-morrow we shall find an opportunity to get away; but now I would not be found out . . . I told mother you weren't here. Go!"

The morrow brought no opportunity for flight. Lily could not leave her room, and it was whispered that the doctors despaired of her life. Then Mike opened his heart to the Major, and the old soldier promised him his cordial support when Lily was well. Three days passed, and then, unable to bear the strain any longer, Mike fled to Monte Carlo. There he lost and won a fortune. Hence Italy enticed him and he went, knowing that he should never go there with Lily.

But not in art nor in dissipation did he find escape from her deciduous beauty, now divided from the grave only by a breath, beautiful and divinely sorrowful in its transit.

Some days passed, and then a letter from the Major brought him back over-worn with anxiety, wild with grief. He found her better. She had been carried down from her room, and was lying on a sofa by the open window. There were a few flowers in her hands, and when she offered them to Mike she said with a kind of Heine-like humour—

"Take them, they will live almost as long as I shall."

"Lily, you will get well, and we shall see Italy together. I had to leave you—I should have gone mad had I remained. The moment I heard I could see you I returned. You will get well."

"No, no; I'm here only for a few days—a few weeks at most. I shall never go to Italy. I shall never be your sweetheart. I'm one of God's virgins, I belong to my saint, my first and real sweetheart. You remember when I came to see you in the Temple Gardens, I told you about him then, didn't I? Ah! happy, happy aspirations, better even than you, my darling. And he is waiting for me; his Maries are about him, but I am his Mary, am I not, dear?"

"You'll get well. The sun of Italy shall be our heaven, thy lips shall give me immortality, thy love shall give me God."

"Fine words, my sweetheart, fine words, but death

waits not for love. . . Well, it's a pity to die without having loved."

" It is worse to live without having loved, dearest— dearest, you will live."

He never saw her again. Next day she was too ill to come down, and henceforth she grew daily weaker. Every day brought death visibly nearer, and one day the Major came to Mike in the garden and said—

" It is all over, my poor friend !"

Then came days of white flowers and wreaths and bouquets and baskets of bloom, stephanotis, roses, lilies, and every white blossom that blows ; and so friends sought to cover and hide the darkness of the grave. Mike remembered the disordered faces of the girls in church; weeping, they threw themselves on each other's shoulders ; and the mournful chant was sung ; and the procession toiled up the long hill to the cemetery above the town, and Lily was laid there, to rest there for ever. There she lies, facing Italy, which she never knew but in dream. The wide country leading to Italy lies below her, the peaks of the rocky coast, the blue sea, the blue-green olives billowing like tides from hill to hill ; the white loggias gleaming in the sunlight. His thoughts followed the flight of the blue mountain passes that lead so enticingly to Italy, and as he looked into the distance, dim and faint as the dream that had gone, there rose in his mind an even fairer land than Italy, the land of dream, where for every one, even for Mike Fletcher, there grows some rose or lily unattainable.

CHAPTER X.

IN the dreary drawing-room, amid the tattered copies of the *Graphic* and *Illustrated London News*, he encountered the inevitable idle woman. They engaged in conversation; and he repeated the phrases that belong inevitably to such occasons.

" How horrible all this is," he said to himself; " this is worse than peeping and botanizing on a mother's grave."

He desired supreme grief, and grief fled from his lure; and rhymes and images thronged his brain; and the poem that oftenest rose in his mind, seemingly complete in cadence and idea, was so cruel, that Lily, looking out of heaven, seemed to beg him to refrain. But though he erased the lines on the paper, he could not erase them on his brain, and baffled, he pondered over the phenomena of the antagonism of desired aspirations and intellectual instincts. He desired a poem full of the divine grace of grief; a poem beautiful, tender and pure, fresh and wild as a dove crossing in the dawn from wood to wood. He desired the picturesqueness of a young man's grief for a dead girl, an Adonais going forth into the glittering morning, and weeping for his love that has passed out of the sun into the shadow. This is what he wrote :

À UNE POTRINAIRE.

WE are alone ! listen, a little while,
And hear the reason why your weary smile
And lute-toned speaking is so very sweet
To me, and how my love is more complete

Than any love of any lover.   They
Have only been attracted by the gray
Delicious softness of your eyes, your slim
And delicate form, or some such whimpering whim,
The simple pretexts of all lovers;—I
For other reasons.   Listen whilst I try
To say.   I joy to see the sunset slope
Beyond the weak hours' hopeless horoscope,
Leaving the heavens a melancholy calm,
Of quiet colour chaunted like a psalm,
In mildly modulated phrases ; thus
Your life shall fade like a voluptuous
Vision beyond the sight, and you shall die
Like some soft evening's sad serenity . . .
I would possess your dying hours ; indeed
My love is worthy of the gift, I plead
For them.
               Although I never loved as yet,
Methinks that I might love you ; I would get
From out the knowledge that the time was brief,
That tenderness whose pity grows to grief,
My dream of love, and yea, it would have charms
Beyond all other passions, for the arms
Of death are stretched youward, and he claims
You as his bride.   Maybe my soul misnames
Its passion ; love perhaps it is not, yet
To see you fading like a violet,
Or some sweet thought away, would be a strange
And costly pleasure, far beyond the range
Of common man's emotion.   Listen, I
Will choose a country spot where fields of rye
And wheat extend in waving yellow plains,
Broken with wooded hills and leafy lanes,
To pass our honeymoon ; a cottage where   •
The porch and windows are festooned with fair
Green wreaths of eglantine, and look upon
A shady garden where we'll walk alone
In the autumn sunny evenings ; each will see
Our walks grow shorter, till at length to thee
The garden's length is far, and thou wilt rest
From time to time, leaning upon my breast
Thy languid lily face.   Then later still,
Unto the sofa by the window-sill

Thy wasted body I shall carry, so
That thou mayst drink the last left lingering glow
Of even, when the air is filled with scent
Of blossoms ; and my spirits shall be rent
The while with many griefs.   Like some blue day
That grows more lovely as it fades away,
Gaining that calm serenity and height
Of colour wanted, as the solemn night
Steals forward thou shalt sweetly fall asleep
For ever and for ever ; I shall weep
A day and night large tears upon thy face,
Laying thee then beneath a rose-red place
Where I may muse and dedicate and dream
Volumes of poesy of thee; and deem
It happiness to know that thou art far
From any base desires as that fair star
Set in the evening magnitude of heaven.
Death takes but little, yea, thy death has given
Me that deep peace and immaculate possession
Which man may never find in earthly passion.

The composition of the poem induced a period of
literary passion, during which he composed much
various matter, even part of his great poem, which
he would have completed had he not been struck
by an idea for a novel, and so imperiously, that he
wrote the book straight from end to end. It was sent
to a London publisher, and it raised some tumult of
criticism, none of which reached the author.   When
it appeared he was far away, living in Arab tents,
seeking pleasure at other sources.   For suddenly,
when the strain of the composition of his book was
relaxed, civilization had grown hateful to him ; a
picture by Fromentin, and that painter's book, *Un
été dans le Sahara*, quickened the desire of primitive
life ; he sped away, and for nearly two years lived
on the last verge of civilization, sometimes passing
beyond it with the Bedouins into the interior, on
slave-trading or rapacious expeditions.   The fre-
quentation of these simple people calmed the fever

of ennui, which had been consuming him. Nature leads us to the remedy that the development of reason inflicts on the animal—man. And for more than a year Mike thought he had solved the problem of life; now he lived in peace—passion had ebbed almost out of hearing, and in the plain satisfaction of his instincts he found happiness.

With the wild chieftains, their lances at rest, watching from behind a sandhill, he sometimes thought that the joy he experienced was akin to that which he had known in Sussex, when his days were spent in hunting and shooting; now, as then, he found relief by surrendering himself to the hygienics of the air and earth. But his second return to animal nature had been more violent and radical; and it pleased him to think that he could desire nothing but the Arabs with whom he lived, and whose friendship he had won. But *qui a bu boire*, and below consciousness dead appetites were awakening, and would soon be astir.

The tribe had wandered to an encampment in the vicinity of Morocco; and one day a missionary and his wife came with a harmonium and tracts. The scene, so evocative of the civilization from which Mike had fled, drew him and held him in a power he could not account for. He told the woman he had adopted Arab life; explaining that the barbaric soul of some ancestor lived in him, and that he was happy with these primitive people. He too was a missionary, and had come to save them from Christianity and all its corollaries—silk hats, piano playing, newspapers, and patent medicines. The English woman argued with him plaintively; the husband pressed a bundle of tracts upon him; and this very English couple hoped he would come and see them when he returned to town. Mike thanked them, insisting, however, that he would never leave his beloved desert, or desert his friends. Next day, however, he forgot to fall on his knees at noon, and outside the encampment stood looking in the direction whither the missionaries had gone. A strange sadness seemed to have fallen upon him; he cared no more for plans for slave-trading in the interior, or plunder in the desert. The scent of the white woman's skin and hair was in his nostrils; the nostalgia of the pavement had found him, and he knew he must leave the desert. One morning he was missed in the Sahara, and a fortnight after he was seen in the Strand, rushing towards Lubini's.

"My dear fellow," he said, catching hold of a friend's arm, "I've been living with the Arabs for the last two years. Fancy, not to have seen a 'tart' or drunk a bottle of champagne for two years! Come and dine with me. We'll go on afterwards to the Troc'."

Mike looked round as if to assure himself that he was back again dining at Lubi's. It was the same little white-painted gallery, filled with courtesans, music-hall singers, drunken lords, and sarcastic journalists. He noticed, however, that he hardly knew a single face, and was unacquainted with the amours of any of the women. He inquired for his friends. Muchross was not expected to live, Laura was underground, and her sister was in America. Joining in the general hilarity, he learnt that as the singer declined the prize-fighter was going up in popular estimation. A young and drunken lord offered to introduce him " to a very warm member."

He felt sure, however, that the Royal would stir in him the old enthusiasms, and his heart beat when he saw in a box Kitty Carew, looking exactly the same as the day he had left her; but she insisted on taking credit for recognizing him—so changed was he. He felt somewhat provincial, and no woman noticed him, and it was clear that Kitty was no longer interested in him. The conversation languished, he did not understand the allusions, and he was surprised and a little alarmed, indeed, to find that he did not even desire their attention.

A few weeks afterwards he received an invitation to a ball. It was from a woman of title, the address was good, and he resolved to go. It was to one of the Queen Anne houses with which Chelsea abounds, and as he drove towards it he noted the little windows aflame with light and colour in the blue summer night. On the carved cramped staircases women struck him as being more than usually interesting, and the distinguished air of the company moved him with pleasurable sensations. A thick creamy odour of white flowers gratified the nostrils; the slender backs of the girls, the shoulder blades squeezed together by the stays, were full of delicate lines and tints. Mike saw a tall blonde girl, slight as a reed, so blonde that she was almost an albino, her figure in green gauze swaying. He saw a girl so brown that he thought of palms and cocoa-nuts; she passed him smiling, all her girlish soul awake in the enchantment of the dance. He said—

"No, I don't want to be introduced; she'd only bore me; I know exactly all she would say."

Studying these, he thought vaguely of dancing a quadrille, and was glad when the lady said she never danced. With a view to astonish her, he said—

"Since I became a student of Schopenhauer I have given up waltzing. Now I never indulge in anything but a square."

For a few moments his joke amused him, and he

regretted that John Norton, who would understand its humour, was not there to laugh at it. Having eaten supper he choose the deepest chair among the clustered furniture of the drawing room, and watched in spleenic interest a woman of thirty flirting with a young man.

The panelled skirt stretched stiffly over the knees, the legs were crossed, one drawn slightly back. The young man sat awkwardly on the edge of the sofa nursing his silk foot. She looked at him over her fan, inclining her blonde head in assent from time to time. The young man was delicate—a red blonde. The wall, laden with heavy shelves, was covered with an embossed paper of a deep gold hue. A piece of silk, worked with rich flowers, concealed the volumes in a light bookcase. A lamp, set on a tall brass rod, stood behind the lady, flooding her hair with yellow light, and its silk shade was nearly the same tint as the lady's hair. The costly furniture, the lady and her lover, the one in black and white, the other in creamy lace, the panelled skirt extended over her knees, filled the room like a picture—an enticing but somewhat vulgar picture of modern refinement and taste. Mike watched them curiously.

" Five years ago," he thought, " I was young like he is ; my soul thrilled as his is thrilling now."

Then, seeing a woman whom he knew pass the door on her way to the ball-room, he asked her to come and sit with him. He did so remembering the tentative steps they had taken in flirtation three years ago. So by way of transition, he said—

" The last time we met we spoke of the higher education of women, and you said that nothing sharpened the wits like promiscuous flirtation. Enchanting that was, and it made poor Mrs.,—Mrs.—I really can't remember—a lady with earnest eyes— look so embarrassed."

" I don't believe I ever said such a thing ; anyhow, if I did, I've entirely changed my views."

" What a pity ! but—perhaps you have finished your education ?"

" Yes, that's it ; and now I must go up-stairs. I am engaged for this dance."

" Clearly I'm out of it," thought Mike. " Not only do people see me with new eyes, but I see them with eyes that I cannot realize as mine."

The drawing-room was empty ; all had gone up-stairs to dance, so, finding himself alone, he went to a mirror to note the changes. At first he seemed the same Mike Fletcher ; but by degrees he recognized, or thought he recognized, certain remote and subtle differences. He thought that the tenderness which used to reside in his eyes was evanescent or gone. This tenderness had always been to him a subject of surprise, and he had never been able to satisfactorily explain its existence, knowing as he knew how all tenderness was in contradiction to his true character ; at least, as he understood himself. This tenderness was now replaced by a lurking evil look, and he remembered that he had noted such evil look in certain old libertines. Certain lines about the face had grown harder, the hollow freckled cheeks seemed to have sunk a little, and the pump-handle chin seemed to be defining itself, even to caricature There was still a certain air of bravour, of truculence, which attracted, and might still charm. He turned from the mirror, went up-stairs and danced three or four times. He remained until the last, and followed by an increasing despair he muttered, as he got into a hansom—

" If this is civilization I'd better go back to the Arabs."

The solitude of his rooms chilled him in the roots of his mind ; he looked around like a hunted animal.

He threw himself into an arm-chair. Like a pure fire ennui burned in his heart.

"Oh, for rest! I'm weary of life. Oh, to slip back into the unconscious, whence we came, and pass for ever from the fitful buzzing of the midges. To feel that sharp, cruel, implacable externality of things melt, vanish, and dissolve!

"The utter stupidity of life! There never was anything so stupid; I mean the whole thing—our ideas of right and wrong, love and duty, etc. Great Scott! what folly. The strange part of it all is man's inability to understand the folly of living. When I said to that woman to-night that I believed that the only evil is to bring children into the world, she said, 'but then the world would come to an end.' I said 'Do you not think it would be a good thing if it did?' Her look of astonishment proved how unsuspicious she is of the truth. The ordinary run of mortals do not see into the heart of things, nor do we, except in terribly lucid moments; then, seeing life truly, seeing it in its monstrous deformity, we cry out like children in the night.

"Then why do we go to Death with terror-stricken faces and reluctant feet? We should go to Death in perfect confidence, like a bride to her husband, and with eager and smiling eyes. But he who seeks Death goes with wild eyes—upbraiding Life for having deceived him, as if Life ever did anything else? He goes to Death as a last refuge. None go to Death in deep calm and resignation, as a child goes to the kind and thoughtful nurse in whose arms he will find beautiful rest.

"It was in this very room I spoke to Lady Helen for the last time. She understood very well indeed the utter worthlessness of life. How beautiful was her death! That white still face, with darkness stealing from the closed lids, a film of light shadow, symbol of deeper shadow. The unseen but easily imagined hand grasping the pistol, the unseen but imagined red stain upon the soft texture of the chemise! I might have loved her. She saw into the heart of things, and like a reasonable being, which she was, resolved to rid herself of the burden. We discussed the whole question in the next room ; and I remember I was surprised to find that she was in no wise deceived by the casual fallacy of the fools who say that the good times compensate for the bad. Ah! how little they understand! Pleasure! what is it but the correlative of pain? Nothing short of man's incomparable stupidity could enable him to dis-tinguish between success and failure.

But now I remember she did not die for any pro-found belief in the worthlessness of life, but merely on account of a vulgar love affair. That letter was quite conclusive. It was written from the Alexandra Hotel. It was a letter breaking it off (strange that any one should care to break off with Lady Helen !); she stopped to see him, in the hope of bringing about a reconciliation. Quite a Bank Holiday sort of inci-dent! She did not deny life ; but only that particular form in which life had come to her. Under such circumstances suicide is unjustifiable.

"There! I'm breaking into what John Norton would call my irrepressible levity. But there is little gladness in me. Ennui hunts me like a hound, loos-ing me for a time, but finding the scent again it fol-lows—I struggle—escape—but the hour will come when I shall escape no more. If Lily had not died, if I had married her, I might have lived. In truth, I'm not alive, I'm really dead, for I live without hope, without belief, without desire. Ridiculous as a wife and children are when you look at them from the philosophical side, they are necessary if man is to live; if man dispenses with the family, he must embrace the cloister; John has done that, but now I know that man may not live without wife, without child, without God!"

. . . .

Next day, after breakfast, he lay in his arm-chair, thinking of the few hours that lay between him and the fall of night. He sought to tempt his jaded appetite with many assorted dissipations, but he turned from all in disgust, and gambling became his sole distraction. Every evening about eleven he was seen in Piccadilly, going towards Arlington Street, and every morning about four the street-sweepers saw him returning home along the Strand. Then, afraid to go to bed, he sometimes took pen and paper and attempted to write some lines of his long-projected poem. But he found that all he had to say he had said in the sketch which he found among his papers. The idea did not seem to him to want any further amplification,-and he sat wondering if he could ever have written three or four thousand lines on the subject.

The casual eye and ear still recognized no difference in him. There were days when he was as good-looking as ever, and much of the old fascination remained; but to one who knew him well, as Harding did, there was no doubt that his life had passed its meridian. The day was no longer at poise, but was quietly sinking; and though the skies were full of light, the buoyancy and blitheness that the hours bear in their ascension were missing; lassitude and moodiness were aboard.

More than ever did he seek women, urged by a nervous erithism which he could not explain or con-

trol.   Married women and young girls came to him
from drawing-rooms, actresses from theatres, shop-
girls from the streets, and though seemingly all were
as unimportant and accidental as the cigarettes he
smoked, each was a drop in the ocean of the immense
ennui accumulating in his soul.   The months passed,
disappearing in a sheer and measureless void, leaving
no faintest reflection or even memory, and his life
flowed in unbroken weariness and despair.   There
was no taste in him for anything; he had eaten of
the fruit of knowledge, and with the evil rind in his
teeth, wandered an exile beyond the garden.   Dark,
and desolate beyond speech was his world; dark and
empty of all save the eyes of the hound Ennui; and
by day and night it watched him, fixing him with
dull and unrelenting eyes.   Sometimes these acute
strainings of his consciousness lasted only between
entering his chambers late at night and going to
bed; and fearful of the sleepless hours, every sensation exaggerated by the effect of the insomnia, he
sat in dreadful commune with the spectre of his life,
waiting for the apparition to leave him.

"And to think," he cried, turning his face to the
wall, "that it is this *ego* that gives existence to it all!"

One of the most terrible of these assaults of consciousness came upon him on the winter immediately
on his return from London. He had gone to London
to see Miss Dudley, whom he had not seen since his
return from Africa—therefore for more than two
years.   Only to her had he written from the desert;
his last letters, however, had remained unanswered
and for some time misgivings had been astir in his
heart.   And it was with the view of ridding himself
of these that he had been to London.   The familiar
air of the house seemed to him altered, the servant
was a new one; she did not know the name, and

after some inquiries, she informed him that the lady had died some six months past. All that was human in him had expressed itself in this affection ; among women Lily Young and Miss Dudley had alone touched his heart ; there were friends scattered through his life whom he had worshipped ; but his friendships had nearly all been, though intense, ephemeral and circumstantial ; nor had he thought constantly and deeply of any but these two women. So long as either lived, there was a haven of quiet happiness and natural peace in which his shattered spirit might rock at rest ; but now he was alone.

Others he saw with homes and family ties ; all seemed to have hopes and love to look to but he— "I alone am alone! The whole world is in love with me, and I'm utterly alone." Alone as a wreck upon a desert ocean, terrible in its calm as in its tempest. Broken was the helm and sailless was the mast, and he must drift till borne upon some ship-wrecking reef! Had fate designed him to float over every rock? must he wait till the years let through the waters of disease, and he foundered obscurely in the immense loneliness he had so elaborately prepared?

Overhead was cloud of storm, the ocean heaved, quick lightnings flashed ; but no waves gathered, and in heavy sulk a sense of doom lay upon him. Wealth and health and talent were his ; he had all, and in all he found he had nothing ;—yes, one thing was his for evermore,—Ennui.

Thoughts and visions rose into consciousness like monsters coming through a gulf of dim seawater ; all delusion had fallen, and he saw the truth in all its fearsome deformity. On awakening, the implacable externality of things pressed upon his sight until he felt he knew what the mad feel, and then it seemed impossible to begin another day. With long rides, with physical fatigue, he strove to keep at bay the despair-fiend which now had not left him hardly for weeks. For long weeks the disease continued, almost without an intermission; he felt sure that death was the only solution, and he considered the means for encompassing the end with a calm that startled him.

Nor was it until the spring months that he found any subjects that might take him out of his melancholy, and darken the too acute consciousness of the truth of things which was forcing him on to madness or suicide. One day it was suggested that he should stand for Parliament. He eagerly seized the idea, and his brain thronged immediately with visions of political successes; of the parliamentary triumphs he would achieve. Bah! he was an actor at heart, and required the contagion of the multitude, and again he looked out upon life with visionary eyes. Harsh hours fell behind him, gay hours awaited him, held hands to him.

Men wander far from the parent plot of earth; but a strange fatality leads them back, they know not how. None had desired to separate from all associations of early life more than Mike, and he was at once glad and sorry to find that the door through which he was to enter Parliament was Cashel. He would have liked better to represent an English town or county, but he could taste in Cashel a triumph which he could nowhere else in the world. To return triumphant to his native village is the secret of every wanderer's desire, for there he can claim not only their applause but their gratitude.

The politics he would have to adopt made him wince, for he knew the platitudes they entailed; and in preference he thought of the paradoxes with which he would stupefy the House, the daring and originality he would show in introducing subjects that, till then, no one had dared to touch upon. With the politics of his party he had little intention of concerning himself, for his projects were to make for himself a reputation as an orator, and having confirmed it to seek another constituency at the close of the present Parliament. Such intention lay dormant in the background of his mind, but he had not seen many Irish Nationalists before he was effervescing with rhetoric suitable for the need of the election, and he was sometimes puzzled to determine whether he was false or true.

Driving through Dublin from the steamer, he met Frank Escott. They shouted simultaneously to their carmen to stop.

"Home to London. I've just come from Cashel. I went to try to effect some sort of reconciliation with Mount Rorke; but—and you, where are you going?"

"I'm going to Cashel. I'm going to contest the town in the Parnellite interest."

Each pair of eyes was riveted on the other. For both men thought of the evening when Mike had received the letter notifying that Lady Seeley had left him five thousand a year, and Frank had read in the evening paper that Lady Mount Rorke had given birth to a son. Frank was, as usual, volutic and communicative. He dilated on the painfulness of the salutations of the people he had met on the way going from the station to Mount Rorke; and, instead of walking straight in, as in old times, he had to ask the servant to take his name.

"Burton, the old servant who had known me since I was a boy, seemed terribly cut up, and he was evidently very reluctant to speak the message. 'I'm very sorry, Mr. Frank,' he said, 'but his lordship says he is too unwell to see any one to-day, sir; he is very sorry, but if you would write ' . . . If I would write, think of it, I who was once his heir, and used the place as if it were mine! Poor old Burton was quite overcome. He tried to ask me to come into the dining-room and have some lunch. If I go there again I shall be asked into the servants' hall. And at that moment the nurse came, wheeling the baby in the perambulator through the hall, going out for an airing. I tried not to look, but couldn't restrain my eyes, and the nurse stopped and said, 'Now then, dear, give your hand to the gentleman, and tell him your name.' The little thing looked up, its blue eyes staring out of its sallow face, and it held out the little, putty-like hand. Poor old Burton turned aside, he couldn't stand it any longer, and walked into the dining-room."

"And how did you get away?" asked Mike, who saw his friend's misfortune in the light of an exquisite chapter in a novel. "How sad the old place must have seemed to you!"

"You are thinking how you could put it in a book —how brutal you are!"

"I assure you you are wrong. I can't help trying to realize your sensations, but that doesn't prevent me from being very sorry for you, and I'm sure I shall be very pleased to help you. Do you want any money? Don't be shy about saying yes. I haven't forgotten how you helped me."

"I really don't like to ask you, you've been very good as it is. However, if you could spare me a tenner?"

"Of course I can. Let's send these jarvies away, and come into my hotel, and I'll write you a cheque."

The sum Frank asked for revealed to Mike exactly the depth to which he had sunk since they had last met. Small as it was, however, it seemed to have had considerable effect in reviving Frank's spirits, and he proceeded quite cheerfully into the tale of his misfortune. Now it seemed to strike him too in quite a literary light, and he made philosophic comments on its various aspects, as he might on the hero of a book which he was engaged on or contemplated writing.

"No," he said, "you were quite wrong in supposing that I waited to look back on the old places. I got out of the park through a wood so as to avoid the gate-keeper. In moments of great despair we don't lapse into pensive contemplation." . . . He stopped to pull at the cigar Mike had given him, and when he had got it well alight, he said, "It was really most dramatic, it would make a splendid scene in a play; you might make him murder the baby."

Half an hour after Mike bade his friend good-bye, glad to be rid of him.

"He's going back to that beastly wife who lives in some dirty lodging. How lucky I was, after all, not to marry."

Then, remembering the newspaper, and the use it might be to him when in Parliament, he rushed after Frank. When the *Pilgrim* was mentioned Frank's face changed expression, and he seemed stirred with deeper grief than when he related the story of his disinheritance. He had no further connection with the paper. Thigh had worked him out of it.

"I never really despaired," he said, "until I lost my paper. Thigh has asked me to send him paragraphs, but of course I'm not going to do that."

"Why not?"

"Well, hang it, after being the editor of a paper, you aren't going to send in paragraphs on approval. It isn't good enough. When I go back to London I shall try to get a sub-editorship."

Mike pressed another tenner upon him, and returning to the smoking-room, and throwing himself into an arm-chair, he lapsed into dreams of the bands and the banners that awaited him. · When animal spirits were ebullient in him, he regarded his election in the light of a vulgar practical joke ; when the philosophic mood was upon him he turned from all thought of it as from the smell of a dirty kitchen coming through a grating.

CHAPTER XI.

DURING the first session Mike was hampered and inconvenienced by the forms of the House ; in the second, he began to weary of its routine. His wit and paradox attracted some attention ; he made one almost successful speech, many that stirred and stimulated the minds of celebrated listeners ; but for all that he failed. His failure to redeem the expectations of his friends, produced in him much stress and pain of mind, the more acute because he was fully alive to the cause. He ascribed it rightly to certain inherent flaws in his character. " The world believes in those who believe in it. Such belief may prove a lack of intelligence on the part of the believer, but it secures him success, and success is after all the only thing that compensates for the evil of life."

Always impressed by new ideas, rarely holding to any impression long, finding all hollow and common very soon, he had been taken with the importance of the national assembly, but it had hardly passed into its third session when all illusion had vanished, and Mike ridiculed parliamentary ambitions in the various chambers of the barristers he frequented.

It was Maytime, and never did the Temple wear a more gracious aspect. The river was full of hay-boats, the gardens were green with summer hours. Through the dim sky, above the conical roof of the dear church, the pigeons fled in rapid quest, and in Garden Court, beneath the plane trees, old folk dozed, listening to the rippling tune of the fountain and the shrilling of the sparrows. In King's Bench Walk the waving branches were full of their little brown bodies. Sparrows everywhere, flying from the trees to the eaves, hopping on the golden gravel, beautifully carpeted with the rich shadows of the trees—unabashed little birds, scarcely deigning to move out of the path of the young men as they passed to and fro from their offices to the library. " That sweet, grave place where we weave our ropes of sand," so Mike used to speak of it.

The primness of the books, the little galleries guarded by brass railings, here and there a reading-desk, the sweet silence of the place, the young men reading at the polished oak tables, the colour of the oak and the folios, the rich Turkey carpets, lent to the library that happy air of separation from the brutalities of life which is almost sanctity. These, the familiar aspects of the Temple, moved him with all their old enchantments ; he lingered in the warm summer mornings when all the Temple was astir, gossiping with the students, or leaning upon the balustrades in pensive contemplation of the fleet river.

But these moods of passive happiness were inter-rupted more frequently than they had been in earlier years by the old whispering voice, now grown strangely distinct, which asked, but no longer through laughing lips, if it were possible to discern any purpose in life, and if all thoughts and things were not as vain as a little measure of sand. The dark fruit that hangs so alluringly over the wall of the garden of life now met his eyes frequently, tempting him, and perforce he must stay to touch and consider it. Then, resolved to baffle at all costs the disease which he now knew pursued him, he plunged in the crowd of drunkenness and whoremongering which swelled the Strand at night. He was found where prize-fighters brawled, and card-sharpers cajoled; where hall singers fed on truffled dishes, and courtesans laughed and called for champagne. He was seen in Lubini's sprawling over luncheon tables till late in the afternoon, and at nightfall lingering about the corners of the streets, talking to the women that passed. In such low form of vice he sought escape. He turned to gambling, risking large sums, sometimes imperilling his fortune for the sake of the assuagement such danger brought of the besetting sin. But luck poured thousands into his hands; and he applied himself to the ruin of one seeking to bring about his death.

"Before I kill myself," he said, "I will kill others; I'm weary of playing at Faust, now I'll play at Mephistopheles."

Henceforth all men who had money, or friends who had money, were invited to Temple Gardens. You met there members of both Houses of Parliament— the successors of Muchross and Snowdown; and men exquisitely dressed, with quick, penetrating eyes, assembled there, actors and owners of race-horses galore, and bright complexioned young men of many affections. Rising now from the piano one is heard to say reproachfully, "you never admire anything I wear," to a grave friend who had passed some criticism on the flower in the young man's button-hole.

It was still early in the evening and the usual company had not yet arrived. Harding stood on the white fur hearthrug, his legs slightly apart, smoking. Mike lay in an easy chair. His eyes were upon Harding, whom he had not seen for some years, and the sight of him recalled the years when they wrote the *Pilgrim* together.

He thought how splendid were then his enthusiasms and how genuine his delight in life. It was in this very room that he kissed Lily for the first time. That happy day. Well did he remember how the sun shone upon the great river, how the hayboats sailed, how the city rose like a vision out of the mist. But Lily lies asleep, far away in a southern land; she lies sleeping, facing Italy—that Italy which they should have seen and dreamed together. At that moment, he brushed from his book a little green insect that had come out of the night, and it disappeared in faint dust.

It was in this room he had seen Lady Helen for the last time; and he remembered how, when he returned to her, after having taken Lily back to the dancing-room, he had found her reading a letter, and almost the very words of the conversation it had given rise to came back to him, and her almost aggressive despair. No one could say why she had shot herself. Who was the man that had deserted her? What was he like? Was it Harding? It was certainly for a lover who had tired of her, and Mike wondered how it were possible to weary of one so beautiful and so interesting, and he believed that if she had loved him that they both would have found content.

"Do you remember, Harding, that it was in this room we saw Lady Helen alive for the last time. What a tragedy that was. Do you remember the room in the Alexandra Hotel, the firelight, with the summer morning coming through the Venetian blinds; somehow there was a sense of sculpture, even without the beautiful body.   Seven years have passe d. She has enjoyed seven years of peace and rest; we have endured seven years of fret and worry.   Life of course was never worth living, but the common stupidity of the nineteenth century renders existence for those who may see into the heart of things almost unbearable.   I confess that every day man's stupidity seems to me more and more miraculous.   Indeed it may be said to be divine, so inherent and so unalter- able is it; and to understand it we need not stray from the question in hand—suicide.   A man is houseless, he is old, he is friendless, he is starving, he is assailed in every joint by cruel disease ; to save himself from years of suffering he lights a pan of charcoal ; and, after carefully considering all the cir- cumstances, the jury returns a verdict of suicide while in a state of temporary insanity.   Out of years of insanity had sprung a supreme moment of sanity, and no one understands it.   The common stupidity, I should say the common insanity, of the world on the subject of suicide is quite comic.   A man may destroy his own property, which would certainly be of use to some one, but he may not destroy his own life, which possibly is of use to no one; and if two men conspire to commit suicide and fail, they are tried for murder and hanged.   Can the mind conceive more perfect nonsense ?"

" I cannot say I agree with you," said Harding ; " man's aversion to suicide seems to me perfectly comprehensible."

" Does it really !   Well, I should like to hear you develop that paradox."

" Your contention is that it is inconceivable that in an already over-crowded society men should not look rather with admiration than with contempt on those who, convinced that they block the way, surrender their places to those better able to fill them; and it is to you equally inconceivable that a man should be allowed to destroy his property and not his person. Your difficulty seems to me to arise from your not taking into consideration the instinctive nature of man. The average man may be said to be purely instinctive. In popular opinion—that is to say, in his own opinion—he is supposed to be a reasonable being; but a short acquaintance shows him to be illumined with no faintest ray of reason. His sense of right and wrong is purely instinctive; talk to him about it, and you will see that you might as well ask a sheep-dog why he herds the sheep."

"Quite so; but I do not see how that explains his aversion to suicide."

"I think it does. There are two forces in human nature—instinct and reason. The first is the very principle of life, and exists in all we see—give it a philosophic name, and call it the 'will to live.' All acts, therefore, proceed from instinct or from reason. Suicide is clearly not an instinctive act, it is therefore a reasonable act; and being of all acts the least instinctive, it is of necessity the most reasonable; reason and instinct are antagonistic; and the extreme point of their antagonism must clearly be suicide. One is the assertion of life, the other is the denial of life. The world is mainly instinctive, and therefore very tolerant to all assertions of the will to live; it is in other words full of toleration for itself; no one is reproved for bringing a dozen children into the world, though he cannot support them, because to reprove him would involve a partial condemnation of the will to live; and the world will not condemn itself.

"If suicide merely cut the individual thread of life

our brothers would rejoice. Nature is concerned in the preservation of the species, not in the preservation of the individual; but suicide is more than the disappearance of an individual life, it is a protest against all life, therefore man, in the interest of the life of the race, condemns the suicide. The struggle for life is lessened by every death, but the injury inflicted on the desire of life is greater; in other words, suicide is such a stimulant to the exercise of reason (which has been proved antagonistic to life) that man, in defence of instinct, is forced to condemn suicide.

And it is curious to note that of all the manners of death which may bring them fortune men like suicide the least; a man would prefer to inherit a property through his father falling a prey to a disease that tortured him for months rather than he should blow his brains out. If he were to sound his conscience, his conscience would tell him that his preference resulted from consideration for his father's soul. For as man acquired reason, which, as I have shown, endangers the sovereignty of the will to live, he developed notions of eternal life, such notions being necessary to check and act as a drag upon the new force that had been introduced into his life. He says suicide clashes with the principle of eternal life. So it does, so it does, he is quite right, but how delightful and miraculously obtuse. We must not take man for a reasoning animal; ants and bees are hardly more instinctive and less reasonable than the majority of men.

"But far more than with any ordinary man is it amusing to discuss suicide with a religionist. The religionist does not know how to defend himself. If he is a Roman Catholic he says the pope forbids suicide, and that ends the matter; but other churches have no answer to make, for they find in the Old

and New Testament not a shred of text to cover
themselves with. From the first page of the Bible
to the last there is not a word to say that a man
does not hold his life in his hands, and may not end
it when he pleases."

"Why don't you write an article on suicide? It
would frighten people out of their wits!" said
Mike.

"I hope he'll do nothing of the kind," said a man
who had been listening with bated breath. "We
should have every one committing suicide all around
us—the world would come to an end."

"And would that matter much?" said Mike, with
a scornful laugh. "You need not be afraid. No bit
of mere scribbling will terminate life; the principle
of life is too deeply rooted ever to be uprooted;
reason will ever remain powerless to harm it. Very
seldom, if ever, has a man committed suicide for
purely intellectual reasons. It nearly always takes
the form of a sudden paroxysm of mind. The will
to live is an almost unassailable fortress, and it will
remain impregnable everlastingly."

The entrance of some men talking loudly of
betting and women stopped the conversation. The
servants brought forth the card-tables. Mike played
several games of écarté, cheating openly, braving
detection. He did not care what happened, and
almost desired the violent scene that would ensue
on his being accused of packing the cards. But
nothing happened, and about one o'clock, having
bade the last guest good-night, he returned to the
dining-room. The room in its disorder of fruit and
champagne looked like a human being—Mike thought
it looked like himself. He drank a tumbler of champagne and returned to the drawing-room, his pockets
full of the money he had swindled from a young

man. He threw himself on a sofa by the open window and listened to the solitude, terribly punctuated by the clanging of the clocks. All the roofs were defined on the blue night, and he could hear the sound of water falling. The trees rose in vague masses undistinguishable, and beyond was the immense brickwork which hugs the shores. In the river there were strange reflections, and above the river there were blood-red lamps.

"If I were to fling myself from this window! . . . I shouldn't feel anything; but I should be a shocking sight on the pavement . . . Great Scott! this silence is awful, and those whispering trees, and those damned clocks—another half-hour of life gone. I shall go mad if something doesn't happen."

There came a knock. Who could it be? It did not matter, anything was better than silence. He threw open the door, and a pretty girl, almost a child, bounded into the room, making it ring with her laughter.

"Oh, Mike! darling Mike, I have left home; I couldn't live without you . . . aren't you glad to see me?"

"Of course I'm glad to see you."

' Then why don't you kiss me?" she said, jumping on his knees and throwing her arms about his neck.

"What a wicked little girl you are."

"Wicked! It is you who make me wicked, my own darling Mike. I ran away from home for you, all for you; I should have done it for nobody else. . . . I ran away the day—the day before yesterday. My aunt was annoying me for going out in the lane with some young fellows. I said nothing for a long time. At last I jumps up, and I says that I would stand it no longer; I told her straight; I says you'll never see me again, never no more; I'll go away to

London to some one who is awfully nice. And of
course I meant you, my own darling Mike." And
the room rang with girlish laughter.

"But where are you staying?" said Mike, seriously
alarmed.

"Where am I staying? I'm staying with a young
lady friend of mine who lives in Drury Lane, so I'm
not far from you. You can come and see me," she
said, and her face lit with laughter. "We are rather
hard up. If you could lend me a sovereign I should
be so much obliged."

"Yes, I'll lend you a sovereign, ten if you like;
but I hope you'll go back to your aunt. I know the
world better than you, my dear little Flossy, and I
tell you that Drury Lane is no place for you."

"I couldn't go back to aunt; she wouldn't take me
back; besides I want to remain in London for the
present."

Before she left Mike filled the astonished child's
hands with money, and as she paused beneath his
window he threw some flowers towards her, and
listened to her laughter ringing through the pale
morning. Now the night was a fading thing, and the
town and Thames lay in the faint blue glamour of
the dawn. Another day had begun, and the rattle
of a morning cart was heard. Mike shut the window,
hesitating between throwing himself out of it, and
going to bed.

"As long as I can remember, I have had these fits
of depression, but now they never leave me; I seem
more than ever incapable of shaking them off."

Then he thought of the wickedness he had done,
not of the wickedness of his life—that seemed to him
unlimited,—but of the wickedness accomplished
within the last few hours, and he wondered if he had
done worse in cheating the young man at cards or giv-

ing the money he had won to Flossy. "Having tasted of money, she will do anything to obtain more. I suppose she is hopelessly lost, and will go from bad to worse. But really I don't see that I'm wholly responsible. I advised her to go home, I could do no more. But I will get her aunt's address and write to her. Or I will inform some of the philanthropic people."

A few days after, he came in contact with some. Their fervour awakened some faint interest in him, and now as weary of playing at Mephistopheles as he was of playing at Faust, he followed the occupation of his new friends. But his attempts at reformation were vain, they wore out the soul, and left it only more hopeless than before ; and he remembered John Norton's words, that faith is a gift from God which we must cherish, or He will take it from us utterly, and sighing, Mike recognized the great truth underlying a primitive mode of expression. He had drifted too far into the salt sea of unfaith and cynicism, ever to gain again the fair if illusive shores of aspiration— maybe illusive, but no more illusive than the cruel sea that swung him like a wreck in its current, feeding upon him as the sea feeds. Nor could he make surrender of his passion of life, and saying—

"I see into the heart of things, I know the truth, and in the calm possession of knowledge am able to divest myself of my wretched individuality, and so free myself of all evils, seeking in absorption, rather than by violent ends, to rid myself of consciousness."

But this, the religion of the truly wise, born in the sublime east, could find no roothold in Mike Fletcher—that type and epitome of Western grossness and lust of life. Religions being a synthesis of moral aspirations, developed through centuries, are mischievous and untrue except in the circumstances and climates in which they have grown up in, and native races are decimated equally by the importation of a religion or a disease. True it is that Christianity was a product of the East, but it was an accidental and inferior off-shoot from the original religion of the race, not adapted to their needs, and fitted only for exportation. And now, tainted and poisoned by a thousand years of habitation in the West, Christianity returns to the East virulent and baneful as small-pox, a distinctly demoralizing influence, having power only to change excellent Buddhists into prostitutes and thieves. And in such a way, according to the same laws, Mike had observed, since he had adopted pessimism, certain unmistakable signs in himself of moral degeneracy.

He had now exhausted all Nature's remedies, save one—Drink, and he could not drink. Drink has often rescued men in straits of mental prostration, from the charcoal-pan, the pistol, and the river. But Mike could not drink, and nature sought in vain to readjust again, and balance anew, forces which seemed now irretrievably disarranged. All the old agencies were exhausted, and the new force which chance, co-operating with natural disposition had introduced, was dominant in him. Against it women were now powerless, and he turned aside from offered love

It is probable that the indirect influences to which we have been subjected before birth outweigh the few direct influences received by contagion with present life. But the direct influences, slight as they may be, are worth considering, they being the only ones of which we have any exact knowledge, even if in so doing we exaggerated them ; and in striving to arrive at a just estimation of the forces that had brought about his present mind, Mike was in the habit of giving prominence to the thought of the demoralizing

influence of the introduction of Eastern pessimism
into a distinctly Western nature.   He remembered
very well indeed the shock he had received when he
had heard John say for the first time that it was better that human life should cease.

   " For man's history, what is it, but the history of
crime?   Man's life, what is it, but a disgraceful
episode in the life of one of the meanest of the
planets?   Let us be thankful that time shall obliterate
the abominable, and that once again the world shall
roll pure through the silence of the universe."

   So John had once spoken, creating consternation
in Mike's soul, casting poison upon it.   But John had
buried himself in Catholicism for refuge from this
awful creed, leaving Mike to perish in it.   Then Mike
wondered if he should have lived and died a simple,
honourable, God-fearing man, if he had not been
taken out of the life he was born in, if he had married
in Ireland, for instance, and driven cattle to market,
as did his ancestors.

   One day hearing the organ singing a sweet anthem,
he stayed to listen.   It being midsummer, the doors
of the church were open, the window was in his view,
and the congregation came streaming out into the
sunshine of the courts, some straying hither and
thither, taking note of the various monuments.   In
such occupation he spoke to one whom he recognized
at once as a respectable shop-girl.   He took her out
to dinner, dazzled and delighted her with a present
of jewellery, enchanted her with assurances of his
love.   But when her manner insinuated an inclination
to yield, he lost interest, and wrote saying he was
forced to leave town.   Soon after, he wrote to a
certain actress proposing to write a play for her.
The proposal was not made with a view to deceiving
her, but rather in the intention of securing their liaison

against caprice, by involving in it various mutual advantages. For three weeks they saw each other frequently; he wondered if he loved her, he dreamed of investing his talents in her interest, and so rebuilding the falling edifice of his life.

" I could crush an affection out of my heart as easily as I could kill a fly," she said.

"Ah !" he said. " my heart is as empty as a desert, and no affection shall enter there again."

An appointment was made to go out to supper, but he wrote saying he was leaving town to be married. Nor was his letter a lie. After long hesitations he had decided on this step, and it seemed to him clear that no one would suit him so well as Mrs. Byril. By marrying an old mistress, he would save himself from all the boredom of a honeymoon. And sitting in the drawing-room, in the various pauses between numerous licentious stories, they discussed their matrimonial project.

Dear Emily, who said she suffered from loneliness and fear of the future as acutely as he, was anxious to force the matter forward. But her eagerness begot reluctance in Mike, and at the end of a week, he felt that he would sooner take his razor and slice his head off, than live under the same roof with her.

In Regent Street one evening he met Frank Escott. After a few preliminary observations Mike asked him if he had heard lately from Lord Mount Rorke. Frank said that he had not seen him. All was over between them, but his uncle had, however, arranged to allow him two hundred a year. He was living at Mortlake, "a nice little house ; our neighbour on the left was a city clerk at a salary of seventy pounds a year, on the right is a chemist's shop, a very nice woman is the chemist's wife ; my wife and the chemist's wife are fast friends. We go

over and have tea with them, and they come and
have tea with us. The chemist and I smoke our
pipes over the garden wall. All this appears very
dreadful to you, but I assure you I have more real
pleasure, and take more interest in my life, than
ever I did before. My only trouble is the insurance
policy—I must keep that paid up, for the two hundred
a year's only an annuity. It makes a dreadful hole
in our income. You might come down and see us."

"And be introduced to the chemist's wife!"

"There's no use in trying to come it over me : I
know who you are. I have seen you many times
about the roads in a tattered jacket. You musn't
think that because all the good luck went your way,
and all the bad luck my way, that I'm any less a
gentleman, or you any less a——"

"My dear Frank, I'm really very sorry for what I
said ; I forgot. I assure you I didn't mean to sneer.
I give you my word of honour."

They walked around Piccadilly Circus, edging their
way through the women, that the sultry night had
brought out in white dresses. It was a midnight of
white dresses, and fine dust ; the street was as clean
as a ball-room ; like a pure dream the moon soared
through the azure infinities, whitening the roadway ;
the cabmen loitered, following those who showed
disposition to pair ; groups gathered round the lamp-
posts, and were dispersed by stalwart policemen.
"Move on, move on, if you please, gentlemen !"

Frank told Mike about the children. He had now
a boy five years old, "such a handsome fellow, and
he can read as well as you or I can. He's down at
the sea-side now with his mother. He wrote me
such a clever letter, telling me he had just finished
Robinson Crusoe, and was going to make a start on
Gulliver's Travels. I'm crazy about my boy. Talk

of being tired of living, my trouble is that I shall have to leave him one day."

Mike thought Frank's love of his son charming, and he regretted he could find in his own heart no such simple sentiments. Every now and then he turned to look after a girl, and pulling his moustache, muttered—

" Not bad !"

" Well, don't let's say anything more about it. When will you come and see us?"

" What day will suit you—some day next week?"

"Yes, I'm always in in the evening; will you come to dinner?"

Mike replied evasively, anxious not to commit himself to a promise for any day. Then seeing that Frank thought he did not care to dine with him, he said—

" Very well, let us say Wednesday."

He bade his friend good-night, and stood on the edge of the pavement watching him make his way across the street to catch the last omnibus. Mike's mind filled with memories of Frank. They came from afar surging over the shores of youth, thundering along the cliffs of manhood. Out of the remote regions of boyhood they came, white crests uplifted, merging and mingling in the waters of life. It seemed to Mike that, like sea-weed, he and Frank had been washed together, and they then had been washed apart. That was life, and that was the result of life, that and nothing more. And of every adventure Frank was the most distinctly realizable : all else, even Lily, was a little shadow that had come and gone. John had lost himself in religion, Frank had lost himself in his wife and child. To lose yourself, that is the end to strive for; absorption in religion or in the family. They had attained it, he had failed. All

the love and all the wealth fortune had poured upon
him had not enabled him to stir from or change that
entity which he knew as Mike Fletcher.　Ten years
ago he had not a shilling to his credit, to-day he
had several thousands, but the irreparable had not
altered—he was still Mike Fletcher.　He had wandered over the world; he had lain in the arms of a
hundred women, and nothing remained of it all but
Mike Fletcher.　There was apparently no escape; he
was lashed to himself like the convict to the oar.
For him there was nothing but this oar, and all the
jewellery that had been expended upon it had not
made it anything but an oar.　There was a curse upon
it all.

He saw Frank's home—the little parlour with its
bits of furniture, scraggy and vulgar, but sweet with
the presence of the wife and her homely occupations;
then the children—the chicks—cooing and chattering,
creating such hope and fond anxiety!　Why then did
he not have wife and children?　Of all worldly possessions they are the easiest to obtain.　Because he
had created a soul that irreparably separated him
from these, the real and durable prizes of life; they
lay beneath his hands, but his soul said no; he desired, and was powerless to take what he desired.

For a moment he stood, in puzzled curiosity, listening to the fate that his thoughts were prophesying;
then, as if in answer. antiphonal, terrible as the an-
nouncing of the chorus, came a quick thought, quick
and sharp as a sword, fatal as a sword set against the
heart.　He strove to turn its point aside, he attempted
to pass it by, but on every side he met its point,
though he reasoned in jocular and serious mood.
Then his courage falling through him like a stone
dropped into a well, he crossed the street, seeking the place Flossy had told him of, and soon

after saw her walking a little in front of him with another girl. She beckoned him, leading the way through numerous bye-streets. Something in the sound of certain footsteps told him he was being followed; his reason warned him away, yet he could not but follow. And in the shop below and on the stairs of the low eating-house where they had led him, loud voices were heard and tramping of feet. Instantly he guessed the truth, and drew the furniture across the doorway. The window was twenty feet from the ground, but he might reach the water-butt. He jumped from the window-sill, falling into the water, out of which he succeeded in drawing himself; hence he crawled along the wall, dropped into the lane, hearing his pursuers shouting to him from the window. There were only a few children in the lane; he sped quickly past, gained a main street, hailed a cab, and was driven safely to the Temple.

He flung off his shoes, which were full of water; his trousers were soaking, and having rid himself of them, he wrapped himself in a dressing-gown, and went into the sitting-room in his slippers. It was the same as when it was Frank's room. There was the grand piano and the slender brass lamps; he had lit none, but stood uncertain, his bed-room candle in his hand. And listening, he could hear London along the Embankment—an occasional cry, the rattle of a cab, the hollow whistle of a train about to cross the bridge at Blackfriars, the shrill whistle of a train far away in the night. He had escaped from his pursuers, but not from himself.

"How horribly lonely it is here," he muttered. Then he thought of how narrowly he had escaped disgraceful exposure of his infamy. "If those fellows had got hold of my name it would have been in the papers the day after to-morrow. What a fool I

am; why do I risk so much? and for what?" He
turned from the memory as from sight of some disgustful deformity or disease. Going to the mirror
he studied his face for some reflection of the soul;
but unable to master his feelings, in which there was
at once loathing and despair, he threw open the window and walked out of the suffocating room into the
sultry balcony.

It was hardly night; the transparent obscurity of
the summer midnight was dissolving; the slight film
of darkness which had wrapped the world was evanescent. "Is it day or night?" he asked. "Oh, it is
day! another day has begun; I escaped from my
mortal enemies, but not from the immortal day.
Like a gray beast it comes on soft velvet paws to
devour. Stay! oh bland and beautiful night, thou
that dost so charitably hide our misfortunes, stay!

"I shudder when I think of the new evils and
abominations that this day will bring. The world is
still at rest, lying in the partial purity of sleep. But,
as a cruel gray beast the day comes on soundless
velvet paws. Light and desire are one; light and
desire are the claws that the gray beast unsheathes;
a few hours' oblivion and the world's torment begins
again!" Then looking down the great height he
thought how he might spring from consciousness
into oblivion—the town and the river were now
distinct in ghastly pallor—"I should feel nothing.
But what a mess I should make; what a horrible
little mess!"

After breakfast he sat looking into space, wondering what he might do. He hoped for a visitor and
yet he could not think of one that he desired to see.
A woman! the very thought was distasteful. He
rose and went to the window. London implacable
lay before him, a morose mass of brick, fitting sign

and symbol of life. And the few hours that lay between breakfast and dinner were narrow and brick-
coloured, and longing for the vast green hours of the
country, he went to Belthorpe Park. But in a few
weeks the downs and lanes fevered and exasperated
him, and perforce he must seek some new distraction. Henceforth he hurried from house to house,
tiring of each last abode more rapidly than the one
that had preceded it. He read no books, and he only
bought newspapers to read the accounts of suicides;
and his friends had begun to notice the strange interest with which he spoke of those who had done
away with themselves, and the persistency with which
he sought to deduce their motives from the evidence;
and he seemed to be animated by a wish to depreciate
all worldly reasons and to rely upon weariness of life
as sufficient motive for their action.

The account of two young people engaged to be
married, who had taken tickets for some short journey
and shot themselves in the railway carriage. "Here,"
he said, "was a case of absolute sanity, a quality almost undiscoverable in human nature. Two young
people resolve to rid themselves of the burden; but
they are more than utilitarians, they are poets, and of
a high order; for, not only do they make most public
and emphatic denial of life, but they add to it a measure of Aristophanesque satire—they engage themselves to marry. Now marriage is man's approval
and confirmation of his belief in human existence—
they engage themselves to marry, but instead of putting their threat into execution, they enter a railway
carriage and blow out their brains, proving thereby
that they had brains to blow out."

When, however, it transpired that letters were
found in the pockets of the suicides to the effect that
they had hoped to gain such notoriety as the daily

press can give by their very flagrant leave-taking of
this world, Mike professed much regret, and gravely
assured his astonished listeners that, in the face of
these letters, which had unhappily come to light, he
withdrew his praise of the quality of the brains blown
out.   In truth he secretly rejoiced that proof of the
imperfect sanity of the suicides had come to light,
and assured himself that when he did away with Mike
Fletcher he would revenge himself on society by
leaving behind him a document which would forbid
the usual idiotic verdict, "Suicide while in a state of
temporary insanity," and leave no loophole through
which it might be said that he was impelled to seek
death for any extraneous reasons whatever. He would
go to death in the midst of the most perfect worldly
prosperity the mind could conceive, desiring nothing
but rest, profoundly convinced of the futility of all
else, and the perfect folly of human effort.

In such perverse and morbid mind Mike returned
to London.   It was in the beginning of August, and
the Temple weltered in sultry days and calm nights.
The river flowed sluggishly through its bridges   the
lights along its banks gleamed fiercely in the lucent
stillness of a sulphur-hued horizon.   Like a nightmare the silence of the apartment lay upon his chest ;
and there was a frightened look in his eyes as he walked
to and fro.   The moon lay like a creole amid the
blue curtains of the night ; the murmur of London
hushed in stray cries, and only the tread of the policeman was heard distinctly.   About the river the night
was deepest and out of the shadows falling from the
bridges the lamps gleamed with strange intensity,
some flickering sadly in the water.   Mike walked
into the dining-room   He could see the sward in
the darkness that the trees spread, and the lilies
reeked in the great stillness.   Then he thought of

the old days when the *Pilgrim* was written in these rooms, and of the youthfulness of those days; and he maddened when he recalled the evenings of artistic converse in John Norton's room—how high were then their aspirations! The Temple, too, seemed to have lost youth and gaiety. No longer did he meet his old friends in the eating-houses and taverns. Everything had been dispersed or lost. Some were married, some had died.

Then the solitude grew more unbearable and he turned from it, hoping he might meet some one he knew. As he passed up Temple Lane he saw a slender woman dressed in black, talking to the policemen. He had often seen her about the Courts and Buildings, and had accosted her, but she had passed without heeding. Curious to hear who and what she was, Mike entered into conversation with one of the policemen.

" She! we calls her old Specks, sir."

" I have often seen her about, and I spoke to her once, but she didn't answer."

" She didn't hear you, sir; she's a little deaf. A real good sort, sir, is old Jenny. She's always about here. She was brought out in the Temple; she lived eight years with a Q.C., sir. He's dead. A strapping fine wench she was then, I can tell you."

" And what does she do now?"

" She has three or four friends here. She goes to see Mr.—I can't think of his name—you know him, the red-whiskered man in Dr. Johnson's Buildings. You have seen him in the Probate Court many a time." And then in defence of her respectability, if not of her morals, the policeman said, " You'll never see her about the streets, sir, she only comes to the Temple."

Old Jenny stood talking to the younger member

of the force. When she didn't hear him she cooed in the soft, sweet way of deaf women; and her genial laugh told Mike that the policeman was not wrong when he described her as a real good sort. She spoke of her last 'bus, and on being told the time gathered up her skirts and ran up the Lane.

Then the policemen related anecdotes concerning their own and the general amativeness of the Temple.

"But, lor, sir, it is nothing now to what it used to be! Some years ago, half the women of London used to be in here of a night; now there's very little going on—an occasional kick up, but nothing to speak of."

"What are you laughing at?" said Mike, looking from one to the other.

The policemen consulted each other, and then one said—

"You didn't hear about the little shindy we had here last night, sir? It was in Elm Court, just behind you, sir. We heard some one shouting for the police; we couldn't make out where the shouting came from first, we were looking about—the echo in these Courts makes it very difficult to say where a voice comes from. At last we saw the fellow at the window, and we went up. He met us at the door. He said, 'Policemen, the lady knocked at my door and asked for a drink; I didn't notice that she was drunk and I gave her a brandy-and-soda, and before I could stop her she undressed herself!' There was the lady right enough, in her chemise, sitting in the arm-chair, as drunk as a lord, humming and singing as gay, sir, as any little bird. Then the party says, 'Policeman, do your duty!' I says, 'What is my duty?' He says, 'Policeman, I'll report you!' I says, 'Report yourself. I knows my duty.' He says, 'Policeman, remove that woman!' I says, 'I can't remove her in that state. Tell her to dress herself, and I'll remove her.' Well, the long and the short of it, sir, is that we had to dress her between us, and I never had such a job."

The exceeding difficulties of this toilette, as narrated by the stolid policeman, made Mike laugh consummately. Then alternately, and in conjunction, the policemen told stories concerning pursuits through the areas and cellars with which King's Bench Walk abounds.

"It was from Paper Buildings that the little girl came from who tried to drown herself in the fountain."

"Oh, I haven't heard about her," said Mike. "She tried to drown herself in the fountain, did she? Crossed in love; tired of life; which was it?"

"Neither, sir; she was a bit drunk, that was about it. My mate could tell you about her, he pulled her out. She's up before the magistrate to-day again."

"Just fancy, bringing a person up before a magistrate because she wanted to commit suicide! Did any one ever hear such rot? If our own persons don't belong to us, I don't know what does. But tell me about her."

"She went up to see a party that lives in Pump Court. We was at home, so she picks up her skirts, runs across here and throws herself in. I see her run across, and follows her; but I had to get into the water to get her out; I was wet to the waist—there's about four feet of water in that 'ere fountain."

"And she?"

"She had fainted. We had to send for a cab to get her to the station, sir."

At that moment the presence of the sergeant hurried the policemen away, and Mike was left alone. The warm night air was full of the fragrance of the leaves, and he was alive to the sensation of the foliage spreading above him, and deepening amid the

branches of the tall plane trees that sequestered and
shadowed the fountain. They grew along the walls,
forming a quiet dell, in whose garden silence the
dripping fountain sang its song of falling water. Light
and shade fell picturesquely about the steps descending to the gardens, and the parapeted buildings fell
in black shadows upon the sward, and stood sharp
upon the moon illuminated blue. Mike sat beneath
the plane trees, and the suasive silence, sweetly tuned
by the dripping water, murmured in his soul dismal
sorrowings. Over the cup, whence issued the jet that
played during the day, the water flowed. There were
there the large leaves of some aquatic plant, and
Mike wondered if the policeman had not rescued the
girl if she would now be in perfect peace, instead
of dragged before a magistrate and forced to promise
to bear her misery.

"A pretty little tale," he thought, and he saw her
floating in shadowy water in pallor and beautiful, and
reconciliation with nature. "Why see another day?
I must die very soon, why not at once? Thousands
have grieved as I am grieving in this self-same place,
have asked the same sad questions. Sitting under
these ancient walls young men have dreamed as I am
dreaming—no new thoughts are mine. For five
thousand years man has asked himself why he lives.
Five thousand years have changed the face of the
world and the mind of man; no thought has resisted
the universal transformation of thought, save that one
thought—why live? Men change their gods, but one
thought floats immortal, unchastened by the teaching
of any mortal gods. Why see another day? why
drink again the bitter cup of life when we may drink
the waters of oblivion?"

He walked through Pump Court slowly, like a
prisoner impeded by the heavy chain, and at every
step the death idea clanked in his brain. All the

windows were full of light, and he could hear women's voices. In imagination he saw the young men sitting round the sparely furnished rooms, law books and broken chairs—smoking and drinking, playing the piano, singing, thinking they were enjoying themselves. A few years and all would be over for them as all was over now for him. But never would they drink of life as he had drunk, he was the type of that of which they were but imperfect and inconclusive figments. Was he not the Don Juan and the poet— a sort of Byron doubled with Byron's hero? But he was without genius; had he genius, genius would force him to live.

He considered how far in his pessimism he was a representative of the century. He thought how much better he would have done in another age, and how out of sympathy he was with the utilitarian dulness of the present time, how much more brilliant he would have been had he lived at any other period of the Temple's history. Then he stopped to study the style of the old staircase, the rough woodwork twisting up the wall so narrowly, the great bannisters full of shadow lighted by the flickering lanterns. The yellowing colonnade—its beams and overhanging fronts were also full of suggestion, and the suggestion of old time was enforced by the signboard of a wig-maker.

"The last of an ancient industry," thought Mike. "The wig is representative of the seventeenth as the silk hat is of the nineteenth century. I wonder why I am so strongly fascinated with the seventeenth century?—I, a peasant; atavism, I suppose; my family were not always peasants."

Turning from the old Latin inscription he viewed the church, so evocative in its fortress form of an earlier and more romantic century. The clocks were striking one, two hours would bring the dawn close again upon the verge of the world. Mike trembled and thought how he might escape. The beauty of the cone of the church was outlined upon the sky, and he dreamed, as he walked round the shadow-filled porch, full of figures in prayer and figures holding scrolls, of the white-robed knights, their red crosses, their long swords, and their banner called Beauseant. He dreamed himself Grand Master of the Order; saw himself in chain armour charging the Saracen. The story of the terrible idol with the golden eyes, the secret rites, the knight led from the penitential cell and buried at daybreak, the execution of the Grand Master at the stake, turned in his head fitfully; cloud-shapes that passed, floating, changing incessantly, suddenly disappearing, leaving him again Mike Fletcher, a strained, agonized soul of our time, haunted and hunted by an idea, overpowered by an idea as a wolf by a hound.

His life had been from the first a series of attempts to escape from the idea. His loves, his poetry, his restlessness were all derivative from this one idea. Among those whose brain plays a part in their existence there is a life idea, and this idea governs them and leads them to a certain and predestined end; and all struggles with it are delusions. A life idea in the higher classes of mind, a life instinct in the lower. It were almost idle to differentiate between them, both may be included under the generic title of the soul, and the drama involved in such conflict is always of the highest interest, for if we do not read the story of our own soul we read in each the story of a soul that might have been ours, and that passed very near to us; and who reading of Mike's torment is fortunate enough to say, " I know nothing of what is written there"?

His steps echoed hollow on the old pavement. Full of shadow the roofs of the square church swept across the sky; the triple lancet windows caught a

little light from the gaslight on the buildings ; and
he wondered what was the meaning of the little gold
lamb standing over one doorway, and then remembered that in various forms the same symbolic lamb
is repeated through the Temple. He passed under
the dining-hall by the tunnel and roamed through
the spaces beneath the plane trees of King's Bench
Walk. " My friends think my life was a perfect gift,
but a burning cinder was placed in my breast, and
time has blown it into flame."

In the soporific scent of the lilies and the stocks,
the night drowsed in the darkness of the garden ;
Mike unlocked the gate and passed into the shadows,
and hypnotized by the heavenly spaces, in which there
were a few stars ; by the earth and the many emanations of the earth ; by the darkness which covered
all things, hiding the little miseries of human existence, he threw himself upon the sward crying, " Oh,
take me, mother, hide me in thy infinite bosom, give
me forgetfulness of the day. Take and hide me away.
We leave behind a corpse that men will touch.
Sooner would I give myself to the filthy beaks of
vultures, than to their more defiling sympathies.
Why were we born ? Why are we taught to love
our parents? It is they whom we should hate, for it
is they who, careless of our sufferings, inflict upon
us the evil of life. We are taught to love them because
the world is mad ; there is nothing but madness in
the world. Night, do not leave me ; I cannot bear
with the day. Ah, the day will come ; nothing can
retard the coming of the day, and I can bear no
longer with the day."

Hearing footsteps, he sprang to his feet, and
walking in the direction whence the sound came, he
found himself face to face with the policeman.

" Not able to get to sleep, sir ?"

"No, I couldn't sleep, the night is so hot; I shall sleep presently though."

They had not walked far before the officer, pointing to one of the gables of the Temple gardens, said—

"That's where Mr. Williamson threw himself over, sir; he got out on the roof, on to the highest point he could reach."

"He wanted," said Mike, "to do the job effectually."

"He did so; he made a hole two feet deep."

"They put him into a deeper one."

The officer laughed; and they walked round the gardens, passing by the Embankment to King's Bench Walk. Opening the gate there, the policeman asked Mike if he were coming out, but he said he would return across the gardens, and let himself out by the opposite gate. He walked, thinking of what he and the policeman had been saying—the proposed reduction in the rents of the chambers, the late inno- vation of throwing open the gardens to the poor children of the neighbourhood, and it was not until he stooped to unlock the gate, that he remembered that he was alive.

Then the voice that had been counselling him so long, drew strangely near, and said "Die." The voice sounded strangely clear in the void of a great brain silence. Earth ties seemed severed, and then quite naturally, without any effort of mind, he went up stairs to shoot himself. No effort of mind was needed, it seemed the natural and inevitable course for him to take, and he was only conscious of a certain faint sur- prise that he had so long delayed. There was no trace of fear or doubt in him; he walked up the long stair- case, without embarrassment, and in a heavenly calm of mind hastened to put his project into execution, dreading the passing of the happiness of his present mood, and the return of the fever of living. He stopped for a moment to see himself in the glass, and looking into the depths of his eyes, he strove to read there the story of his triumph over life. Then seeing the disorder of his dress, and the untidy appearance of his unshaven chin, he smiled, conceiving in that moment that it would be consistent to make as careful a toilette to meet death, as he had often done to meet a love.

He was anxious for the world to know that it was not after a drunken bout he had shot himself, but after philosophic deliberation and judicious reflection. And he could far better affirm his state of mind by his dress, than by any written words. Lying on the bed, cleanly shaved, wearing evening clothes, silk socks, patent leather shoes and white gloves? No, that would be vulgar, and all taint of vulgarity must be avoided. He must represent, even in a state of symbol, the young man, who having drunk of life to repletion, and finding that he can but repeat the same love draughts, says: "It is far too great a bore, I will go," and he goes out of life just as if he were leaving a fashionable *soirée* in Piccadilly. That was exactly the impression he wished to convey. Yes, he would have out his opera hat and light overcoat. He was a little uncertain whether he should die in the night, or wait for the day, and considering the question, he lathered his face. "Curious it is," he thought, "I never was so happy, so joyous in life before . . . These walls, all that I see, will in a few minutes disappear; it is this I, this Ego, which creates them; in destroying myself I destroy the world . . . How hard this beard is! I never can shave properly without hot water!"

As he pulled on a pair of silk socks and tied his white necktie he thought of Lady Helen. Going to bed was not a bad notion—particularly for a woman and a woman in love, but it would be ridiculous for a man. He looked at himself again in the long glass in the door of his carved mahogany wardrobe, and was pleased to see that, although a little jaded and worn, he was still handsome. Having brushed his hair carefully, he looked out the revolver; he did not remember exactly where he had put it, and in turning out his drawers he came upon a bundle of old letters. They were mostly from Frank and Lizzie, and in recalling old times they reminded him that if he died without making a will, his property would go to the crown. It displeased him to think that his property should pass away in so impersonal a manner. But his mind was now full of death; like a gourmet he longed to taste of the dark fruit of oblivion; and the delay involved in making out a will exasperated him, and it was with difficulty that he conquered his selfishness and sat down to write. Fretful he threw aside the pen; this little delay had destroyed all his happiness. To dispose of his property in money and land would take some time; the day would surprise him still in the world. After a few moments' reflection he decided that he would leave Belthorpe Park to Frank Escott.

"I dare say I'm doing him an injury . . . but no, there's no time for paradoxes—I'll leave Belthorpe Park to Frank Escott. The aristocrat shall not return to the people. But to whom shall I leave all my money in the funds? To a hospital? No—to a woman? I must leave it to a woman; I hardly know any one but women; but to whom? Suppose I were to leave it to be divided among those who could advance irrefutable proof that they had loved me! What a throwing over of reputation there would be." Then a sudden memory of the girl by whom he had had a child sprang upon him like something out of the dark. He wondered for a moment what the child was like, and then he wrote leaving the interest of his money to her, until his son, the child born in such

a year—he had some difficulty in fixing the date—
came of age. She should retain the use of the interest
of twelve thousand pounds, and at her death that sum
should revert to the said child born in ——, and if the
said child were not living, his mother should become
possessor of the entire moneys now invested in funds,
to do with as she pleased.

" That will do," he thought ; " I dare say it isn't
very legal, but it is common sense and will be difficult
to upset. Yes, and I will leave all my books and
furniture in Temple Gardens to Frank ; I don't care
much about the fellow, but I had better leave it to
him. And now, what about witnesses? The policemen will do."

He found one in King's Bench Walk, another he
met a little further on, talking to a belated harlot,
whom he willingly relinquished on being invited to
drink. Mike led the way at a run up the high steps,
the burly officers followed more leisurely.

" Come in," he cried, and they advanced into the
room, their helmets in their hands. " What will you
take, whiskey or brandy?"

After some indecision both decided, as Mike knew
they would, for the former beverage. He offered them
soda-water ; but they preferred a little plain water
and drank to his very good health. They were, as
before, garrulous to excess. Mike listened for some
few minutes, so as to avoid suspicion, and then said—

" Oh, by the way, I wrote out my will a night or
two ago—not that I want to die yet, but one never
knows. Would you mind witnessing it?"

The policemen saw no objection ; in a few moments
the thing was done, and they retired bowing, and
the door closed on solitude and death.

Mike lay back in his chair reading the document.
The fumes of the whiskey he had drunk obscured
his sense of purpose, and he allowed his thoughts to

wander; his eyes closed and he dozed, his head
leaned a little on one side. He dreamed, or rather
he thought, for it was hardly sleep, of the dear good
women who had loved him ; and he mused over his
folly in not taking one to wife and accepting life in
its plain naturalness.

Then as sleep deepened the dream changed, becoming hyperbolical and fantastic, until he saw himself descending into hell. The numerous women he
had betrayed awaited him and pursued him with
blazing lamps of intense and blinding electric fire.
And he fled from the light, seeking darkness like
some nocturnal animal. His head was leaned slightly
on one side, the thin, weary face lying in the shadow
of the chair, and the hair that fell thickly on the
moist forehead. As he dreamed the sky grew
ghastly as the dead. The night crouched as if in
terror along the edges of the river, beneath the
bridges and among the masonry and the barges
aground, and in the ebbing water a lurid reflection
trailed ominously. And as the day ascended, the
lamps dwindled from red to white, and beyond the
dark night of the river, spires appeared upon faint
roseate gray.

Then, as the sparrows commenced their shrilling
in the garden, another veil was lifted, and angles
and shapes on the warehouses appeared, and boats
laden with newly-cut planks ; then the lights that
seemed to lead along the river turned short over the
iron girders, and in white whiffs a train sped across
the bridge. The clouds lifted and cleared away,
changing from dark gray to undecided purple, and
in the blank silver of the east, the spaces flushed,
and the dawn appeared in her first veil of rose. And
as if the light had penetrated and moved the brain,
the lips murmured—

"False fascination in which we are blinded.

Night! shelter and save me from the day, and in thy opiate arms bear me across the world."

He turned uneasily as if he were about to awake, and then his eyes opened and he gazed on the spectral pallor of the dawn in the windows, his brain rousing from dreams slowly into comprehension of the change that had come. Then collecting his thoughts he rose and stood facing the dawn. He stood for a moment like one in combat, and then like one overwhelmed retreated through the folding doors, seeking his pistol.

"Another day begun! Twelve more hours of consciousness and horror! I must go!"

None had heard the report of the pistol, and while the pomp of gold and crimson faded, and the sun rose into the blueness of morning, Mike lay still grasping the revolver, the blood flowing down his face, where he had fallen across the low bed, raised upon lions' claws and hung with heavy curtains. Receiving no answer, the servant had opened the door. A look of horror passed over her face; she lifted his hand, let it fall, and burst into tears.

And all the while the sun rose, bringing work and sorrow to every living thing—filling the fields with labourers, filling the streets with clerks and journalists, authors and actors. And it was in the morning hubbub of the Strand that Lizzie Escott stopped to speak to Lottie, who was going to rehearsal.

"How exactly like his father he is growing,' she said, speaking of the little boy by the actress's side. "Frank saw Mike in Piccadilly about a month ago; he promised to come and see us, but he never did."

"Swine. He never could keep a promise. I hope Willy won t grow up like him

"Who are you talking of, mother? ot father?'

The women exchanged glances.

"He's as sharp as a needle. And to think that that beast never gave me but one hundred pounds, and it was only an accident I got that—we happened to meet in the underground railway. He took a ticket for me—you know he could always be very nice if he liked; he told me a lady had left him five thousand a-year, and if I wanted any money I had only to ask him for it. I asked him if he wouldn't like to see the child, and he said I mustn't be beastly; I never quite knew what he meant; but I know he thought it funny, for he laughed a great deal, and I got into such a rage. I said I didn't want his dirty money, and got out at the next station. He sent me a hundred pounds next day. I haven't heard of him since, and don't want to."

"Suicide of a poet in the Temple!" shouted a little boy.

"I wonder who that is," said Lizzie.

"Mike used to live in the Temple," said Lottie.

The women read the reporter's account of the event, and then Lottie said—

"Isn't it awful! I wonder what he has done with his money?"

"You may be sure he hasn't thought of us. He ought to have thought of Frank. Frank was very good to him in old times."

"Well, I don't care what he has done with his money. I never cared for any man but him. I could have forgiven him everything if he had only thought of the child. I hope he has left him something."

"Now I'm sure you are talking of father."

THE END.

04